2

N
W E
S

■ Mackenzie's Campsite
▲ Author's Campsite
----- Mackenzie's Route
—— Author's Route

0   Miles   50

Same scale for all sectional maps

WILLOWLAKE R.

NORTHWEST TERRITORIES

Rae

YELLOWKNIFE R.

ABBITSKIN R.

Yellowknife

MILLS L.

NORTH
ARM

MACKENZIE R.

PROVIDENCE I.

Ft. Providence
FERRY

PROVIDENCE RAPIDS

SULPHUR BAY

GREAT SLAVE L.

BY
TRUCK

H

D1247653

HAY R.

BUF

alacias

ULTIMATE NORTH

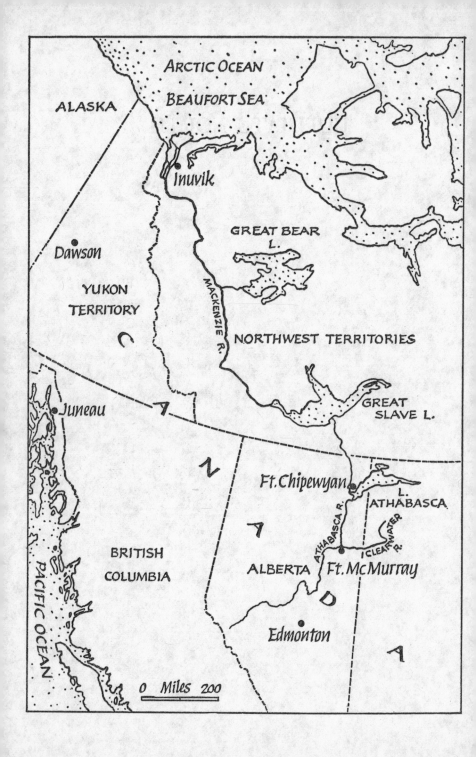

ULTIMATE NORTH

Canoeing
Mackenzie's Great River

ROBERT DOUGLAS MEAD

DOUBLEDAY & COMPANY, INC.
GARDEN CITY, NEW YORK
1976

By the Same Author

Reunion: A Personal History of
the Middle Generation
The Canoer's Bible

Co-author and Editor

Hellas and Rome
New Promised Land
Europe Reborn

Endpaper and interior maps by Rafael Palacios

ISBN 0-385-07252-x
Library of Congress Catalog Card Number 75-35418
Copyright © 1976 by Robert Douglas Mead
All Rights Reserved
Printed in the United States of America
First Edition

For
Thulia
The True Penelope
of This Odyssey

Contents

List of Illustrations

List of Maps

ULTIMATE NORTH

The river is about three quarters of a mile in breadth,
and runs in a steady current. . . .

CHAPTER 1

Last Things

I braked at the edge of the road, shifted into low gear, and eased the station wagon down the bank toward the river: a faint, muddy track among rounded humps of earth shaped as if by a child's exploring hands and lubricated by last night's rain. Here and there a wedge of limestone pushed up, but the bank had been wiped clean of driftwood and grass, first by the departing ice, then by the big spring flood, hardly a week back, that we had been hearing about since our arrival that morning. I stopped the car fifty yards from the water's edge—any farther and we would not get it out again.

After so many jumping-off places, so many beginnings, we had reached the real one: Fort McMurray, on a point of land where two great rivers of the North, the Athabasca and the Clearwater, come together in the northeast corner of Alberta. By now we had driven, my son and I, almost thirty-five hundred miles from our home in eastern Pennsylvania, always north and west: turnpikes and interstates as far as Duluth, then the narrower, winter-armored roads through the forests of northern Minnesota and western Ontario, where deer looked out curiously from among the trees and, once, on a misty early morning, a brown bear ambled at his ease across the deserted highway; then across the limitless wheatlands of Manitoba, Saskatchewan, Alberta, where the earth spreads to the horizons in great rolling swells like a solidified sea, to Edmonton, the metropolis, mother city, of the northland; and finally the three hundred miles straight north to Fort McMurray, asphalt giving way to graded gravel, shoulderless and steeply cambered to ten-foot ditches at either side, where the stripped wrecks of abandoned cars and trucks warn you of the penalties for a moment's inattention, and signs along the road announce the seventy- or hundred-mile stretches that are without "services"—no gas station, telephone, settlement, trapper's shack—and you cautiously steer to the center and flash the headlights on at the occasional dust cloud that means an approaching car or truck, a road gang filling and oiling the ruts and potholes in the short weeks before winter comes again.

It had been a series of jumping-off places, each less known than the last. A hundred yards upstream from where we parked, a steel bridge, painted green, crosses the Athabasca on concrete pylons metered with the river's flood levels, and the gravel road becomes a muddy track, winds on a few more miles along the left bank, and stops. Beyond that, wandering, vanishing, from year to year, older maps show a winter road to a settlement two hundred miles downstream—a cutline through the forest, frozen and usable for trucks and tractors from late October to May, turning to slough with the thaw. But effectively Fort McMurray is the end of the road. Here we leave the car and take to water.

Ahead of us now lay seventeen hundred miles of rivers and lakes, half the distance we had already come by road and, like the roads, leading always north and west; which, traveling by canoe and paddle, I thought might take us anywhere from six to eight or ten weeks, the guess varying with my mood, my latest scanning of the maps, the odd bits of knowledge I had gathered, in the months of preparation for this trip, from others who had canoed parts of our route. The outline was clear enough: down the Athabasca to the lake of the same name, across it to the Slave River, down that to Great Slave Lake and to its western end, where the Mackenzie River begins; then the Mackenzie to its vast delta and, if we could do it, to the shore of the Arctic Ocean. We had simply, I thought, to follow the current. The system we were entering, with its sources in the high Canadian Rockies west of Edmonton, is a kind of north-flowing Arctic mirror image of the Mississippi, not only in size but in the way it has gathered to itself the people, history, geography of the northland. It would carry us to our destination. The time it would take, at that moment of arrival and departure, did not seem to matter very much.

Our goal was a double one: to reach the Arctic—and get back again—under our own power, by canoe; and to follow as closely as we could the route taken by Alexander Mackenzie down the river that bears his name when he made his voyage of discovery, also by canoe, in 1789. There would be differences. Mackenzie had started from Fort Chipewyan on Lake Athabasca, a post named for the Indians with whom he traded for furs, on June 3. We would be starting on June 5 two hundred miles upstream, as far as we could get by road; we would have to try to catch up. The almost two centuries separating our two voyages did not seem to be one of the big differences. Mackenzie's account of his journey, published in the first year of the nineteenth century, is still the truest description of the country and its people, from the seat of a canoe. It and they have not changed much, though just how much was one of the things I hoped to learn, one of the unknowns we were committing ourselves to, as Mackenzie had.

"Time to unload," I said, turning to my son. "Bob Braund will be here in a few minutes."

We got out, unstrapped the canoe from the top of the car, and Jim slid it onto his shoulders, carried it down the river-bank. There were six packs in the back of the station wagon, stuffed with the food, clothing, sleeping bags, tent, and equipment that I hoped would anticipate the unknowns of this trip. We slipped the pack straps over our shoulders, carried them down, and lined them neatly beside the canoe. Not much remained to be done. I had hunted up someone to look after the car till we got back at the end of July or some-time in August, Bob Braund, who with the frontier versa-tility of the North drove a cab, repaired cars, ran the town's only tow truck, leased a fenced yard where the car would be safe from strippers—and would meet us here in minutes to take the car. We had mailed postcards home to let the fam-ily know we'd gotten this far, bought a bottle of Halazone tablets just in case ("We drink it," we were told when we asked about the water) and checked in with the local con-stable of the Royal Canadian Mounted Police to let him know our route and how long we thought we'd take—again just in case. And we had eaten a last restaurant lunch in a cafe, served on the run by a blond, bony, fortyish woman with the kind of manic precision you might learn if you were, say, a Volga German in a Central Asian work camp—the thick north country soup, so, the hot sandwich, the pud-ding, the repeated cups of coffee, the check, so, each with a marionette snap to attention. The Indians have always been here. The whites are from everywhere.

Now there was time to wait. I studied the sky. White clouds edged with black, covering the sun, uncovering it again, neither warm nor cool. Rain? Weather was another of our unknowns, though how important I could not know. Mackenzie had started immediately after the breakup of ice, had seen frozen earth and ice in the sidestreams all down the Slave River, been stopped by ice for two weeks on the lake. I had half expected to camp here on the bank, waiting for the ice to go, but the river now was clear as far as I could see.

The sky darkened. A riffle of raindrops spattered across the river. We slipped our ponchos out of the top of one of the packs and put them on. Bob Braund drove down the bank in his tow truck with a small black mongrel dog in the cab for company.

"You'll wear your raincoats out, taking them on and off, on this river," Bob told us.

Getting ready for this trip had already taken a year. There were, for a start, the maps, beginning with those of Mackenzie and other early explorers, copied from old books. The Canadian government maps of the route came in several different series, to different scales, not all of them complete. I sampled, selected, ordered, waited, studied: nearly fifty altogether, with detailed, large-scale maps of parts of the route, such as the Mackenzie delta, that looked as if they would be difficult to navigate; there were also maps covering side trips I hoped we'd have time for along the way, alternative approaches to the track Mackenzie had followed. None of the road maps I could find showed northern Alberta. Assuming we must be able to drive there, I had written the manager of the Hudson's Bay post at Fort Chipewyan, Mackenzie's starting point, about storing the car for the summer—and had been answered that the road vanished with breakup in early May. Until we were nearly to Edmonton, I was uncertain whether we'd be able to get as far as Fort McMurray or might have to put in elsewhere —farther south and west on the Athabasca, perhaps at some point to the east on the old fur-trade route that led from Montreal across the Great Lakes and up the big lake-and-river systems sprinkled over the northern prairie provinces to Fort McMurray, the traditional traders' junction for the routes to the farthest north.

The canoe itself turned out to be a problem. I had been canoeing since the age of six with my parents, brothers, later with my wife and our sons—and had never in all those years, I discovered, given five minutes' thought to the design of canoes. What would be right? The success of the trip, perhaps our lives, would depend on making the right choice. I collected catalogues, studied specifications, asked friends and acquaintances for advice, drove hundreds of miles to try out possibilities, digressed into research on the bark canoes of the Northwest Indians—surely the canoes they built would suit the conditions. The conclusions were contradictory. With four or five hundred pounds of food and equipment, plus our own weight, the canoe had to have a good carrying capacity—big. But it had to be maneuverable in fast water, light enough for easy portaging where that was necessary. The three rivers we would travel were big enough for serious winds, multiplied by the uncertain variable of the northern summer—we would need a fast-hulled canoe with a low profile to get through them without being worn to exhaustion. On the other hand, the two lakes we had to cross are as big as some of the Great Lakes and have the same reputation for sudden and ferocious storms. Even if we had the luck or wisdom to avoid them, we would need a deep-hulled canoe, high in bow and stern, as insurance against swamping in the rolling swells and crosschop that can build up down three hundred miles of open lake.

Through the winter, on weekends when Jim could get home from college, we experimented. There were days maneuvering through rapids on neighboring streams under cold, gusty, February rain that I hoped was as bad as any weather we'd face in the North. Since most of my past canoeing experience had been on the lakes and short rivers of the Minnesota border country, we took the canoes, loaded, across choppy sections of Chesapeake Bay, the nearest we could come to Athabasca and Great Slave, trying to find out what they would stand, how they would handle. Teaching

ourselves about eddies and riffles and crosscurrents, we traveled to bigger rivers, though again there was nothing we
could get to that would match the ones we had to face.

In the end, with hardly two weeks to spare, I made the
choice, an Old Town Chipewyan from Maine—a lucky
name, though I didn't think of that at the time—made of an
ingenious new combination of plastics that seemed to be
tough; not as big or as fast or as light as I had wanted, but it
had taken us, dry, with a load, through the roughest water
we'd been able to find, and that finally was what seemed
most important. It was what we would be betting on.

Food was a dilemma. On the two- or three-week canoe
trips I was used to, it's hard to go seriously wrong, even if a
bear demolishes the whole lot—there are usually fish to be
had, and at the worst you can reach a settlement of some
kind in a couple of days, on foot if you have to. The two
months or more of our Mackenzie trip would be a different
proposition, though just how different I couldn't be sure.
There would be settlements along our route at intervals of
about two hundred miles, most with a Hudson's Bay store—
perhaps a week apart as long as we had the canoe. I wrote
ahead. Apparently we could count on buying canned stuff,
nonperishables like flour, oatmeal, coffee, sugar, dried milk,
but meat would be chancy, fresh vegetables unlikely. In the
end, I decided to build our food supply around freeze-dried
foods, stews and vegetables, a kind of modern equivalent of
the fur traders' dried corn and pemmican, which they boiled
up into a slurry thickened with flour and whatever meat or
fish they could get. It was a reluctant decision. I've used
freeze-dried food on hikes of a week or two but have always
ended hungry—the portions are niggardly for heavy work,
the calories and proteins skimpy. On a trip of this length, its
main recommendation was that it would keep, was light and
compact (even so, our packs were heavy, filled to bursting,
by the time we set out), but we would have to be lucky
with fishing or, to a degree, we would starve.

Most of the people I talked to about the trip assumed we would carry a gun. I had thought about it. Bears in all circumstances are unpredictable enough to be treated with caution, particularly if they've been made bold by sentimental humans, as at Yellowstone. The bears we were likely to encounter, however, were apparently still thoroughly wild, fearful of man, and over the years I've always been able to keep that kind out of my food supply by one trick or another, chasing off the inquisitive ones, if need be. A gun as a source of food was another matter. Although I don't regard hunting as a sport—it's an unequal contest at best, and I don't kill anything for fun—I have nothing against shooting meat for food, and I enjoy fishing for the same purpose. I investigated further. Bear and moose, I was told, were heavily hunted by the Indians along the Mackenzie itself; going inland after them would mean a day or two of serious hunting, time we might not be able to spare, and, if we succeeded, would leave us with more meat than we could eat or carry. Caribou, wintering in the woodlands east of our starting point and migrating north in the spring, would not be plentiful until we reached the Arctic, toward the end of the trip and, though smaller than moose or bear, raised the same objection: waste. So we would do without a gun, rely on our rods, but even that was doubtful—the fishing was supposed to be good up the small tributaries, uncertain in the big river itself.

A solution had been suggested to me early on, but it was months before I acted on it. A year before we set out for the Northwest, on the way home from a Quetico canoe trip with my two youngest sons, I had stopped off in Ely to visit Sig Olson, one of the great canoeists and outdoorsmen of this century. Forty years ago, as a border lakes outfitter, he had introduced my family to canoeing. In the years since, he had traveled much of the Canadian North—and had written about it. I was starting to think about my own attempt on the Arctic, my mind not yet made up about the route, even about whether the idea was possible. We talked about Sig's travels. Those months on his own in the wilderness, what had he done about food? You couldn't *carry* that much. Hunting?

"Never carried a gun," he said emphatically. "Course, I've nothing against hunting—"

Then fishing—could you count on it?

"Carried a net—little bit of a thing, didn't take up much room in the pack, didn't weigh anything. You know, there are times when you just can't *get* a fish to take a lure—but set the net in an eddy near shore, across a little creek, you're always sure of something, all you need. . . ."

The suggestion stayed in my mind as I planned the trip. As the time for departure approached, I tried to buy a net, found that I couldn't. If we were to have a net, it seemed, we would have to learn how to make one. Hence, over the last weeks before our departure, I spent hours in the basement of our house working with balls of nylon twine strung between two pillars, tying the thousands of knots that eventually, I hoped, would make a usable net. When time and my patience wore out, Jim went on and finished the job, only a few days before we actually left.

Meanwhile, I had been reading Mackenzie's praise of the northern fish, how he and his men had set their nets each night when they camped, what they'd taken. By coincidence, it seemed, we'd hit the right solution. I took it as an omen.

My reasons for these efforts, even after much reflection, I only partly know. That is the way, perhaps, with any emotion strong enough to become a driving force in one's life; known, it evaporates. But the North! Desire of it seemed always to have been in me. I talked about it a little with Sig, that afternoon in Ely. I had just finished the trip with my two boys. They were thinking, I realized, as I had at their age, mostly of what they might have missed while we were away, of nights in motels and meals in restaurants on the way back—of *going home!* For my part, though, I felt barely warmed up, in the swing. I was ready to load up the canoe and head out again, north, as far as I could go, following the lakes and rivers—Hudson Bay, the Arctic, what could stop me? But—a family to nurture if you can, sons to get through college, the wide web of obligations constraining you: at forty-five a lot of things begin no longer to be possible.

"Why"—Sig was almost scornful "—I was older than *you are* before I made my first trip to the Arctic. *Of course* you can do it!"

I remembered an evening, long past, on a Quetico lake, the northern lights pulsing high in the heavens and my father pointing out the stars and constellations he knew. He had been about the age that I was now. The North Star—Hudson Bay lay that way, you could start from where we were and get there by canoe, how far, a thousand miles? Men had done it. Indians—farther, there was no limit . . .

It was years later before I learned much more about the canoe routes engraved across the geography of the northland by the last ice age, the Indians who used them for hunting and trade, the *coureurs des bois* and *voyageurs* who followed. They led me, finally, to Mackenzie, the most dauntless, in that summer of his voyage to the northern sea, among many dauntless men, and the pull of a remote past was bonded to that of a distant North: If you could re-experience that voyage of discovery, follow that route with his informed eyes, perhaps you could enter into his time as well. Romantic? An escape from a threatening present? And yet—

Family legend traces our origins to a Norse shore I have never seen. But it would be like the Quetico: a few elements —the gray-green granite of the Canadian Shield frosted with a thin brown loam of rotting pine needles, the mothering water, food source, leading everywhere, the pines, black and red, interspersed with birch—sorted in infinite combinations. The North: It called to me like a lost homeland, almost remembered. I would know it when I reached it. My father had said, only half joking, he wanted to die there, be buried there.

And the North, Sig, what was it like? I had images of harshness, bleakness, frozen earth—

"It's *one country*, same as this, the whole way. Rock banks along the rivers. Pine and birch and aspen—course, they get to be little bits of things by the time you're past the Arctic Circle." With his hands he shaped their size in the clear northern light. I began to see them.

I would have to get there for myself.

In the final weeks before our departure, the tempo of preparation accelerated. I was determined to get away by Memorial Day, May 27, in the hope of getting to our put-in point, wherever that turned out to be, by June 3, Mackenzie's date—for the sake of symmetry, let us say; for luck.

I have lived with deadlines of one kind or another most of my life, though never without the sense of being driven by them to the end of what I am capable of, or beyond; pain. Yet there is mercy too in such arbitrary conclusions: They set limits to what you can attempt to learn, know, do. As the end of May approached, I had assembled most of the scraps of history and current fact that I could find and on them had erected a rickety structure of expectation, projected from my own past experience. I had studied, for instance, monthly temperature reports for the whole length of the Mackenzie valley but could not be sure what they told me about weather. *One country*, Sig had said. I knew the sky and wind and currents of the Quetico, the kinds of weather they combined in that a canoeist must live with, allow for. The Mackenzie would be like that, I thought, the differences those I had found in Mackenzie's own careful notes on canoeist's weather two centuries back—between our start and the middle of June, I more than half expected to be stopped by ice jams, as he had been.

In Minnesota we drove half a day off our route to talk to another canoeist who, years back, had crossed Lake Athabasca: practical questions of routes through the Athabasca River delta, prevailing winds on the lake and the combers that might build in front of them, confirmation about food he (had taken a gun, but in the two months of the trip had time to kill only a couple of ptarmigan, the northern quail—which, he said, made a tasty but not filling stew). I expected to amplify all this at Fort McMurray but found no one who had ever canoed the river—what little they knew was from power boats, and even that was fragmentary, misleading. Fort McMurray, I thought, would be a town on the order of Ely, perhaps with more cabins, fewer houses, but still a railhead pointed toward the same northern wilderness, stoically decaying while old livelihoods declined—mining and logging it had been at Ely, fur trading and barge transport at Fort McMurray, the supply point for the remote water routes Mackenzie himself had been the first to map. Instead, it turned out to be a city in the midst of an oil-based land boom—a population of perhaps a couple of thousand, but a city nonetheless, and new-built on its old site in the past three or four years: cement sidewalks and apartment buildings and suburban-looking ranch houses on the paved street leading into town, a row of gas stations and car dealerships; big new elementary and high schools; a Hudson's Bay Company branch that proved to be not the traditional trading post but a department store on a new shopping plaza; three new motels that could take their place without a second glance on the outskirts of any North American town.

The last week before we left was feverish. I was trying to get everything in order for my wife, who, for the next two or three months, would have to manage our dual enterprise—the house with its cycle of costs and upkeep, the garden, the comings and goings of the three remaining boys—on her own; in twenty-three years of marriage, we had never been more than a few days apart. There was money to be sorted out, accumulated bills to pay, leaving her clear, several forms of insurance to deal with, an off-hours visit to the family doctor for tetanus shots, prescriptions for some all-purpose antibiotics, advice on medical emergencies in a land where there would be fewer doctors than settlements. Both cars went through a series of overhauls. Fire lighters, insurance against wet days when no wood would start, turned out to be something the local hardware stores stocked only in winter and took a day's hunting. So did gasoline cans, which might be essential to carry us the long jumps between functioning service stations in that first year of the fuel short-age—while I had been studying northern maps, others had cannily made the rounds and bought them up.

I take one thing at a time, put everything else out of mind till that is done. Hence it was not till the night before we left, with everything done that could be done, the packs all filled and lined up, ready to load into the car, that I got around to reducing the canoe trip to a detailed itinerary. Until that moment, it had not seemed important. The only boundaries were my son's finishing one semester at college and starting the next, three and a half months, mid-May to the end of August; the route itself was determined by geog-raphy, for us as it had been for Mackenzie. We would have to be able to take time where we needed it to explore the unknown, the unexpected, the lucky accidents of canoe travel as of any other. But there might be emergencies at home—my wife, I realized, would have to be able to com-municate with us at points along the way, and to do that she had to know where we'd be, and when; getting her letters in any case seemed suddenly vital, a tenuous link with home. I unpacked the maps again, ran off distances, guessed at daily mileages, arrivals, and departures. My original estimates of distance, it turned out, were wildly out for the Athabasca

River but improved as we got farther north. I did a little better on the time. I figured to take it easy at the start, on the Athabasca, be stronger and faster-moving by the time we reached the Slave River with its more vigorous current, slow down again crossing Great Slave Lake. The only thing I made no allowance for was weather. I had never in the Quetico been stopped by rain or wind. It had been a point of honor—take the weather as it comes, but don't let it stop you.

I typed up the itinerary and left it on top of the pile of things my wife had to know about. The copy went into the back of my notebook, a reminder of where to look for mail.

I refolded the maps, put them back in their case, went down to the basement, and slipped the case down one side of the plastic pack where, with the cameras, film, emergency medicines, the tape and epoxy for repairing canoe, tent, or packs, it would be safe from damp. I studied the packs, thinking through what was in each. What had we forgotten? In my briefcase there were lists of things we still had to get, mostly staple foods like flour and sugar and dried milk and oatmeal, when we crossed into Canada, to avoid the irritating Canadian duty on food (17 per cent—I had gone so far as to protest to the responsible minister in Ottawa and had received a bureaucratic answer with a packet of further regulations, including one that apparently allowed the customs office to demand a deposit on a "boat" as insurance against selling it in Canada without paying the appropriate import duty). There was also a mass of correspondence with people I wanted to see on our way out or back—a few friends, a lot of business contacts with whom I had to check details of a book I'd been trying all spring to finish.

I went upstairs and sat down at my desk again. It was late by now, the rest of the house asleep—we would be trying for an early start. What else remained to be done?

All through this past week, the sense of finality had been building. It was a feeling that everything I did, I did for the last time—the feeling of ending and farewell that you have at the moment of moving to a new house, a new place, a different job, a changed life; or, more strongly, the feeling at the end of a responsible life of having put one's affairs in order, of leaving behind for one's descendants no more than the irreducible confusions and absurdities, the accumulated baggage of human living and aging. Therefore, after the list of serial numbers—credit cards and traveler's checks, cameras and lenses, the canoe, another final duty, insurance against loss—as the first heading in my journal of the trip I wrote: Last Things. I meant both all the random finalities of preparation for long absence and man's end and the world's: Death, Judgment, Heaven, and Hell. It was less portentous than it sounds. Indeed, ironic: I was not afraid, but there were enough unknowns in the months ahead to be sobering, best faced with not too much sense of one's importance. But seriously too: The family's motto is *Semper Paratus*, a Latin cliché borrowed by the Coast Guard that means first of all a readiness for death—living in preparation for that first of the Last Things.

Somewhere in the weeks before we left I had dreamed of our departure by canoe: a steep rocky bank, at the bottom a big river boiling in torrent, the canoe loaded and waiting, a crowd of people behind us and no choice but to attempt what is beyond us; we step in, push off, are dumped, all lost. I do not dream much and take the dreams all the more seriously for their rarity. I would be watching for that particular configuration of flowing water and solid ground, would know it when we came to it. For those in life, death is a symbol, meaning transformation. We could not make this trip, my son and I, without much change.

I followed Bob Braund to the storage yard where the car would stay till August, rode back with him in his truck. We exchanged telephone numbers, his so I could give him warning to get the car ready for our return, mine "in case."

I studied the Athabasca, miles of rapids up above the bridge somewhere, the Clearwater coming in among low islands a mile or so down: fast enough but smooth, not a riffle in sight. Five miles an hour of current, Bob said, though he had never been on it in a canoe; Jim, with his pocket slide rule, calculated it at a mile and a half. This was not the place I had dreamed.

We loaded the canoe, filled it with the packs, for the first time. We held it, floating, shifted the load minutely: trim now, though the big pack, with the tent and sleeping bags, the cargo of books, looked top-heavy; we could adjust as we got the feel of it.

Jim got in at the bow, holding the canoe with his paddle. I stepped in at the stern, pushing off with a trailing foot, wary of the rocks along the bank. We looked back, waved. Just out of sight of the bridge, I steered into the eddy below one of the islands, and we went ashore to have a look at the mouth of the Clearwater, take some pictures: white sand, mud ankle deep from the flood sucking at our boots, a core of willow shrub in the middle, holding the island together. The dark clouds crossed the sun with a momentary shower, cleared. The rain garments, dignified as a doctoral robe, came off again and slid under the flap of one of the packs. We were on our way at last; on our own.

Being endowed by Nature with an inquisitive mind and enterprising spirit, a constitution equal to the most arduous undertakings, I was animated by the desire to undertake the perilous enterprise.

CHAPTER 2

For the Sake of Furs

Late in the morning of June 3, 1789, a Wednesday, four canoes struck out from Fort Chipewyan on Lake Athabasca, skirted the swampy, log-jammed delta of the Athabasca River, and headed the twenty miles north to the outlet of the lake, Rivière des Rochers—"rocky river," named by the French-speaking canoemen for the pink granite that forms its banks, a western outcrop of the Precambrian Shield. In the lead, in the biggest canoe, was Alexander Mackenzie, a twenty-five-year-old wintering partner of the North-West Company, in command of the fort and of the expedition that was now beginning.

Their weather that morning was the half-sunny kind that follows the early-June breakup of ice at the west end of the lake, neither hot nor cold, darkening at moments as the sun darts among clouds. Their goal was a great river rumored to lie somewhere to the north and west, possibly—it was no more than a hopeful guess compounded from scattered bits of geographic fact and gossip—a route through the Rockies to the Western Ocean, the Pacific: a solution to the riddle of

the Northwest Passage that had haunted the nations of
northern Europe and above all the English for nearly three
centuries. Ice was the limiting factor. They would have to
get to the end of the great river, wherever it led, and back
by late September or early October, when the lakes and
rivers would freeze again and put an end to the comparatively easy travel by canoe. The penalty for failure would be
to winter in unknown country through months of subzero
darkness, unprepared by the summer of fishing and hunting
that made it possible for the Indians of the Athabasca region to survive; as for some of them it still does.

The fort that Mackenzie left behind was no more than a
few log huts, built the year before: the most distant outpost
of the fur-trading organization based in Montreal twenty-
five hundred miles to the east, as the canoe routes ran; a
depot for the guns, knives, axes, the gunpowder and shot,
the bolts of cloth and tubes of glass beads manufactured in
England and traded here for the furs—beaver above
all—hunted by the Indians all through the northland. In
Mackenzie's absence his cousin Roderic Mackenzie, brought
over from Scotland, would be in charge with perhaps ninety
men.

With Mackenzie in the lead canoe were four Canadians—
French *voyageurs* from Montreal or possibly Quebec; a German; and the Indian wives of two of the Frenchmen, which
a tolerant North-West Company helped them bargain from
the local Indians and fed through the winters, along with
their brats. Among other things, the women would clean,
butcher, and stew whatever fish or meat was taken in the
course of the voyage; scrape and wash the hides, chew them
soft, cut and stitch them into soft moccasins, leggings, as the
men needed replacements; probably also they would put up
the tents at night, this being a woman's responsibility
among the Chipewyans, though they were not the caribou-
skin teepees of these northern Indians but white men's tents
of canvas, with sapling ridgepoles to be cut each night, guy
lines, stakes.

Another big freight canoe would accompany Mackenzie three hundred miles north for a summer of trading with the next Indian tribe, at the limit of explored territory. In charge was Laurent Leroux, a clerk—a subordinate, a junior officer in the half-military hierarchy of the North-West Company: a man under contract at a modest annual wage and, unlike his chief, with no share in the considerable profits to be made from furs, though with the spur that he too might in time rise to partnership.

Counterbalancing the two canoeloads of Europeans were two of Indians: a Chipewyan chief with his two wives and two young men, either or both of whom may have been his sons; and two hunters, the chief's followers. The chief had traveled much of the North, knew English, several Indian languages, had traded on his own account as a middleman between the whites and the more remote tribes. His function would be to translate, interrogate, negotiate with the Indians met along the way (neither he nor Mackenzie knew, when they set out, that the succession of languages they would encounter were all closely related members of the same family, more or less mutually intelligible, as, say, one dialect of Italian to another). The hunters' task was demanding in a different way: to provide meat for themselves and the eight men and four women of Mackenzie's complement; which meant tracking game on foot through the woodland, muskeg, and half-thawed tundra along the riverbanks and at the same time *keeping up* with canoes driven by their leader's determination and the desperate shortness of the season. Both functions, information and meat—the canoes could not carry enough food to last the summer—were indispensable to the success of the expedition, yet the Indians' position in the party was ambiguous. Their chief, Ageena, was the successor to another Chipewyan, Matonabbee, who twenty years earlier had salvaged a British overland expedition to the Arctic and became more than any other the model for Rousseau's Noble Savage. A great man among his people: not—with his two canoes, his white man's tent, his wives, his men—a subordinate to Mackenzie; but not an equal, either.

All four of the canoes were made of birch bark: not the papery outer bark but with the tan inner rind turned out, naturally waterproof with the juices of the living tree, (assisted, sometimes, by an application of red ocher), darkening with age to a deep brown. The bark was formed over a framework of spruce, stitched together at bow and stern with *watape*, the tough, pliant roots of the black spruce, and—since birch big enough to cover a canoe with a single piece of bark was rare, particularly in the North—stitched also along the sides where sections of bark were pieced together and gussets cut out to shape it to the canoe's elegant curves. These seams were sealed with black, sticky spruce gum that never fully hardened—one of the canoemen's almost nightly tasks was to melt a mass of resin over the cook fire and regum the canoe; in rough weather they might have to stop several times in a day, unload, and patch with gum. Apart from the seams, good-quality birch bark is both flexible and quite tough—but nevertheless to be treated with caution, particularly in the absolute wilderness. Rough-hewn planks, preferably cedar, would be laid lengthwise along the bottom of the canoe to distribute the weight of the cargo and keep it out of the water in wet weather. Where the banks were rocky, the water rough, the current swift, the men leaped into the water waist deep to unload and land the canoe, protecting its bark skin from puncture.

Mackenzie's and Leroux's canoes were both big ones: about twenty-seven feet in overall length, fifty-seven inches abeam, twenty-seven inches deep amidships; when they started out, more heavily loaded for the long voyage ahead than Mackenzie liked, his canoe probably drew close to twenty-four inches, leaving no more than a hand's breadth of freeboard. (The proportions of these basic dimensions were identical with those of the deep-hulled seventeen-footer I chose for Mackenzie's route, another lucky sym-

metry; most modern canoes are narrower and less deep—
and carry less and are wetter in rough water.) Both the
traders' canoes had the high, rounded bow and stern rising
as much as five feet above the keel line, borrowed, probably,
from Iroquois war canoes white traders first encountered far
to the east more than two centuries earlier and now traditional. The high bow and stern provided space for a painted
company mark, perhaps a Union Jack, or simply a decora-
tive emblem to suit the builder's taste, circular and geometric in the manner of the hex signs of the Pennsylvania
Dutch. They were also functional: turned over, with a tarp
stretched to the nearest pair of trees, the canoe made a shelter nearly high enough to stand in, protecting the cargo
from overnight rain, providing a place where, normally
when on the road, the canoemen could sleep out of the
weather.

Such a canoe weighed around three hundred pounds, and
on portages, when it was carried upright, bow and stern
resting on padded shoulders, it was considered a reasonable
load for two not very big men (the thrifty Scots who ruled
the Company did not favor heavy eaters—food was a cost to
be managed like any other); the *avant* and *governail*—
foreman and steersman to the English-speaking traders,
more skilled, experienced, better-paid than the *milieux*—
were responsible for portaging the canoe. It was the type
known as a North canoe, *canot du nord,* although a foot or
two longer than normal, built for the wild rivers, with their
hundreds of rapids, west and north of Grand Portage, the
great trading junction at the Pigeon River on the northwest
shore of Lake Superior; east of there to Montreal, the trade
goods were carried in Montreal or *maître canots,* usually
about ten feet longer than Mackenzie's but occasionally as
much as forty feet—the physical limit for a keelless boat
with a nonrigid frame. Probably Mackenzie's two canoes
had been built at the factory set up for the purpose at
Grand Portage—in the harsh conditions of the north, a bark

canoe lasted only about a year, and the brigades bringing
the furs out from their winter posts were likely to need new
canoes as well as the bundles of trade goods and sacks of
corn supplied for their return journey. They could, however,
have been built at Fort Chipewyan; there was an adequate
supply of birch and spruce, and canoe building, a couple of
days' work for a crew, was one of the skills a *voyageur* was
expected to have.

A paddle was each *voyageur's* personal possession, hand-
carved from heart of birch, the grip, throat, and blade tip
painted red or black, the blade itself often white—easier to
see in the murky water of muddy rivers like the Athabasca.
It was made thick in the blade for shoving off rocks in fast
water, the blade no more than four or five inches wide for
the quick stroke, sixty per minute, that the canoemen favored, timed to the rhythms of their songs (one who sang
well could sometimes earn a bonus for his voice). The
milieux, seated on the thwarts close to the water in the
deep-laden north canoe, needed paddles no more than four
or four and a half feet in length. The *foreman* and *steersman*
—together, the *bouts*, endmen—normally used six-foot paddles in the high bow and stern, but each carried a spare as
much as nine feet long for levering the canoe through
rapids, which they took standing. The northern Indians preferred a paddle with a bigger blade, often decorated with a
geometrical emblem that was also its owner's mark.

The Indians' canoes were not much over half the length
of Mackenzie's and proportionately sharper in bow and
stern, narrower-beamed—fast enough, except in the
roughest weather, to keep up with the big canoes and their
four or five paddlers. The hunters' canoe would have been
14 or 15 feet long, light enough for a man to carry miles
through the brush to a distant lake for the sake of game.
Ageena's would have been big enough to carry his women
and the two half-grown braves—18 or 18½ feet, at least 40
inches wide amidships. Both would have had the low profile

at bow and stern and the sharply rockered bottom favored by the Chipewyans—design features that make a canoe less vulnerable to the winds that sweep across the big lakes of their country, capable of the fast turns a canoe must make to live in rapids or in heavy seas.

Three thousand pounds, in addition to crew and passengers, was calculated as a standard load for a north canoe (four tons for a Montreal canoe, including a crew of eight to twelve), but stretching it a few inches all around—length, beam, depth—could add another thousand. The canoe Mackenzie chose for his expedition was on the big side, carrying nearly two tons of cargo. That would have included the canoe's basic equipment—its *agrès*, the Canadians called it: a square sail, with its topyard, underyard, and mast, which was stepped in a hole drilled through a forward thwart for the rare days of following wind; a roll of bark for patching the canoe, with a bundle of *watape* and a slab of resin; a pair of reddish canvas tarps, made moderately waterproof with a mixture of tallow and ocher; and a sponge for bailing (in the worst weather, the brass cookpot, too big to pack, did service as well). The canoemen's personal effects would easily fit within the customary forty-pound limit—like air passengers, they were required to travel light: a pair of blankets and a change of shirt and trousers, provided by the Company as part of their keep; a knife, ax, gun; and tobacco for the clay pipes, which helped make the sixteen hours a day of paddling bearable (there were regular breaks every hour or so for smoking, every four or five miles, and distances were sometimes reckoned in pipes). Mackenzie, in command, had, besides, a tin-lined, iron bound box with beveled lid, water- and animalproof, to hold his log books, the supply of ink and pens with which he wrote them, the navigational instruments with which he would plot and map the course. The Indians along the St. Lawrence, first seeing such a chest to protect the traders' goods, had called it a *wangun*, meaning that it contained things to sell, a name that among some canoeists has stuck; to the Canadians it was simply a *cassette*, a little box.

For his own use and for periodic pledging of friendship with natives along the route, Mackenzie carried one or two nine-gallon kegs of rum, ninety pounds each. Powder and shot to last the journey may have run to another five kegs; there were big nets such as served on Athabasca for fishing, thirty feet or more long and proportionately deep. Goods for trade—and for sealing terms, creating demand among men who had never seen the like—were few and light: knives, awls, beads, ninety-pound coils of Brazil tobacco, small kettles, bolts of printed cotton cloth from Manchester; no heavy guns, powder, lead; no bulky metal pots to replace the baskets of bark or woven spruce root that were still the norm for the tribes of the Northwest (the baskets were watertight; meat was cooked, when that was possible, by dropping hot stones into the water until it boiled, a tedious process). The rest of the cargo, perhaps a ton, was food: pemmican made up in standard packs of eighty-five or ninety pounds; a supply of fat; possibly flour; and a few packs of dried corn, hauled the previous fall from Grand Portage, which they saved for emergencies and rarely touched. The pemmican was jerked meat, probably caribou —cut in strips, sun-dried and smoked, then crumbled and mixed with an equal volume of liquid fat and stored in deerskin sacks. A durable and concentrated food reserved for long journeys, as it still is: With the sauce of appetite, it could be relished just as it came from the packs, but berries, if the season afforded them, improved it; boiled, thickened with flour, it made a palatable slurry when fresh fish and meat failed. Yet even a ton of pemmican, twenty or more packs, was at best emergency food. Mackenzie reckoned three pounds per person per day as the minimum to keep them going, half a pack for the party—more than twice what they could carry for the hundred and more days of the season. They would depend on the hunters and the nets; or they would starve.

Except for their moccasins, Mackenzie's canoemen were probably *not* dressed in the fringed buckskins of American frontier folklore: wool breeches strapped over knee-high stockings to keep out mosquitoes and flies, held up with a long, colorful sash wrapped around the waist, the end trailing, a *voyaguer's* most prized possession, along with his pipe; a wool shirt, a bandanna tied around the neck, another protection against bugs, a broad-brimmed hat to keep off the rain, fan a reluctant fire. Mackenzie himself wore, in addition, the kind of long, broadcloth traveling coat, with a hood, that the English called a capot, borrowing the French word (there were several spares in his kit); possibly the gentleman's and officer's tricorne of the period; and a sword on his belt, largely symbolic, though it could be a useful inspirer of respect in hostile Indians (at intervals along the route, he thrust his sword into the thawing earth and made note of the depth of the permafrost, rarely more than a foot). The traditional dress of the subarctic Indians had been caribou-hide leggings (sewed to high-topped moose-hide *mukluks*—overshoes—in cold weather), breechclout, a long-tailed, loose-fitting shirt, moose-hide mittens hung around the neck on a long string of green skin. Wool trousers (or the cloth to make them), however, were among the desirable goods the Indians bought from the traders with their furs—wool does not turn cold and soggy when wet—and Ageena's men must have had them, though they kept the traditional leather shirts and mittens, indispensable for paddling when the weather went cold. Probably as a matter of dignity the chief dressed much like Mackenzie, though Ageena had no capot of his own till late in the voyage the trader gave him one as an inducement for continuing.

Mackenzie was not among the paddlers in his canoe, though in a pinch he could turn to with the best of them. Partly, it was simply not a form of labor befitting the expedition's leader, but also he had more important work to do.

As the party worked its way across Lake Athabasca, he would be already comfortably seated in the bottom of the canoe, leaning against a pack, his log book open on his knees, his pen busy recording the course: compass directions, distances estimated from time and average speed and line of sight, the portages around rapids, when they came, paced off unloaded and noted down, described; at night, alone in his tent, he added the day's events, the character of the country he had passed through, though some of his accounts of the Indians counseled with along the way are so full, detailed, and accurate that they seem as if written on the spot. Periodically he went ashore to fix latitude and longitude with his navigation instruments and the pocket watch that served him as chronometer. He knew also how to estimate the compass deviation but never allowed for it in his log of the course. Compass deviation is the angle between true north and the magnetic pole. In places, along Mackenzie's route, the deviation would have been as much as forty degrees to the east: when his compass, headed by the bow of the canoe, showed a course as due north, it was actually northeast; his west was northwest. Both the compass and his hopes of finding a way through to the Pacific gave a consistent westerly bias to his directions.

Years afterward, Mackenzie's log was edited and published, bulked out with a description of the fur trade of the Northwest as he knew it, to the glory of British commerce; a manuscript copy of the original, evidently an intermediate stage toward publication, has survived in the British Museum. Both documents are strikingly reticent. Except by chance implication, they tell us almost nothing of the practical circumstances of the journey, perhaps from the natural human difficulty in recording or even recognizing the everyday and familar, what they ate and wore, what the canoes were like, how made—those kinds of facts we must piece out from other sources. Nor, except for Leroux, a colleague in training, did Mackenzie ever mention any of his companions by name. The crew was simply the four Canadians and the odd German. Ageena was recorded as the English Chief —he had traveled the six hundred miles overland (the water route down the Churchill—English—River and across Lake Winnipeg was unhealthy for a Chipewyan, blocked by the hostile Crees) to trade with the English at the Hudson's Bay Company outpost of York Factory in the mouth of the Hayes River; he was so known among his people. Two years after Mackenzie's voyage, a young employee of the rival Hudson's Bay Company, Peter Fidler, came prowling through the Athabasca country, met the English Chief and Mackenzie's canoemen, and reported their names to his superiors as a bit of commercial intelligence that might prove profitable. The Frenchmen's names were François Barrieu, Charles Ducette, Joseph Landry, Pierre de Lorme; the German was Johann Steinbruck, the first name Anglicized to John.

Directly, the journal tells us even less about the questions that for a modern reader come first. What combination of motives would induce a young man to hazard his life traveling across an unmapped continent where the known dangers were almost certainly less formidable than the unknown? What personal qualities would persuade or compel his fourteen disparate companions to share those risks? What kind of man would drive himself and them sixteen or eighteen hours a day toward so doubtful a goal? The heading Mackenzie put at the start of his log, when he copied it out to submit to a London publisher, provides answers of a sort: What followed was a

Journal of a voyage performed by order of the N.W. company, in a bark canoe in search of a passage by water through the N.W. continent of America from Athabasca to the Pacific Ocean in summer 1789.

To make sense of Mackenzie and his motives, we must piece out that beginning with the circumspect and single-minded hints in the journal itself, with what we know of his life and of the fur trade in which it was lived—a commercial response to the European obsession with the rich and exotic that in the eighteenth century flooded in from the limits of the earth, in particular the furs provided by the wild men, *sauvages,* of North America.

The North American fur trade had its beginning around 1500 in the casual conjunction of a pair of cultural necessities, Indian and European. The Europeans needed a new source for furs, already becoming scarce in the cold lands bordering the Baltic: furs of many kinds to trim luxurious garments, of course, or to be made up into warm robes and cloaks against killing winters more severe in the fifteenth and sixteenth centuries than at any time since; above all, beaver fur, prized in felt for its color, its thickness, its glossy sheen. (The felting process, in which the soft underfur is scraped from the hide, separated from the coarse outer guard hairs, and pressed between rollers to form a smooth, tough, matted fabric, was still fairly new, at least in northern Europe; the first occurrence of the word "felt" in English is dated 1450. The discovery of this process and of an abundant new source of the raw material created a demand for beaver hats that was both immensely profitable and very nearly insatiable.) The Indians, for their part, were equally bent on obtaining the manufactured goods that the white men could supply. There were no traditional weapons or tools as effective as the guns, axes, knives, awls, the brass or copper pots, the flint and steel for making fire, the woven cloth, that replaced them. Cutting down a big birch, for instance, the first step in building a bark canoe, is nearly impossible with a stone ax: The trunk was banded with clay low down, a fire built around it, the weak point thus made slowly chipped at—a method that with much repetition would eventually fell the tree. Cooking in a pot of bark or basketry was so slow that meat was most often roasted directly over the fire and eaten half raw.

What followed from this mutual discovery of the two cultures, in the immense territory that became Canada, was the reverse of what happened to the south but in the end no less destructive for the Indians. Wherever the land and climate suited farming and fixed settlements, the fishing and hunting of the nomadic tribes was necessarily excluded. In Virginia and Massachusetts, and over and over as the settlers pushed west across the continent, with the realization of this hard fact, the uneasy welcome of the first encounters gave way to warfare that continued until the Indians had disappeared—killed off, removed, or in some places assimilated, creating a new racial stock no longer purely European. In the northern lands, on the contrary, where the Europeans came as traders, the needs of the two peoples seemed to be complementary. Although a few whites learned to hunt and trap, merging into the Indian life, it was generally their interest and profit to stand apart, cultivating the tribal organization that produced furs, encouraging and rewarding the proficient hunters. Warfare was that of tribe against tribe, fighting, as they always had, over territory, more bitterly now that control of productive land meant more successful commerce with the Europeans; the traders' role in these wars was that of peacemakers—warring Indians brought in few furs. Where there was Indian violence against whites, it was usually not to drive them out but to compel them to set up trading posts—or, once established, to remain.

The earliest traders were Breton fishermen off the coast of Newfoundland, who went ashore for water or fresh meat to vary the shipboard fare of salt pork and beef, hard biscuit, and exchanged trinkets for furs provided by the local Indians. Early on, the fishermen discovered the economy of preserving their catch by sundrying and smoking, Indian fashion—it cost less than the older method of salting—and for that purpose regular summer camps were set up that presently became permanent bases for fishing; and for trading in furs.

The early fishing camps fitted a pattern that was general among the nomadic Indians. Those that depended on game scattered in small bands during the winter, when meat was scarce, but in summer came together by the hundreds at places where the hunting or fishing was good and produced stocks that, dried and smoked, would help them survive the winter. These summer gatherings had long been opportunities for trade among the tribes. Those like the Hurons along the St. Lawrence, whose land was poor in game, traded their corn or tobacco for furs. By the same process, native copper from deposits up the Saguenay and along the south shore of Lake Superior—pure enough so that people who knew nothing of smelting could coldhammer it into tools, valuable ornaments—traveled down the Hudson River or Connecticut River and penetrated New England. By the end of the sixteenth century, French ships were being fitted out exclusively for the Indian trade, with no thought of fishing. The Indians, at first innocent of the value of what they had to sell and of the goods they acquired, became sharp bargainers but often quite literally sold the clothes off their backs; they had learned that their beaver robes commanded a better price than the raw furs—the pelts had been trimmed and scraped, the guard hairs worn away, leaving only the valuable underfur, a saving in the manufacturing process for which the feltmakers of Paris and Amsterdam and London were ready to pay.

The cities of Quebec (where Cartier had wintered as early as 1535) and Montreal were established early in the seventeenth century as fortified trading posts at traditional summer gathering places of the Indians. There was no sharp distinction between trade and exploration. The French King and Government were as avid for profits—both directly and in the form of varied and ingenious taxes—as for discovery, and provided the troops to protect the commerce. By the 1650s, French explorer-traders had followed the Indian canoe routes up the St. Lawrence and Ottawa rivers, across the Great Lakes and through the border lakes country to Lake Winnipeg and the Red River. A pattern had been set that was to be repeated all across the continent to the Pacific Ocean and the Arctic.

For the Indians, guns were decisive among the European goods they acquired. Before, hunting with bows, spears, snares, they had lived in balance with their sources of meat and clothing, often by deliberate restraint; if they broke into a beaver lodge where seven or eight animals might be spending the winter, they customarily left a pair to breed again in the spring. Now the slaughter became indiscriminate. Moreover, as the Indians, encouraged by the demand for furs, ranged beyond their tribal boundaries, the old constraints no longer applied. The beaver, dependent on streams that he can dam to maintain the constant water level that protects the entrance to his house, does not migrate. Consequently wherever trade was established, the beavers, the heart of the commerce, disappeared, and the Indians became doubly dependent on the Europeans. Those who had relied on beaver for clothing and food became middlemen, trading European manufactured goods with more distant tribes for furs and meat. A succession of inter-tribal wars was fought—by the Iroquois, Huron, Fox, Assiniboine, Cree, Chipewyan—as those who had made earlier contact with the traders sought to protect their position and prevent their neighbors from gaining the advantage of guns, powder, shot. The once migratory hunting tribes tended, in turn, to gather around the trading posts, which were now sources of food of a sort—European grains, fat, salt meat, perhaps hominy—as well as manufactured goods. Credit supplied food through the summers, ammunition for winter hunting—and became a spur to efficient fur collection; the Indian wives who solaced the French canoemen, including Mackenzie's, were often women who had been sold by their fathers or husbands to pay off impossible debts owed to the traders. Wherever guns became available, the Indians promptly abandoned their traditional weapons—not only stopped using them but in a few years forgot how to hunt with them or even how to make them. Hence, when furs for trading were scarce or unobtainable or wars in Europe interfered with the flow of goods, the Indians simply starved—they could not buy European food, and without powder and lead they no longer knew how to get it for themselves.

The Indians' infatuation with alcohol also began early. Rum or brandy was less often traded than given: It reciprocated the tribal feast that welcomed a trader's arrival and served to soften the natives' wariness of sharp bargaining. Cultural traits, the tribal personality, varied greatly from tribe to tribe, from the cheerful, open-hearted Chipewyans to the Iroquois, harsh and obsessive, murderously submissive to violence counseled in bad dreams. A few tribes shunned drink, at least at first, the Chipewyans among them; more often, they took to it with the same abandon they showed for most other things European. The result was that those nearest the trading posts, where liquor was cheapest and most accessible, became progressively less useful, for hunting or for anything else.

What had been begun by the loss of difficult but workable means of livelihood, by novel and unhealthy food, by chronic drunkenness, was completed by diseases to which the Indians had little immunity. Across the centuries and down almost to the present, waves of smallpox, influenza, measles swept through the tribes, exterminating whole peoples as they came into contact with the traders; syphilis, though slower, seems also to have been endemic.

It was this combination of forces—exhaustion of the earlier fur country, decay of a native population that was both a market for European manufactures and a source for an important raw material—that drove the traders ever farther west and north. So far as the Indians were concerned, the effects were heightened by competition among the Europeans.

Among the French, the fur trade was powered by individual enterprise. Working for their personal profit, alone or in shifting alliance with other traders and with the merchants in Montreal and Quebec who marketed the furs and secured the European goods that bought them, the traders pushed as far into the heart of the continent as canoes could carry them within the limits of a season, seeking always fresh sources, fresh markets, where the furs were better and more abundant, the prices demanded by the natives, least. By the early eighteenth century, Frenchmen so motivated had established bases on all the Great Lakes; had pushed down into Wisconsin and northern Illinois, down the Mississippi; had worked their way up the Missouri and, from what is now Duluth, west to the headwaters of the Mississippi; and had crossed the Canadian prairies, following the Saskatchewan River upstream almost to its source in the Rockies, near the western border of what is now the province of Alberta. Throughout these early centuries, the interest of the French Government in the trade was indirect. It sought to control the supply of furs by licensing the traders putting out from Montreal in the spring, exacting a substantial fee for each canoe. It attempted also to fix prices for the benefit of the French industries that supplied the trade goods, collecting taxes in both directions. A string of forts shielded the French traders from British penetration of the markets —from New York and Albany, from the south shores of the Great Lakes; and, increasingly, from Hudson Bay.

British involvement in the North American fur trade was later than the French and opposite in method. North of New England, the British claim rested on Henry Hudson's unfortunate final voyage in quest of the hoped-for Northwest Passage through or around the continent to China and India. In

1510, the explorer sailed through the strait named for him
north of Newfoundland, down the east shore of the great
bay, and spent a starving winter, his ship locked in the ice.
In the spring, a furious crew mutinied and set their captain
and his sons adrift in a small boat; no more was heard of
him.

It was more than sixty years before the British pursued
this claim. In the 1660s, two disaffected French traders who
had worked their way west by canoe to the Lake Winnipeg
area or beyond turned up in London with a scheme for
exploiting the rich continental interior by way of Hudson
Bay: le Sieur Pierre Esprit Radisson and his brother-in-law,
Médart Chouart, Sieur de Grosseilliers. In 1668, they persuaded a group of London merchants to send a shipload of
goods and establish a post at the mouth of the Rupert River
in James Bay, the southern extension of Hudson Bay. The
profit from the furs that came back the next spring was
handsome. In the spring of 1670, Charles II granted a royal
charter to "The Governor and Company of Adventurers of
England Trading into Hudson's Bay"—the Hudson's Bay
Company. Its terms of incorporation were similar to those of
the highly profitable East India Company established at the
beginning of the century. It was to have a monopoly on the
trade; within its territory, it would have responsibilities for
exploration, settlement, and government, as well as trade.
Since that territory was defined as all the land draining into
Hudson Bay—including, for instance, Lake Winnipeg and
the Saskatchewan as well as all the rivers flowing north from
Quebec and emptying along the east shore of the bay—
conflict with the French was inevitable.

By the end of the seventeenth century, the British had
ringed Hudson Bay with rivermouth trading posts as far
north as Fort Churchill, on the dividing line between Cree
and Chipewyan territory. York Factory was the central supply and collection point, although actual operations were
managed by the directors in London—the factor at each

post kept a detailed journal, a running report transmitted periodically home, whence instructions on policy and operations were sent back. The Company's functionaries—its servants—were a secure bureaucracy, modestly paid, with none of the French traders' incentive of profit to draw them inland in search of new markets; nor, with few exceptions, did they have the energy or the wilderness skills of their competitors—when, in the eighteenth century, they made their first tentative efforts to establish upriver posts, they relied not on the swift, light canoes of the French and Indians but on heavily built rowboats manned by dour boatmen hired over from the Orkney Islands in the far North of Scotland.

The British style, then, was to wait at the coastal trading posts for the Indians to come to them. It was an unventuresome approach, but it worked surprisingly well. Low wages and comparatively cheap transportation—direct by ship along the short northern route, neither the risk nor the expense of the long-distance lake and river routes inland—meant lower prices: fewer beaver skins for a rifle, a keg of shot or powder. Moreover, the English goods were often of so much better quality than the French that the Montreal merchants who supplied the traders were obliged to smuggle their goods in from England or New York in order to compete. As a result, native leaders like Mackenzie's Ageena would travel hundreds of miles to trade with the Hudson's Bay Company, a season-long journey that, if made overland, in winter, might use up whatever supplies had been obtained and leave the Indians worse off than they began. For the shareholders, who had assembled an initial capital of £10,500, the profits were impressive. In an early year of the Hudson Bay trade, goods worth £650 yielded a shipload of furs that brought £19,000 at auction in London —not all profit, certainly, but enough to pay handsome dividends year after year while doubling and tripling the Company's capital.

The French response was to carry the trade farther and farther west and north and, from their strategically placed forts, to prevent the Indians from traveling to trade with the British, or vice versa, when necessary by attacking and burning the outposts of the Hudson's Bay Company. What followed, beginning in 1689, was a series of European wars, each with its New World counterpart. The issues in Europe were complex; the rival national claims in North America were so contradictory, so obscured by geographic uncertainty, as to make the legal rights and wrongs unresolvable —but among all the issues, none was more important than access to the fur country. The climax of this prolonged conflict did not come until the war Americans know as the French and Indian War, ending with the capture of Montreal and Quebec and the Treaty of Paris, which in 1763 ceded all of New France to the British and gave the continent west of the Mississippi to Spain.

The change of regime in Canada had little effect on the operation of the fur trade. From its posts on Hudson Bay, the Hudson's Bay Company continued its cautious probing of the interior, no longer hindered by French troops. The Montreal-based traders—"peddlers," the gentlemen of Hudson's Bay contemptuously called them—still worked on their own account or in shifting partnerships, though their primary fur market was now London, not Paris; and for that reason their names were more often Scots or Irish than French, but they were French-speaking, more or less, since their canoemen were still the same hardy *voyageurs* recruited in Montreal or Quebec. Among the new men who with the return of peace took over the trade from the French, there was also a sprinkling of Americans who had ventured north from the declining fur country of upper New York, Wisconsin, or Minnesota, following the long-established pattern—success in any area soon exterminated the beaver, which were the basis of the trade. The most interesting of these American traders who moved in after the French and Indian War was Peter Pond. It was Pond's discoveries that made Mackenzie's possible, Pond's ideas that stirred his Scottish partner to his tremendous effort.

Pond was a Connecticut shoemaker who forsook his father's trade to run off to the army in the last years of the French and Indian War; tried sailoring to the West Indies; and, in the 1760s, soon after the French capitulation, went West to enter the fur trade. "The same inklanation and sperit that my ancestors profest run thero my vanes," he wrote toward the end of his life, though the martial ancestors he imagined were Puritan tradesmen who had been in the country since 1630. "I found tareing at home was too inactive a life for me. . . ." The voice of that fragmentary memoir written in old age is that of an eloquent but semiliterate man: a talker with a persuasive presence, a "projector," to use the eighteenth-century term, a dreamer of grand schemes that, while he talked, became real and convincing to others; and, in that same recollection, with an immense physical energy as well, probably a big man for the time, powerfully built, capable of thriving summer-long and winter-deep in the remotest continental wilderness. He was also, contemporaries remembered, "odd in his manner"— abrupt, moody, violent when thwarted, unpredictable enough to be dangerous.

By the mid-1770s, Pond had reached the headwaters of the Churchill River in the far northwest of what is now Saskatchewan. There he formed a loose partnership with other traders who gave him the responsibility for opening up new territory to the north. In 1778, he succeeded on a grand scale. In that year, Pond found his way across the previously unknown Methye (or La Loche) Portage— twelve miles with canoes and the traders' ninety-pound packs, broken in the middle by a small pond, ending in a killing descent to the Clearwater River. It was the height of land separating the Churchill system, draining east into

Hudson Bay, from an entirely new watercourse flowing in the opposite direction, west and north. A new era in the fur trade and in the exploration of the far Northwest had begun.

Pond pointed his canoes down the Clearwater, survived a fearsome sequence of rapids, and entered the easier Athabasca River. A hundred and forty miles downstream, on a high bank just below the point where the meandering Embarras River branches off into the west end of the Athabasca delta, he threw together a couple of cabins and settled in for the winter. By the following spring, he had collected twice as many furs in this virgin territory as his canoes could carry out to Grand Portage. It was a fortunate beginning.

Peter Pond remained in the Athabasca area for another ten years, trading and exploring. In the end, it was Mackenzie who provided the occasion for his departure.

Alexander Mackenzie was still a schoolboy when Pond established his trading post on the Athabasca. Mackenzie had been born in 1764 at Stornoway, a port on the landward side of the island of Lewis in the Outer Hebrides—about the same north latitude as Fort Chipewyan. His mother died when he was ten. His father packed up the children and emigrated to New York, where he had a brother well set up in business. The American Revolution intervened. Mackenzie's father and uncle joined a New York regiment raised to suppress it, and the boy was sent away for safety, first to Johnstown, then in 1778 to Montreal to finish his schooling. The next year, his father and uncle both dead of disease, Mackenzie was apprenticed at the age of fifteen to Gregory, McLeod & Company, a firm of merchants specializing in the fur trade. Five years later, he had put together enough cash to finance a canoeload of goods to trade at Detroit.

Meanwhile, about 1780 Pond and his partners had formalized their relationship in a new firm they called the North-West Company, an ambitious organization that aimed to cover the whole of the West and Northwest that

Pond had opened up and to do business on a scale to rival the Hudson's Bay Company. The possibilities were limitless, and Peter Pond, counseling with his partners in the summer gathering at Grand Portage, would have put them in the most glamorous light.

It was after the organization of the North-West Company that Pond began to range more widely in his explorations of the Athabasca region, perhaps in an effort to justify the bombastic claims he had made for the new territory. He seems to have canoed down the Slave River to its outlet in Great Slave Lake, where he set up a trading post under a clerk. He also went up the Peace River, which joins the Slave near its beginning, and started another subpost. Probably snowshoeing cross-country in winter—the Indians of the area knew the use of snowshoes and tobogganlike sledges, hauled by their women, but did not yet have the dog sleds of the Eskimos, the Arctic Indians, and the Crees to the east—he reached the west end of Great Slave Lake where the huge river Mackenzie was to explore flows out to the west; he may also have followed that river to the point where the Liard enters it from the western mountains. From distant Indians, Pond heard more about the great river and another, flowing west beyond the mountains, that must have been the Yukon—it was impossible to tell whether the reports had to do with one river or two; also from the Indians (it seems unlikely that he ever got there himself), he learned of another big lake, Great Bear, two hundred miles north of Great Slave, ending in a west-flowing river that emptied into the great river.

While Pond was piecing together these bits of geographic guesswork, he heard of a new discovery that made electrifying sense of what he had learned. Captain James Cook, whose mappings of unknown coasts from Newfoundland to New Zealand, Australia, and the Antarctic were the most thorough and accurate yet made, was sent in 1776 to explore the Bering Strait, known from a Russian expedition thirty-five years earlier. His object was the old British dream of finding the Northwest Passage, this time from the west. Cook sailed north along the west coast of North America, west along southern Alaska, then through the Aleutians to the Bering Strait, north along the coast till stopped by the summer ice pack. Heading south again, he wintered in the Hawaiian Islands, meaning to try again the following summer; and early in 1779 was killed in a scuffle with the islanders. Along the way, he had surveyed the large bay on the south coast of Alaska that today is known as Cook Inlet. Shallows and bad weather prevented him from getting to the head of it, but from the driftwood and alluvial mud flats he encountered he assumed it must be the mouth of a large river. When his journals and maps were published two years after his death—and for many years afterward—it was so named: Cook's River.

Peter Pond evidently knew this journal of Cook's last voyage—or at any rate the gist of what it reported. The latitude of Cook's River, which was accurate, seemed to match Pond's for the great river that flowed out of Great Slave Lake, which was not. With a further mistake in longitude—and the leap of imagination of a hopeful, boasting, energetic, unlearned man—Pond concluded that the two rivers were the same, the distance from the source in Great Slave Lake to the mouth on the Alaskan coast no more than a few hundred miles: the Northwest Passage. He began making maps to buttress his belief.

It seems likely that Peter Pond needed a discovery of such magnitude both as a matter of personality and for the practical purpose of strengthening his position with his partners. In 1780, they had made the serious mistake of dividing Pond's responsibility for the Athabasca district with Jean-Étienne Waden, an inoffensive Swiss. For Pond it was not a tolerable arrangement. In the course of the winter, he quarreled repeatedly with Waden, finally put a pair of rifle balls through him, and left him in his cabin to bleed to death.

Eventually, there was a trial for murder in Montreal, ending inconclusively with uncertainty as to whether a British court actually had legal jurisdiction in the ungoverned territory thousands of miles north and west. Despite the outcome, Pond's partners were uncomfortable; such violence was bad for trade. In 1785, the North-West Company reorganized itself, offering Pond a share in the partnership that he considered demeaning. For a time, he stayed out, talking grandly of starting a rival company, getting support for his plan of exploration from the British or American government, from the Russians, who already had a trading post in the Aleutians. He made new versions of his map, submitted one to the Continental Congress, then unpredictably rejoined his partners in the North-West Company and returned to Athabasca. In the meantime, however, Mackenzie's old employers, Gregory and McLeod, had formed a new trading organization to compete, the Montreal Company, enlisted Mackenzie as a partner, and had set about establishing rival trading posts wherever the North-West Company was already doing business. The gentlemen of the North-West Company reacted with fury. Rival traders were beaten, their cabins burned; one of the Montrealers, Alexander Ross, sent to the Athabasca area, died—at the hands of Peter Pond's men if not of Pond himself.

It was a destructive situation for both the companies. In 1787 they merged, and Mackenzie was taken in as a partner and sent to Athabasca—ostensibly to assist Pond in his scheme of exploration but in fact with the same dividing of authority that had proved unhealthy for Waden.

It is not easy to imagine two more different men. Mackenzie, born to the harsh conditions of another northland, had also the clansman's sense of the supremacy of the group, the tribe, and a corresponding modesty, tact, circumspection, restraint; the Scots readiness to sink himself in the abstract pursuit of profit as an end in itself, a national trait nonetheless real for being proverbial. Even at the age of twenty-three, when he first followed Pond's route to Athabasca, he had qualities that the Indians and the French canoemen acknowledged with a willingness to follow him to the ends of the earth: handsome, ruddy, tireless, quick, with an abundance of coppery hair, penetrating eyes, a smiling, even disposition—he could be angry when the occasion required, his rebuke could reduce these rough men to tears, yet his anger was always purposeful and controlled, never sinking into the brooding, murderous irritability of his older partner. Where Pond was careless and approximate, working by guess and intuition and luck, Mackenzie was thorough and systematic—businesslike: Coming out from Montreal, he kept a log of the route that years after reappeared in his history of the fur trade—distances and compass bearings, the name, number of paces, and often the latitude and longitude of each of the hundreds of portages; his descriptions of the several Indian tribes have the comprehensiveness and exactitude of an anthropologist's field notes, though their motive was not scientific curiosity but single-minded furtherance of the trade; his vocabularies of the Indian languages—the words needed to do business—represent days and weeks of patient question and answer with many informants. Even in the hasty record of his original journals, Mackenzie showed a sense of phrasing that was written, not oral, the product of a basic if spotty education, self-improved.

The two men spent one winter together, perhaps two, within the confines of Pond's post on the Athabasca River. There could hardly have been any aspect of style or personality, of simple fact, on which they did not differ, beginning with Mackenzie's common-sense assumptions about the responsibility for the two deaths, but they survived each other. Pond talked; Mackenzie listened, forming his own conclusions, perhaps here and there inserting an ironic but respectful hint. Pond grew more expansive. From the mouth of Cook's River, they would point their canoes along the Alaskan coast to the Bering Strait, cross over to Siberia, head west up the Asian rivers to Europe and Russia's Baltic capital! For men capable in a season of crossing North America by canoe and of surviving its eight-month, subzero winters, the idea was less extravagant than it sounds. Pond, who had come to think of himself in terms of governments, heads of state, prepared a map for presentation to the Empress Catherine the Great. Mackenzie may tactfully have stowed it among his effects.

In the end, such was Mackenzie's diplomatic silence, his self-assured singleness of purpose, that Pond was persuaded to return to Montreal under the impression that the younger trader, actually an equal partner in the Company, was staying behind to carry out his orders. Negotiating with the several governments that might be interested in his discovery better suited Pond's dignity; the discovery itself, in the years he had been thinking about it, had passed from a hopeful supposition to a certainty safely entrusted to a man he took to be a competent underling provided by a helpful Company. Besides, at forty-eight, Pond was old for the killing life of a wintering partner. It was time for him to go back into civilization and enjoy a little of the ease he had earned.

While this delicate exchange of responsibilities was being worked out, Mackenzie strengthened his own position by bringing out from Scotland his cousin Roderic, with the double loyalty of blood and clan, to take charge in his absence. He also set about undoing most of what Pond had done in the ten years since his arrival in the Athabasca region. Pond's base, he concluded, was poorly sited and would have to be abandoned; Roderic spent the winter building a new one on the southwest shore of Lake Athabasca, near the river's mouth, which he named Fort Chipewyan for the local tribe. Pond's outlying posts he also closed (and later rebuilt in different locations). Indeed, the few references Mackenzie made to Pond when he published his account of his voyages seem designed to erase his predecessor's name from the record. Pond's "innocence" of the two deaths "was not so apparent as to extinguish the original suspicion." Mackenzie's Fort Chipewyan was "much better situated for trade and fishing" than Mr. Pond's "Old Establishment." Even Pond's place names were "erroneously" applied. His Athabasca River was really the Elk; Lake Athabasca was the Lake of the Hills. (Athabasca, meaning "place of the willow swamp," is apt enough for the west end of the lake; names vary in these languages with the aspect emphasized or the person addressed—ask the name of something and the answer will depend on the exact form of the question.) Nevertheless, Pond's names stuck. His presence, otherwise forgotten, is spread across the Northwest in names he was the first to use.

Altogether, by the time Mackenzie set out on his voyage, the slate was clean. Whatever discoveries he made would be his own.

Mackenzie's log of his voyage was not a private document —that is the first reason for its reticence. It would be studied by his partners in the North-West Company as a basis for policy; it would guide later traders along the route. That is the purpose of the descriptions of the country and its people, of the careful record of distances, compass bearings, hazards in the form of rapids, weather, scarcity of food. To Mackenzie's partners, the purpose was known, defined, and did not need repeating, but his silence about his motives was politic as well: Success, if it came, would be self-evident and would belong to the man who achieved it; failure would be imputed to the man who for years had been promoting the expedition, Peter Pond, provided Mackenzie could preserve an air of dutiful noncommitment to his older colleague's speculations.

Yet the possibilities that might follow from the expedition's success—from actually finding a way through the mountains to the Pacific—were grand enough to dazzle any trader, particularly a young man who, like Mackenzie, had only two years earlier been taken in from a despised rival company. For the small number of proprietors, the profits from the fur trade were still fabulous. The year after Mackenzie's voyage, the North-West Company marketed £88,000 worth of furs produced from trade goods bought in England for £16,000. It was not the astronomical increase of the early Hudson's Bay Company years; expenses were high—for ships out from England and back, transportation from Montreal by canoe (the canoemen's wages and food were the least expense), interest on the considerable capital needed to buy trade goods that would not bring a return in furs for three or four years (a year from order in Montreal to delivery; another for sorting, packing, and shipping to the interior trading posts; at least a third year for collecting the furs, sorting and packing them, then shipping them to the London auction). Nevertheless, in the 1780s and 1790s this cumbersome process regularly yielded £6,000 per share for the partners in the North-West Company: Mackenzie's one share was worth fifty or a hundred times the yearly wage of a senior clerk of the Hudson's Bay Company (the hirelings of the North-West Company did slightly better)—say $50,000 or $100,000 in modern terms; a few partners had two shares; the Montreal trading firms that were also in the partnership had several.

Since these profits depended on the vulnerable beaver, they could only be maintained by continuous expansion—new territories where the animals were once again abundant, new tribes to buy the trade goods with their furs. A route to the Pacific would assure that, but it would also open an even grander prospect: direct trade with China, already an important market for North American furs by way of London and the long, expensive sea route around the Cape of Good Hope. Cheap manufactured goods from Manchester and Birmingham filtered through the Northwest in exchange for furs, which might then be shipped west to Chinese ports to come home again to Europe in the form of precious silks, porcelain, tea, all carried in the Company's ships: The riches to be gained, if they could bring it off, were beyond estimating.

Yet the prospect of colossal wealth—and of the power beyond wealth that might fall to whoever could open up and control a vast new land, a new mode in the commerce of the world—was not the only or perhaps even the chief of the forces that impelled this poor boy from Stornoway. Cook's discoveries had made him one of the heroes of the age. His fame owed as much to skill, thorough preparation, and new navigational instruments and techniques, as to old-fashioned valor; and to a public hunger for facts about the remote places of the earth that his journals fed. Cook's journals provided the model for Mackenzie's own, which go beyond the requirements of commercial intelligence or his partners' limited and pragmatic imaginations. Whether or not at the outset he ever permitted himself such an ambition, they became in time the foundation of a fame not inferior to Cook's. A kind of secular immortality, both public and personal: It is not a motive often acknowledged in our time or apparently much valued. For the men of the eighteenth century, however, it remained as powerful a drive as it had been since the beginning of the Renaissance, and so it must have been for Mackenzie also, scaled to his time and place, the immediate opportunity, the modesty and constraints of his personal history.

Mackenzie and his canoes made an easy first day of it. Crossing Lake Athabasca, they were untroubled by the big waves that often torment that end of the lake, building up behind winds blowing the hundred and fifty miles of its length. They camped early, with three hours of daylight to spare, about eight miles down the Rivière des Rochers, probably at the point where the three channels in which it flows out from the lake come together in one. It was the season, then far more than now, when the spring sun is repeatedly shadowed by flights of birds—geese and ducks in many species, pelicans, the majestic cranes—bound for nesting grounds all through the Mackenzie Valley, in places as far north as the Arctic coast. Ageena's Indian hunters brought in a goose and a pair of ducks to add to the stew pot for dinner. As they landed, one of the canoemen pulled out his gun, brought down another vagrant duck, and in the enthusiasm of setting out, the canoes being all unloaded and beached, leaped into the chilly water and swam for it. The months of preparation were past, the enlisting of men for the venture, collecting of supplies, cautiously negotiating with difficult men like Peter Pond and the Company's phlegmatic, earthbound partners. Now was the time for doing.

CHAPTER 3

The Place of the Willow Swamp

A mile or two below Fort McMurray, the wind was blowing hard against us from the north, pushing the river current up in two- and three-foot waves; hard paddling. Before we shoved off again from the willow island opposite the mouth of the Clearwater, I shifted the packs, laying them flat to be out of the wind, lowering the canoe's center of gravity in case the day got rougher. It was the first of many small adjustments as I tried to learn the style of this north country we had embarked on.

I had loaded the canoe as we did in Minnesota's border lakes country where from childhood up—with my parents, brothers, later my wife and our sons—I learned most of what I know about canoeing. The lakes are small, five or ten miles long, glacier-scoured in the Precambrian Shield, connected by portages of a quarter or half a mile, and twenty miles of distance with four or five portages is a good day. You load the packs upright in order to swing them into the canoe and out, onto your shoulder, in one motion, saving time and effort on the portages. That was simply the way I did these things; one of the ways. But on these endless northern rivers and lakes, there would be no portages. "One country," Sig Olson had said of it—yes, in a sense. It was not that I did not see the differences; my whole past—those summer canoe trips in the gentler northland the *voyageurs* called *le Beau Pays*—hung like a veil between my mind and the actual country we had entered and would have to master.

We pushed on. Sprinkles of light rain bedewed us, minutes at a time, and ceased as a dark cloud hovered between the river and the sun, not enough to wet, and we no longer bothered with the raincoats. Another adjustment: The border lakes weather revolves in regular cycles, from cloudless and bright to overcast to half a day or a day of heavy, settled, drenching rain; and begins again. I had read about the limited rainfall of the North, the scanty winter snows, but such statistics do not mean much; weather must be felt, lived. It was seven o'clock, still full daylight, before we found a possible camp, the best on the river, as it turned out: a wide, flat shelf of white limestone beach, separating in layers to reveal fossil shells like miniature scallops, up the bank behind it a clearing big enough to hold a hundred tents. A trapper's establishment may have stood here once— cabin, storehouse, drying racks for meat and skins, the row of heavy stakes driven into the earth for the dog team— perhaps even a succession of minimal settlements going back to a trading post in Mackenzie's time, but now, other than the clearing itself, no human sign remained. The trees along these northern rivers—pines, spruce, aspen, birch, all bordered with the half-dozen varieties of the impotent, indomitable willow—grow meager in their short seasons and, once cut, come back slowly; centuries afterward, you can tell where men have cleared and built, from the difference in growth.

Along the river on that first day, the banks had been shaped by the sharp geometry of spring, sheered by ice breaking loose and the flood that succeeded: too steep and thickly greased with mud to climb, too tightly grown with trees above to clear—hours of ax work—for a night's camp. Our camps would be the mud-coated sandbars at the point of a river bend, the clearings around an abandoned trapper's cabin.

It was ten-thirty before we had the tent up, had cooked dinner on the limestone beach, cleaned up, and slipped into our sleeping bags for the hour of obligatory note-making on the day: still light enough to see by in the long northern twilight but later than I liked. My father's style of camping, which became mine, was one of early-morning starts, early stops. Again, it was a condition of a connected but different country where the shorter days penalize the late traveler and—stumbling over rocks and roots trying to make camp, cook, and eat, swarmed with mosquitoes, by a flickering firelight, before crawling exhausted into sleep—you learn what it means to be benighted. So you travel early and, besides avoiding a ragged end of day, have time for a before-dinner swim, an hour of sunset fishing when the fish seem as hungry as at dawn; the usual morning calm assures the canoeist of at least a few hours of travel, even if the wind comes up hard enough by noon to blow him onto shore. It was a rhythm I kept pushing for—working into the final darkness, struggling out of the tent at four or five in the morning to light the breakfast fire—but rarely achieved; it was not the rhythm of the place and season, but that too I was slow in learning.

In my last-minute plotting of our itinerary, I had figured the distance down the river from Fort McMurray to Lake Athabasca and Fort Chipewyan at about a hundred and fifty miles. Taking it easy, helped by the current, we would be there in four or five days, holding down to thirty miles a day as we put the finish on our winter's training; later we would be tougher, would move faster. The official distance turned out to be forty miles longer—another day and a half —and a recheck of the maps agreed. A slight annoyance at the miscalculation—where else had I gone wrong?—yet it did not matter much: Mail, if it got there, would wait; there was not likely to be any emergency message from my wife. In those first days, we were still fresh, unworn: The months ahead stretched forward like a boy's vision of his life, infinite possibilities framed by unlimited time to try them out. There was no need to push. A day or two could not matter much.

When Mackenzie came down the Athabasca River on his way to take charge of Peter Pond's trading post, the route was already ten years old, well known and without hazard, the final familiar leg of the long journey out from Grand Portage; no need to describe it. His interest did, however, light for an hour or so on a local curiosity twenty miles downstream from the Clearwater:

> . . . Some bitumenous fountains, into which a pole of twenty feet long may be inserted without the least resistance. The bitumen is in a fluid state, and when mixed with gum . . . serves to gum the canoes. In its heated state it emits a smell like that of sea-coal. . . .

Mackenzie's "bitumen" is a thick petroleum pitch such as had been imported to England in small quantities from the Middle East since the Middle Ages. "Sea-coal" he remembered from boyhood in Stornoway: soft coal washed up from exposed veins on the sea bottom and used by cottagers who could afford nothing better, stinking in the grate with all the sea salts and minerals that had leached through it. He had taken the time to probe one of these deposits with a long pole, had tried heating it in a kettle, tossing a blob onto the fire to see if it would burn—and had found no more use for it than the Indians: mixed with spruce resin, it could be used in the never-ending task of sealing the seams of a birchbark canoe.

In most places along the river, the banks have not changed much in the two hundred years since Mackenzie noticed them: sandy yellow clay streaked with black veins of pitch. In the years since World War II, however, several American companies, modestly encouraged by the Canadian government, have realized that Mackenzie's bitumen was actually an immense surface reservoir of oil—billions of barrels of it, perhaps, no one really knows or will admit how much; and have begun to look for ways of getting it out. Hence, in that first summer of the oil shortage, when the whole world had awakened to the discovery that petroleum is a scarce and precious commodity, the means not merely of wealth but of limitless political power, the place Mackenzie described had become Tar Island, the heart of what is now the Athabasca Tar Sands. The banks rise two hundred feet, black with oil, and have been carved into terraces. Along them, high up, in silence, trucks trundle back and forth, hauling loads of the black sand to the new refineries built side by side along the river; "an oil *mine*," the oil men call it. As we drifted past, plumes of steam wreathed the tops of the first clean, white fractionating towers that were going into production that summer, emblems of the industrial future that was finally coming to the fur trader's wilderness.

Oil—the hope that these tiny new refineries would soon be producing on a colossal scale—was the force that had changed Fort McMurray from the decaying, log-built road end I expected to a 1970s boom town. A few miles downstream from Tar Island, we tied the canoe to a floating dock made of small logs lashed together and climbed the steep, muddy bank to Fort McKay: Fort McMurray as it was till three or four years ago, a dozen Indian cabins sprawled around a Hudson's Bay Company post established there a century earlier; a school, a tightly locked church; "M'kye" they call it in the hard Scottish vowels and consonants of the earliest traders that lie across the local speech, Indian and white, like a geological stratum. The place seemed deserted. The late afternoon had settled into a steady, soaking drizzle, driving the people indoors behind lightless, curtained windows. Near the school, four brown-faced little boys appeared and danced around us, laughing and shouting, perhaps at my son's bearded face and shaggy head. Among these beardless people, with our pale skins and capelike green raincoats, we were exotics but no longer strange enough to fear. "Got a penny, mister?" one bold little boy shouted, dancing up to my son with his hand out. "Got a penny?"

We made for the only building where there was light, which turned out to be the village cafe, built not of logs but of weathering boards, painted white: a single room with a Formica-topped counter along one wall, a big stainless steel coffee maker, a soft-drink cooler, a few tables and chairs; in the middle of the room, a tall Indian youth played a solitary game of pool. We bought cans of Coke, an unexpected luxury on this second day, from the Edmonton Scot who ran the cafe—"Or there's coffee, if you like"—and sat down at a table to dry out, warm up, and answer a string of questions: Where were we from and how were we traveling and where, what kind of a canoe and how big, what was it made of? The outside world we came from began only twenty-five miles upstream at Fort McMurry, but the real distance, more truly measured in decades than in miles, is greater; for those born to it, a lifetime. The settlement was on the point of drastic change. That week, the provincial government and the oil companies had announced the future. On the wall of the cafe, a large map in several colors showed how the land was to be divided up among oil claims, refineries, an extension of the road, a new town to be built inland to house the people brought in to create these things. The presence of an advance guard—geologists, surveyors, truckers, vice presidents who arrived in company jets from Philadelphia and Dallas for a few days' fishing and on-site inspections; men like the cafe owner come to make money on food and drink and mineral rights and get out again—explained the hands-out boldness of the little Indian boys.

For their parents and older brothers, none of this was likely to make much difference: The skills to grade the roads and build the houses, refine and pump the oil, would be brought in from that remote other world in the south. Even the land, neatly mapped for buying and selling, would do nothing for them. Officially in the place called Fort McKay, the Indians were squatters on government land. The land they owned by law and a fifty-year-old treaty was the few acres across the river still shown on the map as a Chipewyan "reserve" but abandoned fifty years ago when the Hudson's Bay Company rebuilt its post on this side and the Indians followed, pulling down the cabins and floating them across.

The afternoon was getting late: time to move on. I drank the last of the Coke, put out the cigarette. Farewells and good luck. The rain was beginning to let up. The small boys had vanished. We slithered down the bank again to the canoe, leaning back as if on skis to keep from falling. Canoes and boats were pulled up on both sides of the dock. With the coming of the oil men, a road had been cut through most of the way from Fort McMurray, but the people here were still turned toward the river—highway, source of food—as they always had been, and it would take more than oil to change them. One of the boats, an aluminum one with a big outboard on the stern, was elaborately painted along one side in the multicolored lettering inspired by Peter Max. As we pulled out into the current, I squinted to make out what it said. The message was "Kiss My Ass."

Fort McMurray is the Athabasca oil project in the present tense, Fort McKay its future, in embryo. A few miles farther brought us to Bitumont, the earliest phase of the experiment, named, one would think, by a classically educated oil publicist. Here, twenty-five years ago, the first attempt had been made at mining the oil sands, separating the petroleum, barreling it, and shipping it out on barges. A cautious effort, but it had worked; Tar Island was the sequel. One man was left, I had heard, an old man who had worked there and stayed on as a tolerated half-official watchman over nothing worth guarding, knowing, it was said, as no one else now seemed to, the river ahead of us, the route beyond. I steered the canoe over toward the bank. It was late and the rain and wind had tired us. Across the river a few miles farther, there was supposed to be an open cabin that promised a night's easy shelter. This man, if we found him, could give us an exact heading. If you miss an objective and go below it, the current, caressingly gentle when you're traveling with it, is strong enough to make getting back up again an ordeal for two men in a canoe; with the darkness coming, it would be impossible—hours, perhaps, before we'd find a feasible camp site.

We left the canoe floating, roped to a willow clump, and started up. A ramp, carved from the steep bank, led back from the remains of an earthwork jetty to a group of sheds, weathered board walls sagging, the truck-size doors hanging from their hinges, the corrugated iron roofs starting to crumple and come loose. In this country where a few thousand whites and natives form a human veneer spread across millions of miles, nothing has changed much in thousands of years. Things decay slowly; whatever human that has been abandoned is indeterminately past, as ancient as Rome or the Pyramids even when its life is measured not in centuries but in decades, years.

The whole bank was crusted in layers and rolling waves of a black, rock-hard asphalt, as if a volcanic seam had burst; a test, perhaps; or simply a useless waste product of the experiment in oil production. As we climbed, an old man came down to meet us: slow, leaning on a stick whittled from a birch sapling, small, frail and lightly built, in a checked wool shirt with a scarf tied around his neck. He paused to cough into a handkerchief as we came up, rheumy eyes overflowing with moisture, but famished for talk; from the top of the bank, he could have watched us for miles down this straight stretch of river. Americans? And what did we think of that President of ours and what would happen with the congressional investigation—but we had cut loose from all that, and his news was fresher than ours; he came from listening to the radio. And since we were from Philadelphia, there was the city's hockey team to talk of with its improbable championship, the star a boy from a place only a couple of hundred miles east, a local hero. And where were we bound for, the Mackenzie delta, Aklavik—in that little thing? He pointed at the canoe with his stick, and we enlarged on it; it had taken us already through two days of rough weather. His canoe had been a big freight canoe with a forty-horse kicker, but someone had stolen the motor—not the Indians, trust them, but new people brought in by the oil; the country was changing. I looked for his boat but did not see it—he could not have hauled it up the bank—and wondered but did not ask what he did for food. Cans left off from passing boats? Had we come to fish? He talked about the whitefish on the Slave River, Lake Athabasca—only in nets, never take them with a plug; in the fall they came up the river to spawn. And the birds, the flights of geese and ducks overhead, heading north? Late this year—had we seen them?

I asked about the cabin and he pointed the channel through the midriver islands, couldn't miss it. We said good night and started down, leaving him: a small old man who had spent most of a lifetime in the North, working at one job and another, whatever would have him. Now what was left was a shack among the rotting, abandoned machines, the radio and the occasional passing boat or barge for conversation, the silence of the migratory birds; he would die here, not long. At the bottom, loosing the canoe and shoving off, I turned and waved. He raised his stick.

Explorers of the North from Mackenzie on have reported mineral wealth on the scale of Athabasca's oil. Most were men who had learned to live in the country, survive it, take pleasure in it and their own adequacy, but it was not the wilderness that drew them. Coming over the high ground of the Methye Portage, Mackenzie had looked down on the valley of the Clearwater River—the true gateway to the North, the beginning of the immense system of waters draining toward the Mackenzie River and, ultimately, the Arctic Ocean—and put down a record of what he saw:

> The valley . . . is confined by two lofty ridges of equal height, displaying a most delightful intermixture of wood and lawn, and stretching on till the blue mist obscures the prospect. . . . Nor, when I beheld this wonderful display of uncultivated nature, was the moving scenery of human occupation wanting to complete the picture. From this elevated situation, I beheld my people, diminished, as it were, to half their size, employed in pitching their tents in a charming meadow, and among the canoes, which being turned upon their sides, presented their reddened bottoms in contrast with the surrounding verdure. At the same time, the process of gumming them produced numerous small spires of smoke, which, as they rose, enlivened the scene, and at length blended with the larger columns that ascended from the fires where the suppers were preparing. It was in the month of September when I enjoyed a scene, of which I do not presume to give an adequate description. . . .

It is, I think, a double vision such as a highlander might have experienced descending the hills around Glasgow or some other outpost of eighteenth-century manufacturing: the smokestacks of the Industrial Revolution signaling the coming of prosperity to an impoverished land. It was a human vision that led Mackenzie across the divide: of an empty land to be transformed and made productive, humanly useful and valuable, by a human presence, by human activity; the future penetrating the present.

That transformation seems still as remote in most of the North as it was for Mackenzie. Mineral deposits are dotted all across the land from the Athabasca River to the Arctic—

oil, coal, zinc, lead, uranium, gold—in a magnitude still only sketchily known. Periodically, for reasons in the outside world that have little to do with what is actually in the ground, there is a flurry of prospecting, claims are surveyed and staked, bought and sold, mines opened, worked for a few years, abandoned. Succeeding Canadian governments over the past sixty years have been ambivalent about whether to exploit the wealth of the North—and how and at what cost—or to preserve it untouched as an endowment for an indefinite future. This uncertainty is first of all human: There are not many inducements strong enough to lure skilled men from the settled parts of the country or to keep them in the North once they have come. Like the first Europeans on the shores of North America, they recoil from such emptiness until they can remake it into something like their remembered home; not many, like the old man at Bitumont, stay long enough to become part of this land, incapable of leaving it, no longer fitted for the crowded, nervous, ordered civil life of cities. There are perhaps forty thousand people in the whole of the Northwest Territories—the figures are as vague as the records of known mineral deposits—and half of them are Indians and Eskimos, passively worked on by social theories devised in Ottawa, caught between a past no longer recoverable and a future they have not yet learned to live in.

The first night out from Fort McMurray, we tried the net. Neither of us had much notion of how to manage it. We hooked floats along the top, lead weights along the bottom, tied one end to a rock on shore and pushed off in the canoe to anchor the other end out in the current. In the morning, the weeks of effort that had gone into making it were rewarded with a big northern pike which, filleted, made a hearty breakfast. "Setting the nets" had been an almost nightly incident on Mackenzie's voyage, and he kept track of the number and kind of fish hauled in each morning and of the men's mending of the nets—the fish, caught in the meshes, wind the net in a tangle, breaking the strings but rarely getting out; constant retying is part of the work. Nevertheless, I felt inhibited about using the net—someone had told me it was against the law—and decided, after trying it out, to save it for emergencies.

Hence, I was curious, two nights later, when we found a big net strung across a small stream that flows into the Athabasca. Up on the bank was another cabin we'd been making for, figuring there'd be enough open space around it for us to camp. But the cabin was a wreck—thirty feet above the river, the spring flood had floated it off its foundation and set it down again, broken-backed—and the level ground around it was occupied by a pair of tents; tied to the bank was a big freight canoe with two motors mounted on its square stern. The man who owned it came down to meet us, a big fellow in the green coveralls of a trucker or mechanic, one of the new oil workers, perhaps, a face as Scottish as his name. We exchanged the ritual cigarettes. Out for the weekend from McMurray (it was Friday by now)—his wife, he said, the woman reclining in a deck chair in front of one of the tents, dark glasses over her eyes, a broad-brimmed hat shadowing her face, gazing at us in silence. Our canoe did not much impress him. In his own, with the big motor, he made it from McMurray in four or five hours, twenty miles an hour, where for us it was three days, now. He had a still bigger one on order—$1,500 it came to these days.

I asked about the net staked across the stream mouth. His? Consternation ruffled his square, honest-guy face. No, no, that was illegal for a white man, an Indian fisherman had come by in the afternoon to set it up. Indians could net all the fish they wanted, but only for their own use, not to sell: "They feed them to their dogs."

It is one of the things every white man of the North knows about the Indians, invariably spoken with an edge of bitterness; the fish are mostly whitefish, slow-growing in these cold waters but big and abundant, and they can be taken only in nets. It is also true—but only in the sense that the dogs, thick-furred and wolflike, perpetually clamoring for food, eat whatever their masters eat and anything else they can scavenge, down to an unguarded pair of boots or the leather straps off a pack. (There are cautionary tales against defecating upwind from a dog; an explorer noticed that his beard, roughly trimmed with a knife when it became cumbered with his frozen breath, was immediately gobbled up and reappeared the next day after passing through the dog's intestines.) The fish, gutted, split, sun-dried, and smoked, will keep through the winter, though by cutting holes and using long poles it's possible to set the nets under the ice. Brown and oily, the fish can be eaten in that form, filling and pretty good, if monotonous; or it can be boiled up into a stew; some of the older people still pound it into a meatless pemmican, as a concentrated food for travel and hunting.

We finished the cigarettes, said good-bye and good luck, and pushed off toward a small island a mile or two downstream, little more than a high sandbar held together by a nape of willow. Unpromising, but there was space enough to pull the canoe out, put up the tent, build a fire; we were beginning to learn. I used a paddle shovel-fashion to dig a hole that would shelter the fire; Jim cleared some stubs of willow and with another paddle leveled a spot just out of reach of the river for the tent.

In the months ahead of us, we would hear and qualify by skeptical observation the few other things the whites know of the Indians: that they are maintained in idleness by the government—by "welfare"; are paralyzed by alcohol; and are chronic thieves, though the Indians themselves, warning you never to leave a canoe or pack unguarded, blame the children. The situation was not fundamentally different from the one the fur traders had created, nor did it seem blameworthy, on any side. The traders—and Mackenzie was a just, observant, and tolerating man among many who were at least careful about money—had seen real needs, having to do with easing the conditions of life, and had acted on them for their own abundant profit; the functionaries who devise social policies do much the same. Neither has been capable of connecting action with reaction, effect with effect; which for the Indians, on the whole, has been destructive. We shall come to particulars.

All this came later and slowly. In our week down the river, the most striking thing about the natives was their absence. Until the end of World War II, the river was still the beginning of the high road to the North. Now, although government-subsidized dredges kept the channel open and a few barges still carried heavy freight to a couple of sawmills and two or three roadless villages on Lake Athabasca, the axis of transportation had shifted west, to a road and railroad built since the war. The people had departed; or had gathered into settlements like McMurray and Fort McKay. Hence, although we passed a dozen trappers' cabins (and in one place several, the nucleus of a settlement assembled around one strong family, good fishing, abundant meat and furs), none was occupied. At one, a hungry cat growled to be fed while it waited for its absent owners. Most of the cabins were long since abandoned, the doors hanging open, the oakum leaking out of the chinks between the logs. The flood had hastened the process, undercutting the banks until the houses built on the cleared ground at the top had begun to slump, to fall in and be carried off in a later spring. The areas marked and numbered on our maps as reserves were all, like the one opposite Fort McKay, deserted, though older men still came out in winter from the settlements to trap; it was their land, habitual.

It was not till near the end of the river that we found any people actually living on it. By now it was beginning to be important to find someone who could tell us about the course through the delta. A few miles farther, the map showed the river dividing into three or four big channels, many smaller ones, all swamp between. The channels spread like the fingers of a hand, emptying into a bay at the end of Lake Athabasca. The difference between finding the right channel or not was as much as ten miles of open water from river mouth to Fort Chipewyan on the other side of the bay; we'd had enough warnings about the danger of crossing it in a canoe to make us cautious. Although we had not yet reached the dividing point, we had already had a taste of the delta. The river had slowed and narrowed, under the bright June sun it meandered in lazy arcs like a tidal stream in the far South, and the canoe hung bewitched on the mirrored surface like Coleridge's "painted ship upon a painted ocean"; the sun had burned my hands the color of old oak, drying them to the texture of parchment. The night before, we had camped on a narrow beach between the river and a willow swamp, swept clean of wood and coated with mud; hunting something to burn along the edge of the willow thicket, I had broken through the dry crust and sunk to my boottops in soft ooze, and for a panicky moment I wondered if I would be able to pull out again.

Toward noon we reached a cabin that looked occupied: a log dock built that spring, two or three boats, a canoe. Dogs staked back from the shore set up their wolflike yipping as we tied up; a man came down from the cabin, small, brown, and slight, gray-headed, to see who had come. I asked about the way through the delta. He could show us, he said, if we had maps.

The cabin was small, with a narrow entranceway built on at the front: a scoured wood table on one side, three chairs, a cast-iron stove, the room behind filled up with a bed. We sat down at the table, our backs to his wife, a handsome, black-haired woman who took her place in a corner by the stove; propriety—with strangers, it was for the man to talk. I offered cigarettes, spread the map out on the table. Now, the route? We wanted to come out onto the lake as far west as possible, follow the edge of the bay around to Fort Chip, but from the map I couldn't tell which channels were passable—we'd been warned—

"The canoe channel," his wife suggested. He studied, hunted a pair of steel-rimmed glasses, followed a branching channel with a fingernail, remembering—no, blocked by a logjam now; it was a long time since he'd been that way. Yes, the canoe channel, he had it now, and showed me, several turnings to catch—tricky; I marked them with my ball-point pen.

His wife got up, offered to make coffee, the universal sign of northland hospitality, and shoved a wad of paper into the stove, lit it. The paper flared, smoked, burned out. "Wet wood," she explained, and sat down again.

I asked questions, cautiously, not ready to leave yet. Conversation in the white man's sense of talking at random, for the pleasure of it, for the sake of civility, is a kind of impropriety, unworthy of a serious man; the purpose of talk is question and answer, information, negotiation—otherwise, silence. Did they, I tried, live here all year round? We had seen the abandoned houses along the river. . . . No, this was his *trap line*—they had a house in Fort Chipewyan, came out here for the summer, he alone for parts of the winter, for the furs; there was only one other family on the river now, cousins.

I had been wondering about a place name that occurred several times in the area: there was the winding Embarras River branching off several miles up, a settlement marked on the map as Embarras Portage, of which all trace had vanished; and a place called simply the Embarras, a great bend in the river around a hundred-foot clay cliff, which we had climbed—and found only a sawmill and a fat millhand who had never heard of the name ("Eddies," he had said with an air of special knowledge, warning us about canoeing the river; "we call them 'eddies.'"). *Embarrass*, I asked, saying the word in English: What did that mean? It was, I thought, an old French word for a tangle of driftwood that might collect at the river bends in the spring, an obstacle to be broken up or portaged around.

Ah, *embarras,* the woman said, pronouncing the words in French, *Embarras Portage?* I found her speech clearer to follow than her husband's, mission-taught, strongly Scottish like the whites' but with the lilting music of her Indian tongue; and under that was another layer of language as she said the French words with the soft, archaic *r*'s of the eighteenth-century canoemen who had given the names. She shifted into Chipewyan, still talking to her husband's back, explaining the question, discussing possible answers. No, she said at length, they did not know what the word meant. Simply, it was what these places were called. They had always been.

Again she offered to make coffee and lighted a ball of paper in the stove, watched it go out: wet wood. The gesture had been made, but I was getting hungry and it was time for leave-taking. We said our thanks, farewells. The man came with us down to the canoe and waved us off.

I had expected to get out to the end of the river, where we could see the lake, by late in the day, then camp for the night if it looked too rough to cross and go on in the morning calm. The country did not give us that choice. Once we had entered the maze of channels, there was no stopping, no turning back. The channels wound through overflowing swampland held together by thick-growing willow shrubs that stretched as far as we could see with no solid ground. The wind was blowing in hard from the lake now, so strong it was impossible to tell whether we were traveling with the current or against it, in the right direction or completely turned around as we followed the twistings and turnings of the route the Indian had told us. For hours in the distance ahead I could make out the open space that must be the lake, but we seemed never to come nearer. An Indian and his son in a big plywood scow were headed the same way. They would pass us, smiling and waving, stop, idling the motor, to pull in a net, go on. Finally, toward the end, we caught up with them where they had cut the motor and seemed to be waiting.

"Fort Chipewyan across that way?" I shouted, pointing—by now, with the wind and the constant veering of the channels, I was no longer sure just where we'd come out. The man nodded. "You worried about crossing?"

"I'm worried about *you*," he answered. "Big wind out there, big waves."

"We're not going to cross. We can follow the shore around."

He looked dubious: "No good in a canoe. Dangerous." He started the motor again, eased the boat out into the channel, and was gone.

The willow spread all around us, golden as a field of ripe wheat, moving in waves with the wind. We could just see the lake down at the end; probably it was as rough as the Indian had said. We tried pushing through the willows, which were shelter—if we could get through to the head of the bay there might be some place to camp and wait for a calm—but except in the channel, kept clear by the comings and goings of the fishermen, the way was blocked by big logs of driftwood laced together like jackstraws; the meaning, finally, of *embarras*. I remembered: The Minnesota friend who had canoed this way had mentioned the logs, tightly packed miles out into the lake; in a bigger canoe than ours he had swamped trying to cross this same large bay—it had not looked bad from the shore, but then the waves were pouring over the stern, filling the canoe to the gunwales.

To be free is to have choices, even if they are all bad; compulsion is enraging—or so for me. But here there was no choice. We could not get through without going out into the lake; we could not go back up the river to the solid land at the beginning of the delta—the day was late, it would take hours even if we could find the way again in the half darkness of the northern summer night; we could not wait where we were—the canoe was too tightly loaded to sleep in. We would have to chance it.

We paddled on out to the end of the channel. The waves were coming straight at us from far down the lake, lost in distance. Then we were in them. I swung the canoe around to the left, heading north across the bay. We would take them obliquely at as tight an angle as I dared. They were bigger than I had been able to see, three and four feet, twice the depth of the canoe at its deep bow and stern, but rolling and wide-spaced: Paddling hard to keep ahead, we rode down, then up and over. The wind roared in my ears. I could barely hear to shout directions, congratulate us and the canoe that we did not seem to be taking much water. My arms were getting stiff and tight with fatigue, bruised tender where I braced the paddle against the gunwale, ruddering; it was all I could do. No stopping to rest now: A moment's hesitation and the canoe would swing around into the trough, the waves would dump us, everything lost.

Hours of this, endless. And then we were across and driving along the edge of a little cove that half broke the wind. I steered in among some big floating logs and tied up. We lay back, resting. I looked back. It was hard to see just where we had come, the sun, that way, was near setting, the shore line a band of black. Fort Chipewyan must be only a few miles ahead now, but I could not make it out, the dark mass of a group of islands was in the way, and all between thick fields of willow growing in the shallows like reeds, flooded by the driving wind and waves. We stood up to urinate over the side of the canoe, dug some cheese and sausage and bread out of a pack, a chocolate bar to split. It was nine or ten o'clock by now, not dark yet but too late to find our way through the willows to the settlement. We headed for an island that, if we'd read the map right, must be about half-

way, winding among darkening channels through the
willows. It was after midnight before we reached it, full
dark.

The island, after the hard crossing, the days of camping
on the mud flats along the Athabasca, was an immense relief: high and rocky, topped with pines, with a shelf of
clean, bare rock along the water—a piece of the *Beau Pays*
transplanted from the border lakes country, welcoming, embracing; a kind of homecoming. We unloaded, pulled the
canoe out. Jim carried the tent up to set up on soft, level
ground among the trees. I lay down, too tired to move. But
we still had to eat something. I found a can of beans, emergency food, as yet untouched, the little gasoline stove we
carried for the same purpose; it was too dark to find wood, I
was too exhausted to collect rocks for a fireplace, build a
fire. But I could not seem to get the stove to light; or the jet
sputtered with a smoky flame feeble as a candle. I took it
apart, cleaned it, emptied the tank and refilled it; nothing. I
became more and more depressed, and the feeling doubled
back: self-disgust that so small a thing could bother me so
much. Drop me anywhere in the wilderness, I had boasted,
with a knife and a box of matches and I'll manage, I'll survive and get out again. Perhaps; yet now that self-reliance
seemed contemptible, as if all my life I had depended not
on myself but on things, a series of tiny defenses against no
longer having a choice, one more thing that I could do to
postpone failure and despair. I had worshiped them as truly
as a savage the magic carried in a pouch at his breast, and
when they failed me I was lost. And we were still only at the
beginning of the trip, the sixth day out—the easiest
part. . . .

We ate the beans cold, out of the can. I dipped up a jar of
sluggish water from among the willow stems and mixed
some lemonade.

While we ate, I noticed a glowing orange light across the
lake where we had come from. A big building, burning? But

there was nothing over there. I studied it through binoculars, unable to think—and realized finally that it must be the moon coming up, the first time we had seen it, but diminished through the sharp angle of the northern atmosphere; remote, a stranger.

In the night I woke, cold, and crawled out of the tent for an hour of diarrhea, mosquitoes swarming in the chilly darkness, pricking at my tender skin like burning needles. It was only fatigue made worse by rage and hunger, but it seemed the beginning of the final defeat: We had merely been settling the silt out of the water, not treating it, but with the flood it must be poisoning us. I took a couple of the all-purpose pills the doctor had prescribed before we left, another white man's talisman, and went back to bed.

It was late in the morning before I managed to wake, feeling dried out and transparent with fatigue. The wind was beginning to blow again, nattering at the tent. I got a small fire going, mixed up some Tang, heated coffee—all I felt able to take in, keep down. Lobstick was the odd name of the island we had got to, one of a group guarding the town which from this side we still could not see; the word for a tree trimmed of its branches so as to leave only a tuft at the top, a sign the *voyageurs* learned from the Indians—"we are camped here" or "come this way." We had headed right.

Getting to the place had become unexpectedly important: mail from home, letters to write, film to send off for processing; certainly a rest from the struggle with the delta, perhaps a chance for a meal cooked by someone else, eaten at a table. Above all, it seemed, I needed to be among people again. It was another small discovery about myself. One way or another, my life has insulated me against the human herding instinct, gladly, on the whole; a writer's work is necessarily done in solitude. Now, the week on a river whose people had departed had shifted the balance—and I needed them after all. Being with my son was not much help. Despite radical differences in temperament, we are enough alike in attitudes, in the ways we think, the things we mean by the words we use, so that talking to him is like talking to myself, like being alone; and, constrained by our sense of our respective roles, we do not talk much. I needed to be with other people; he too, of course.

We finished the lukewarm coffee, packed up slowly, loaded the canoe, and pushed out through the willows. Rounding the island, I caught the first sight of Fort Chipewyan across the two miles of choppy water: a row of little houses, painted white, lining the beach like an English fishing village but rougher, poorer, closer to its harsh beginnings; a green hill behind, surmounted by the radio tower that meant communication with the world to the south. At one end was the glum bulk of the mission school, built of gray stone. Near the center, aligned with the shore, the wooden church faced east, its New England meetinghouse spire pointed at the sky.

The whole of the party were now employed in taking the baggage and the canoe up the hill . . . . The men and Indians were very much fatigued. . . .

CHAPTER 4

We Are Not Dead but Live

The morning we paddled into Fort Chipewyan, Indians on the beach were cutting up driftwood with a chain saw, a hugh pile of sections of tree trunk several feet across, cut to fireplace length and ready for splitting. As we tied up at a small dock pushing out from the beach, boats followed us in, towing whole trees gathered in the Athabasca delta across the lake; it was what kept the channels open. That must always have been where the people got their firewood. The sandy soil around this end of the lake is a thin frosting on the underlying granite; the wood it supported could never have been big or abundant.

After the sober warnings against thievery, I left Jim to guard the canoe and packs and headed for the town's one dirt street, looking for the Hudson's Bay store—"The Bay," as it likes to call itself. Even here, although the road led only to the new airport a couple of miles around the point, there were pickups and a few cars hauling up and down, an ancient tank truck crawling in low gear to settle the yellow clouds of summer dust. There would be mail there, perhaps with luck an opening to the famous hospitality of the North

—a place to stay or at least pitch our tent for the night. I was not ready to go on.

I found my way back past the checkout counters, the grocery department, the clothes and furniture and guns and hardware to the office at the back of the store. "*Mister* Shelton," the manager firmly and formally introduced himself, a rubicund, industrious Scot in a tweedy business suit, the same man I had innocently written the previous fall to ask about the road to Fort Chipewyan. My arrangements for mail turned out to be another mistake: In the most recent book I'd been able to find about the Canadian North, the Hudson's Bay man was still everywhere the postmaster as well, that was simply what you did about your mail—a misapprehension that provided us with at least one introduction in every settlement we stopped at for the rest of the summer. No, Mr. Shelton explained after pulling a letter from his in basket—"I was wondering what to do about it": The mail was one of the vestigial functions of government that the Bay was at last divesting itself of. No profit in it—and he launched into a disquisition on the high cost of doing business in the North.

I asked if there were anyone who could put us up for the night. Nothing! Here were government people coming and going, prospectors, engineers—this unspoiled village, magnificent lake, grand scenery, splendid fishing—and nothing in the way of hotel or restaurant. A natural resort: It was an ungrasped opportunity; it stirred him with a moral fervor. (Nearly all the Hudson's Bay managers and clerks turned out to be, like Shelton, fellow tribesmen of Mackenzie, spiritual descendants—"We don't seem to mind the climate or the small-town atmosphere," one of them modestly explained; the company advertised regularly in the Glasgow and Edinburgh papers, the little weeklys scattered across the Highlands. To the Scots, this land of many deprivations was pure opportunity; Shelton himself had started out in a post farther north, had worked himself up and south, and seemed destined to continue the climb to Fort McMurray, Edmonton, perhaps even the northern headquarters in Winnipeg.) Still, although a satisfactory hotel and restaurant were yet to be built, there *was* a sort of motel, a cafe with three or four rooms built onto it, but they were always full—

I headed down the street to the Delta Inn, the sort of truck-stop diner that sprouts next to the gas station at any American country crossroads—a room divided by a counter with a row of stools, refrigerator, sink, and stove on one side, three or four tables on the other—but without the trucks; a nonfunctioning jukebox stood in one corner, the country rock music of the CBC's Northern Service blowing steadily from a radio behind the counter. Near the door, like the *patron* guarding the *caisse* in a provincial French cafe, the innkeeper sat with a cashbox and an adding machine, a slow and amiable man with long face framed by bushy, graying sideburns, a well-fed belly hanging over his belt: fifteen cents for coffee, twenty-five for ice cream; he punched the keys, pulled the lever for the total, and—forty cents, with an air of wonder—these machines!

I wondered about a room, just the one night; the possibility of a bed having offered itself, it had become essential. Ah! His rooms, unfortunately, were all occupied. Still—I explained that we had canoed from McMurray, we were tired: Perhaps . . . yes, something could be arranged. His looks, his gestures, his speech, not the local Scottish but French perhaps: archetypal, I had met this man a thousand times in bars and small shops in Paris and the little towns of central France, and—V*ous êtes québécois, monsieur?* I asked. *Ah, non!*—his only French. His grandfather was from there, Québec. A touch of Indian then, I thought. Fort Chipewyan had grown around a trading post built to replace Mackenzie's twenty miles across the lake: 1800, the oldest settlement in Alberta continuously occupied, time enough for mingling; the grandfather might have been a Nor'wester, a canoeman, a clerk. The Indian languages—did he speak them? Ah, Cree—not so bad. He gestured: his wife, a Cree, dark, broad-faced, and heavy-set, in a long black skirt, sat at a table in a room off the kitchen, knitting; their daughter, Indian as her mother but lithe and pretty, worked behind the counter. And the other language, Chipewyan? No, impossible—another gesture; no one could learn it.

We carried the packs up to the inn, piled them in the basement—easy building here, not far enough north yet for permafrost—where we would sleep that night, in our sleeping bags, on the unmade beds of two Indian serving girls, curtained off; last, the canoe, and set it down beside another at the back of the building—safe there, the innkeeper said, no one would bother it. We settled at the counter for a late lunch of scrambled eggs. Still feeling delicate, I asked for milk. The girl carefully poured out a large glass of cream from the refrigerator. *Milk?* There was no milk.

Now that we had a bed for the night, the pressing question was the river ahead—rapids unmarked on our maps and the course through them or around, other hazards, possible camp sites we could aim for; after our struggle crossing the delta, I was cautious. Above all, there were the big rapids near Fort Smith a hundred miles down the Slave River, the only real barrier between us and the Arctic coast fifteen hundred miles distant: 15 or 16 miles of rapids, a drop of 110 or 115 feet, like a Niagara laid on its side (exact figures, like all others in the North, are hard to come by and vary from source to source; on another river 150 miles due west, the same geology has created two spectacular falls measured at 109 and 50 feet, respectively). We had had plenty of warnings about the rapids but all from boatmen, no one who could tell us the actual routes or the portages; Mackenzie's own notes were not full or detailed enough to trust.

Mr. Shelton, who never traveled by water himself, had suggested I talk to one of the wardens—"rangers," in American—of Wood Buffalo National Park. Mackenzie had mentioned the buffalo in the high plains west of the river, a

different species from those of the American plains, bigger;
the herds, killed off, were reintroduced in the 1920s and
now roam a park sprawled across northern Alberta and the
Northwest Territories, a rough rectangle a hundred miles
wide, two hundred miles long, bounded by the Athabasca
and the Slave. The park management, flooded out, had
pulled back to the two towns, Fort Chipewyan at one end,
Fort Smith at the other.

A warden, Ian Tempany, another Scot, cautioned me cir-
cumstantially about a rapids halfway down the Rivière des
Rochers, the name given the three-channeled outlet of Lake
Athabasca in the thirty miles before it joins the Peace River
and becomes the Slave; I marked my map. He did not know
the big rapids at Fort Smith, but there was a man there who
could probably tell me about them, a kayaker who had explored the river, was interested in its history; I could telephone. We swapped bear stories. The wardens packed their
meat and bacon in a metalbound *cassette* any time they
traveled into the park, but still an occasional raiding bear
broke in, made bold by hunger and the delectable smells (I
was counting on a fiberglass *wangun*, an experiment, to do
the same job). While we talked, a small, aging, heavily
muscled man came up and was introduced, a tanned,
crinkly-smiling face, eyes narrowed by long looking across
bright water into the sun, a rich-burred voice transmitted
unchanged from the heart of the Highlands: Simon Fraser.
For any canoeist he was a living monument to an epic history. In 1808, his grandfather and namesake, Mackenzie's
trading successor, had started from here, crossed the
Rockies, and descended the river that bears his name, to the
Pacific, the first white to survive it by canoe; possibly the
most difficult and dangerous stretch of water on the continent that is reckoned as more or less canoeable.

That night, from the pay phone in the cafe, I telephoned
the number in Fort Smith, a complicated exercise in northern technology that apparently involved routings through

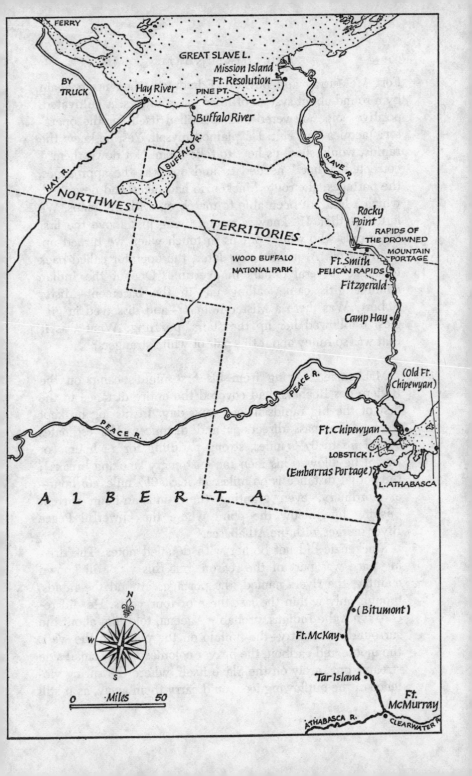

Fort McMurray and possibly Edmonton, then north again by a round-about system of microwave towers. A cultivated, positive voice answered and identified itself for the operator: Jacques Van Pelt. I explained myself. Yes, he knew the rapids, would show us how to take them. Not down them, I corrected. What I needed to find out was the approaches, the portages: the route Mackenzie had taken and described, which I had not been able to match up with my maps. We left it at that. He knew someone living just above the first big rapids who would put us in touch when we turned up. We rang off. A quarter hour later, the operator called back to collect several dollars in overtime. One of the Indian counter girls came calling me in the basement—Mister Robert? Was there a Mister Robert?—and dissolved in giggles. I followed her up the stairs, puzzling: What was it that was so funny about this pair of white strangers?

Mackenzie, starting from his first night's camp on the Rivière des Rochers, had covered the entire distance to the first of the big rapids in one long day. In his log he kept track of compass directions and distances. His estimates added up to 67½ miles, strong paddling for 14 hours (or less, if he allowed his men the customary smoking breaks); the actual distance is 90 miles, at least 6½ miles an hour—extraordinary, even granting the 2-mile-an-hour current pushing him below the point where the powerful Peace River merges with the Athabasca.

Mackenzie did not bother with detailed notes. The driving pace was part of the reason, but this was still known country, the rivers named, the portages around the rapids, though only within the last three or four years. He did record what the Indians, probably Ageena, told him about the surrounding country—the buffalo on the plains to the west, the moose and caribou, the beaver colonies up the small side streams but rarely on the Slave itself, where the spring violence of the outflowing ice would carry them away, as it still does. He knew also of the salt springs and deposits of pure, clean salt west of the Slave; the Chipewyans ranging the territory, Ageena among them, brought salt to the post to trade, a commerce that, if they were like Indians everywhere else with a commodity their neighbors lacked, must have been long established before the fur traders arrived. (More than once, passing the mouth of one of the streams flowing in from the west, I caught a mysterious whiff of the sea—and remembered; the salt pools. Yet the streams were not salt enough to affect the plant life growing along their banks, above all the ubiquitous willow that, in the absence of the water grasses and reeds and wild rice farther south, feeds the moose.) The riverbanks were thick with water birds—geese, ducks, swans, an occasional beaver exploring beyond the safety of his normal domain; so many, the trader noted, that "without suffering the delay of an hour . . . we might soon have filled the canoe with them, if," he considered, "that had been our object"; as of course it was not.

Mackenzie's one long day took us three and a half. We did not keep his hours—I was late to bed in the midnight twilight, struggling awake toward six with the sun full up—but the weather slowed us and we took time for exploring. I did not yet feel the urgency of the season. The summer stretched limitless ahead.

We camped early the first night on a high, rocky island that breasted the current, as welcoming as Lobstick back on the lake; there was a look of rain in the sky, and we got into the tent just as it began. We were trying the net again, and within minutes I heard the thrashing of a good-sized fish and went out in the rain to pull in and clean another northern pike. The rain sputtered on through the night and all the next day. In the morning, to shelter the fire, I hung a big sheet of plastic I'd brought for such days, the one time we used it the whole summer, and we ate a leisurely breakfast, waiting for the rain to stop. In the Quetico we made it a point of honor never to accede to weather, but packing up in the rain means that everything gets wet, takes days to dry. Toward noon, it let up and we hastily loaded the canoe and pushed off. The rain came on again, blinding and cold. With the wind against us, blowing the river into rough chop and baffling crosscurrents, it took us three hours to go a couple of miles.

By the next morning the weather had turned around: bright sun, hot, the river stirring like molten glass with enormous eddies that gripped the canoe and passed it from one to the next in lazy zigzags. At the end of a watering trail, a huge black bear sat on his haunches eyeing us, cooling his feet in the water. There were birds to observe and photograph, though not the abundance Mackenzie had seen: a pair of eagles sporting in the treetops; a whistling swan that splashed along the water ahead of us, taking off; swarms of bank swallows darting in and out of nests dug into the bank; pure black ducks, scoters; on a rocky outcrop in midriver, a big gull's nest of sticks and grass with three brown-speckled blue eggs, the adult birds swooping and screaming defensively overhead. Halfway down, jutting out into the river, we climbed the one landmark Mackenzie had mentioned, "an huge rock" rising above the low banks: La Butte, not rock but a steep crumbling hundred-foot hill of sandy clay held together by sparse heath; and wondered how it survived each spring's onslaught of ice and flood.

Late that afternoon we went ashore at a group of cabins, plaster-chinked, the logs painted red. A neat sign facing the river identified it as Hay Camp, a buffalo-management center, but "management" had been an abandoned experiment in turning the buffalo into marketable meat, signified by a big log slaughterhouse in the middle of the camp; Indians, hired in for the summer from Fort Chipewyan and Fort Smith, occupied the cabins, waiting for forest fires. (If you have the cash—$150 for a nonresident license, $100 a day for the mandatory guide—you are allowed to hunt any

buffalo that wander outside the park, a sport not much
livelier than shooting steers in a feed lot.) I asked about the
chances of seeing the herds. A warden, another Ian, said
they usually came into camp about this time of day, and he
offered to drive us along a work road, looking for them;
down to ten thousand in the last helicopter survey—four
thousand trapped and drowned in the flood—hadn't we seen
the carcasses dumped along the riverbanks? (We hadn't.
Feeling clammy, I resolved to be more careful about boiling
the water.) We climbed into a truck. Several Indians got in
behind—for the ride, the breeze that would blow the
mosquitoes away, to push us through wet spots in the road;
the road, greased with rain, spongy in the hollows, was
blocked off, officially closed. We drove for miles, slithering
uphill, coasting cautiously down. An immense black bear,
tall as a bull, ambled across the road, but we found no
buffalo; the heat—they had retreated to the cool of the hills.

The rapids the Fort Chipewyan warden had warned
about had proved to be innocent, at least at this water, a big
riffle stretching across the half-mile breadth, a momentary
fast-water break in the monotony of paddling. Thirty miles
farther, we came to another that looked more serious, tangled with driftwood; forgotten by the warden, though
Mackenzie had mentioned it. I cautiously pulled out on a
rocky island above. We ate lunch, inspected the channels,
thought about crossing to the far bank where it looked
easier, and decided to chance it. But pushing down we hit
the edge of the chute, slopped an inch of water over the side
of the canoe, and came out just above another drop, below
the island, which I'd not been able to see, and paddled
furiously to keep out of it. Safely across, I put in on a
muddy, willow-thick bank, and we painfully unloaded the
canoe and dumped the water; a cautionary incident. There
were still, as it turned out, three other short bits of fast
water, none big enough to be marked on our map, but we
managed them all without taking water. On the last,

though, only a couple of miles above the first of the big rapids, I pulled over to a rocky bank for a look; Jim slumped in the bow as if not knowing what to do, the canoe started to drift out into the current, and I jumped for the bank— and slipped on the slime at the water line, went in up to my waist, and scrabbled out sputtering with rage. Further instruction.

The changing routes around the rapids sketch a small-scale history of the North. Mackenzie had avoided the rapids by following a series of small channels on the east side of the river, connected by half a dozen strenuous portages. That solution lasted into the 1820s, when the North-West and Hudson's Bay companies ended their rivalry in merger and York boats manned by Orkneymen (later, Indians) replaced the canoes. The water route shifted to the west side of the river, more open but rougher. Empty, the boats were stout enough to chute down the rapids, be poled or tracked up, except at one point, the Mountain, a steep, sandy point where the men harnessed themselves to the boats like horses to haul them the two hundred feet up and over, scattering as the boats sledded down on the other side (Mackenzie had named a Mountain Portage, but on the opposite bank and farther upriver); the trade goods and furs were still loaded in ninety-pound packs and carried on men's backs, as in Mackenzie's time, across the five main portages that resulted. In 1874, the Hudson's Bay Company had built the post it named Fort Smith at the north end of the rapids (we arrived in the midst of its centenary) and cleared an oxcart track along the west bank the whole length of the rapids. A decade later, the rowboats gave way to steam-powered paddle-wheelers and heavily built wooden barges, one steamer working up from Fort McMurray to the rapids, the other north from Fort Smith and eventually down the Mackenzie River to its Arctic delta. The barges, built farther south, could be pulled apart at the end of the

season and profitably sold as lumber; the steamboats were
small enough to be hauled up on the banks, out of reach of
the winter ice. That system lasted with little change till after World War II, the oxcarts giving way to steam tractors
and finally to trucks. A thriving town, Fort Fitzgerald, grew
from the haulage, at the south end of the rapids.

The old system began to die in the late forties, when a
road was pushed north to Great Slave Lake and eventually
inched circuitously east to Fort Smith. The distance from
Edmonton, the commercial capital of the North, was close
to a thousand miles by truck but cheaper and faster than by
water. Except for an occasional fishing boat chugging up
from Fort Chipewyan and three or four families of trappers
in the whole of its three-hundred-mile length, the Slave was
now deserted. At Fort Smith, government replaced trading
and transportation as a livelihood. Fitzgerald became a
ghost town.

All this I pieced together months later from a dozen
sources. As we paddled across the final stretch of rough
water to Fitzgerald, I knew only what I'd been able to work
out from Mackenzie's hurried notes; and what I hoped to
learn from Jacques Van Pelt.

We tied up at Fitzgerald in midafternoon: a couple of
cabins, a white frame house with peeling paint, a ruined
board church spread across an open hillside where thirty
years ago there had been a hundred houses, two hundred;
all gone now, dismantled, burned. ("The kids!" someone
said later of the church. "Setting fires—nothing to do!") At
a guess, the man who was to put us in touch with Jacques,
Bob Stevenson, would live in the house, not one of the
cabins. We climbed the dirt road to the top of the hill.

Several little towheaded children were playing in front of
the house—chopping up wood, building a fire. Mrs. Stevenson, a blond woman in shorts, her feet bare, answered my

knock in a voice that my ears, after the varieties of Scots, heard as Irish (British Columbia, I gathered later as we talked, where her husband had gone to college, there being none nearer). Jacques had said something about some people in a canoe, but her husband was still asleep, and would we like some tea while we waited? We went in: screenless windows open on the warm afternoon; in corners of the room, a couple of mosquito coils burning—slow, like punk, with a heavy incense smell that in time dispels the bugs. We drank the tea, talked, waited.

Bob Stevenson woke, came out of the bedroom, and sat groggily at the table with us to drink a cup of tea, waking up. A nephew was visiting from the south, he had taken the children up the river in his boat, the motor had broken down, and it had taken all night to paddle back. He was a tall, big-boned man of thirty with a long scowling face dark with stubble around the chin; only his hair, straight, shiny-black and shoulder-long, looked Indian. The talk grew fitful, languished. It was Saturday, getting late, I had things to buy in Fort Smith; I restrained myself. But could we perhaps telephone this man in Fort Smith, or—

No, he would drive us in, had to go anyway about the motor. He drew himself up from the table, collected his regalia from around the room—black pointed riding boots, a short denim jacket to match the jeans, a high-crowned black sombrero with a hawk's feather in the band; going to town. Our stuff? We got in his car, coasted down to where we had left the canoe. I loaded the packs into the trunk, the back seat. My son carried the canoe up the hill; we would leave it, come back to get it the next day. Bob stopped to pull a couple of guns, a new ax, from the green plywood scow tied up a little farther along the beach: the kids!

His wife decided to come in with us. We climbed in: a new two-door Ford but battered by the roads, the windshield spiderwebbed with cracks from flying gravel, like every car

1. Early June on the Athabasca River was spring and summer in one, bright sun and clear skies, warm air, and the sense of infinite space. Here, Jim lies back in the canoe and rests, drifting with the northward current.

2. Spring floods, heavier than normal, had layered the Athabasca's sandy banks with mud, and we sank into it as we shoved out into the river.

3. Tar Island, a few miles north of Fort McMurray, is the center of an oil field first noticed by Mackenzie. Here, the high banks of the Athabasca have been cut in terraces and the oil-rich sand is hauled to refineries by trucks such as the tiny dot at the center of this picture.

4. Fort Chipewyan, oldest continuous settlement in Alberta: the Athabasca cafe, where Chipewyans, Crees, and whites mingle in the long spring daylight.

5. The deep-ridged bark of a bamagoulia, or black poplar, tree, trapped with other driftwood in a minor rapids on the upper Slave: our first lesson in the power of the river.

6. The end of the Pelican Rapids, part of the series by which the Slave River, midway down, drops more than a hundred feet to the level of Great Slave Lake.

7. A gull chick in a rookery offshore in Great Slave Lake. New-hatched and unable to swim to safety, it has no other defense but to crouch down and imitate a rock.

8. Our tent billows in the gale that held us for two days at the end of Pine Point on Great Slave Lake. Earlier storms had bared the driftwood skeleton of the beach.

in the North. We roared off, the radio tuned to country rock from the one station in Yellowknife, three hundred miles north on the other side of Great Slave Lake, the air conditioner turned up high, not to cool but to blow the dust and mosquitoes back through the open windows. Sixty, seventy, seventy-five, the car swaying in the ruts—I started to say we weren't in that much of a hurry, stopped myself; a test, a dare. I lighted a cigarette, another for his wife between us on the front seat.

Back in the house, with an appearance of complaint, he had talked about the burden of his travels—Edmonton, Saskatoon, Ottawa; meetings, discussions, planning, *talk*, time taken from serious work. I had answered questions, identified ourselves. Now, curious, I asked: What did he *do*? The car slowed a little. He was, he said, the district representative of the native peoples in the territorial government. It explained: the self-conscious style, constructed, not inherited, of a public figure; and the travel, the car, the guns, the big motor on the boat, the expensive camera on a table in the front room of the house; steady money. The district was the Mackenzie District of the Northwest Territories, although Fitzgerald itself was technically in Alberta, just below the sixtieth-parallel border. My mind caught on the word "native," an all-embracing official term: treaty Indians—with a recognized legal connection with a tribe, tribal voting rights; Eskimos in the Delta and along the coast; half-breeds in dozens of combinations, some of them living a life that was tribal in style but unofficial; and the Métis, descendants of the canoemen, with that half-French inheritance, set apart from the Indians by mutual feelings of superiority, a people distinct enough to have raised a western civil war a century ago but now coalescing as the Indians became like them. And what would they do, the native people, to survive? What were the policies? Bob talked vaguely about restoring a traditional life on the land, but connected somehow with the actual world; about reviving Fitzgerald—he had been born there, his memories were of hundreds of people living there that made its present intolerable. It was to be a dual life such as he had been gifted with by the chance of an election and by birth: a *half-breed* —a not quite offensive word, almost identifying a people, a pride. He flew by jet to attend the council chambers in the cities but also took the boat down the Mackenzie to squat by trappers' fires, confabulating; a famous dancer, someone told me later, and you could see it in the hard, athletic body —Indian dance, the shuffling, stamping, leaping celebratory mime of hunt and death to a tuneless chant around the fires, danced to exhaustion.

The car slowed again, coming into town, and—"Hey, *man!*"—stopped. A young Indian couple came over to ask a favor of the public man, Indian also in a style that had been perfected on a college campus somewhere: beaded headbands binding the lank black hair, new buckskins, brightly colored nylon jackets; on his back the young man carried a baby in a nylon carrier mounted on a tubular aluminum frame with padded shoulder straps. On the radio the music had been succeeded by announcements: personal messages, lost dogs, family visits, finally a list of movies—*fillums*, the trained, accentless announcer's voice called them, over and over—playing or to come in Fort Smith, Hay River, Yellowknife. We said good-bye to the two young Indians. The car moved on.

"Executive acres!" Stevenson announced and swung into a wooded tract of new small ranch houses and split levels that might have been transplanted from any North American suburb; and stopped at one that was unlike any of the others —a Swiss chalet in its red-earth-toned stain, overhanging roof and deck, the details of its windows and trim; but octagonal. An unusual man would live here. We unloaded the packs, said our thanks. I left Jim to introduce himself and rushed off on foot to cash a last-minute traveler's check, buy some odds and ends of food, a can of bug spray, whiskey.

"And what do you think of the *mosquitoes?*" Jacques asked. He was younger and less quirky than he had sounded on the round-about long-distance telephone: a narrow face lengthened by a curly, neatly trimmed beard, the loose-fitting coveralls and rubber boots of those few Indians who still lived from the river. It was a question we had heard or would hear from nearly every white we met in the North, always more or less gleeful. Or if not the mosquitoes, then the deer flies, the bulldog flies that with a slash of their jaws could draw blood and leave a lingering, spreading bruise; or the billowing dust clouds in the towns; or, depending on one's notions of civil amenities, the nearly total absence of newspapers, magazines, books, music, conversation; or the high prices of food, beer, liquor; or the scarcity of skilled mechanics (engines were regularly flown to Edmonton for repair); or the rickety transportation system; or simply the interminable summer light and winter dark. Mackenzie had noticed a similar quality in the Chipewyans: their "querulous disposition . . . which they express by a constant repetition of the word *eduiy*, 'it is hard,' in a . . . plaintive tone of voice." The mosquitoes, indeed, were thick in the towns and swarmed as hungrily in bright sun as in chilly dawn, both new experiences for me; but I answered mildly that, except for that, they did not seem any worse than in Minnesota, and the same remedies worked as well here as there.

The two little girls had gone to bed. Jacques and his wife, my son and I, were sitting around a welcome fire in the circular fireplace, hung from the high ceiling of the tightly screened, angular living room. Outside, the slow twilight was turning to dark; getting late. We had been asked to stay for dinner, spend the night, a luxurious break in our labors on the river. We had spent the evening looking at the town, then driving back along the road to Fitzgerald, pulling off to inspect the rapids from the high riverbanks.

After three hundred miles of paddling, we had arrived in the Northwest Territories. Locally, I noticed, it is simply "The Territory." Here, if you have any shame to run from, any vision of quick and muscular profit to be made, you can still, as in Mark Twain's America, "light out for The Territory"; and many are so drawn. Fort Smith, like Fort McMurray, was a surprise, all new, despite the centennial, in the past three or four years: the houses, a motel, a hospital, a museum, a teachers' college, a hockey rink, a new-built Hudson's Bay store, offices for half a dozen government agencies, a territorial liquor store with elderly drunken Indians falling down the high steps in front, begging for drinks; and older, a cathedral, fieldstone-Gothic, whose bishop attempts to shepherd the entire North from here. There is a chamber of commerce that talks hopefully of virgin timber for lumbering, hydroelectric power from the rapids (distasteful to the few like Jacques who value them simply because they are there, because they are beautiful), transportation, industry, tourism. All this is potential. The economic reality is government, paid for in Ottawa—a reality that seven years earlier had made Yellowknife the first territorial capital and decreed a series of regional administrative centers, of which Fort Smith was one of the fortunate; a town of perhaps three thousand with the lineaments of a city.

Meeting Jacques and seeing his house, I had guessed architecture as a livelihood, and wondered—not much call. Actually, it was government again, but at a remove: a succession of research projects, currently a study of pelicans in their most northern nesting ground, the Pelican Rapids. (The name was as old as Mackenzie and I had wanted to know why but, knowing the white, big-billed birds only from winters along the Florida coast, had not thought of the obvious. The summer nesting area of the fifty or so surviv-

ing whooping cranes was likewise not far off, in Wood Buffalo National Park.) That evening, stopping along the riverbank, we had used Jacques' telescope to study the pelicans
on their rocky colony in the middle of the rapids.

We talked about the route ahead: the second half of the
Slave River; two hundred miles of Great Slave Lake to cross,
rougher by reputation than Lake Athabasca, before we
reached the beginning of the Mackenzie; and then still more
than a thousand miles on the great river to the sea and journey's end. Jacques had canoed parts of the river. In the ten
years since he came North to teach in a government school,
his work had taken him up and down the whole valley, he
knew someone in nearly every settlement. (Ten years is a
long time here; many of the people he knew had gone elsewhere, whole communities had vanished.) We talked too
about the rapids, the portages. He had studied the Hudson's
Bay Company haulage routes—old photographs, documents,
maps; I marked my map. It did not look like the route
Mackenzie described—narrow channels choked with logs
and ice, starting from a camp by a stream on the east side of
the river. No, no, Jacques was positive, whatever he said,
Mackenzie *must have* taken the fur-trade portages on the
west; there *was* a way on the other side but he had never
tried it, only a few old Indians ever used it. At the time, I
hadn't the information to dispute him, and I let it pass.

"But you really *ought* to try it, you know," Jacques said
persuasively. I said again that my whole training had been
to avoid rapids, go around them; I remembered as a boy
chafing at my father's caution, portaging small rapids in the
Quetico that I wanted to run, daring him—and in my turn
imposing the same middle-aged restraint on my children.
Maybe, I said finally; perhaps if he would *show* us the
approaches, since he knew them, lead us through the rough
spots. . . .

It was late, time for sleep. In the night, a couple of
mosquitoes penetrated the house's defenses. By now, I had

grown almost indifferent to mosquitoes in clouds, but a single insect singing in my ear was a torment. I did not sleep much.

In the morning, the house woke late. We waited around. Jacques worked in his vegetable garden, an indispensable support of the householder's life in the North; I washed some socks and underwear and hung them on a line. Around noon, "Well, are you ready?" he challenged. "It's getting late." I tossed some sausage and bread into the camera pack for lunch. We climbed into the Minibus and headed down the road to Fitzgerald to retrieve the canoe and paddles.

"So these are the two fellows that are going to commit suicide!" Bob Stevenson greeted us, in a heavy, lugubrious voice. He had just waked. I demurred; he repeated the line —he liked it, he had been polishing it. He told us a story of a couple of young priests a few years back who had started toward the first of the big rapids, Cassette, in a canoe, been dumped in what looked like easy water in sight of Fitzgerald, their bodies never found. There was a monument on a high point opposite the place. *He* would not go near the rapids in a boat, *he* did not want to die. We had heard other stories by now, to the same point: of, for instance, a party of athletic Germans only a year or two ago who had tried to run the whole sixteen miles in kayaks, and were prevented by drownings. It was another touch of northern *schaden-freude*, as old as Mackenzie. At one point, he noted laconically, one of his Indians' canoes had gone through the rapids and been smashed, but "the woman who had the management of it, by quitting it in time, preserved her life, though she lost the little property it contained." The last portage on his route—the comparatively easy one on the east side of the river—already bore the name it still carries, Portage des Noyés: Three years earlier, bound like us for Great Slave Lake, "five men were drowned, and two canoes and some packages lost, in the rapids on the other side of the river. . . ."

We loaded the canoe onto the car and drove off. Jacques had a plan for us. We would start from an old farm, abandoned, the halfway house on what had been the Hudson's Bay cart track. From there a trail led down to the river, to a rocky point on the second major rapids, Pelican. We would put in there, skirt the edge of the rapids, round a small point, cross another bay, and carry over the Mountain Portage, which we had driven to the night before. From there, it was only a couple of miles of fast water to a point within carrying distance of his house—unless, of course, we had time to push on through the final section, the Rapids of the Drowned. An exciting afternoon!

Near a ruined barn just off the road, Jim took the canoe, and I swung the pack over one shoulder. Jacques came with us to the edge of the clearing, where the trail began. He would leave us now. Wasn't he going to come with us to the end, at least show us the starting point? I had thought . . . No, he was quite definite; tempting, certainly, but this was a day reserved for his family. He bade us a grave farewell, shaking our hands, and turned back to the car.

Under the trees, mosquitoes thronged. The trail was over a mile, up and over a sandy ridge, then petering out as it descended toward the river among thick woods. We walked fast, in silence, sweating. Halfway along, Jim looked tired and I took the canoe.

We came out on the rocky point. I got some raisins out of the pack and sat down to study the course; we could eat a little more when we got to the portage—time was beginning to press. The river here was close to a mile across. A short distance upstream, it slid down a smooth slope of six or eight feet, the last big drop in the Pelican Rapids, but not sharp; and that was above us. Across the river and below us, the water boiled with continuous whitecaps, but it did not look like the place I had feared in my dream. The point we had to make for was a mile and half down. I looked at it through the glasses but could not tell much: Fast, it looked, I could not see how rough. All we had to do, Jacques had said, was keep to the shore of the bay between here and the point, a widening in the channel that, in my experience of rivers, would mean a slowing of the current, probably big eddies running back along the edge; we could pull out, he said, short of the point if the passage looked rough. To get a better look at it, I decided to approach the point in a wide, outward arc, cut in toward the shore well back from the point, pull the canoe out, and walk out to the end before attempting it. Prudence, I thought. It was a serious error.

For the first time since the beginning of the trip, we strapped on the life jackets. "*Sure,*" I remembered the advice given another canoeist in the North, "*always* wear your life jackets. It makes the bodies easier to find."

I said a quick prayer, in silence, and pushed off. Halfway across the bay, still inside the two points, I realized we were not going to be able to see much. I pointed the bow toward the shore. "Put some muscle into it!" I shouted to my son. There was more current than had seemed possible.

I had picked a clump of boulders on the bank, lined up with the bow, as a steering point, half a mile, a quarter mile, ahead. We did not seem to be getting any closer. Then I realized that the current was drifting us slowly out into midriver, the heart of the rapids; we were not going to make the point. "*Paddle as hard as you can!*" I shouted. "I *am!*" Jim called back, aggrieved, as if I had insulted him. I dug in hard, gasping with the effort, my lungs moaning. I could not let it happen.

We could just about hold our own, but for all our effort the current, cold, powerful, and pitiless, was inching us out into the wild center of the rapids. It caromed off the point as if fired from a gun. I had never in my life been so gripped by such force, and there was nothing I could do about it, no alternative. We were even with the point, now twenty-five yards out past it, fifty, sliding toward the line of white water. "We're going to have to do it! *Get down!*"

The year of my birth, 1928, had made me not quite the right age for any of the wars of my lifetime. I had never, therefore, been faced with the common experience of men of my generation: that of being deeply frightened; not afraid, anxious, worried—I was not *afraid*—but, given all the tales we had heard, credibly threatened with the prospect of death. My mind, I noticed, was clear, working fast, as it is said to. At the least we stood to lose the cameras, perhaps the canoe, paddles. End of trip, humiliation—the money; I could not replace them. I wondered if the camera pack would after all float, and for how long; I had never tested it as my wife had urged—what good would it do to know it was useless, I argued, when there was nothing else? Or my son—sweet Jesus, my son, the seal of all my promises to my wife! Or—what words would Jacques contrive to tell my wife what had happened? Would he even figure out where to write? And who else would give a damn? My aging parents? A couple of publishers, owed money?

I had the camera pack standing upright near the stern, but there were not going to be any pictures now. I laid it flat, shoved it amidships—I did not want it falling over, throwing us off balance—and slipped forward onto my knees. My hat: a vision of myself, pulled out days later with the hat still clinging to my head, flashed across my mind, a final ignominy. I pulled it off and shoved it back into the stern.

We had reached the edge of the rough water, pulled by now a hundred yards out from the point. I swung the bow downstream, dug in, and we were in it. Two strong currents collided, two sets of bow-high waves, and there was no way to take them except straight along the trough. The canoe, riding high and loose without its normal load, tipped wildly, and a big wave sloshed over the side. "Change sides!" I shouted, and I switched, sliding farther forward. It began to rain, hard—flashes of lightning, thunder. The bottom of the canoe was several inches deep by now, the water pelting from side to side and throwing the gunwales closer to capsizing every time a wave struck. One more and we would be over—

And then we were through it, past the point, and into the next bay, the high isthmus of the Mountain Portage straight ahead. I cut sharply toward the muddy bank, thanking God. No eddy; even here, along the edge, the current ran stronger than any we had hit on either river—it would have been chancy, getting out above the point, even if we'd been able to get near it. We tied up, climbed, up to our boottops in black mud, to the trees at the top of the bank, to get out of the rain, and hunched down on a wet log.

I lighted a cigarette. We would get across to the portage, I decided, another mile, and get out. No more of this! The next stretch was likely to be worse.

The rain passed. We paddled slowly across the bay, keeping close to the bank—no more! I could see the low point in the ridge where the portage had to be but not the trail itself. The approach was blocked by big logs, fifty feet out from shore. I pulled up beside one that looked solid. Jim sat. In a fury I got out and felt the log slip, sink under me, and I was up to my waist again. I climbed out, balanced on another log, pulled my boots off, and began to wring my socks out. Jim started dragging the canoe across the logs. I shouted at him to wait, God damn it, and I'd help—I didn't want the canoe damaged. I pulled the wet socks on again, laced my boots.

We were not through with it yet. I could not find the trail, only a hundred-foot slope of deep, soft sand, wet now with the rain. We were arguing about the canoe. My fight was up, I was going to take the God-damned thing up the hill. Jim insisted, shouting too for once. He got it up, started off, and I grabbed the pack. We hiked along the shore, looking for the trail. Then something strange was happening: the ground seemed to be shifting under me at unpredictable angles; this was staggering, it seemed, dizziness, a new experience—something wrong with my equilibrium.

"I've got to stop!"

I slipped the pack off, sat down. Still not right; I would have to get down flat on the ground. I lay back, my mind clear, shuffling through the card file of possibilities: simply being cold, say, the idiotic plunge trying to land, or the lack of a proper meal, or simple fright, what exactly was the physiology of shock, the therapy? Wrap in blankets, keep warm. Was I trembling? Or a stroke of some kind, an "episode," and the momentary dizziness while the blood vessels found their bypass in the brain and a small and not very important part of your consciousness is closed off and begins to die? I remembered portages on trips with my father, taking the heaviest loads to spare him, running back to keep him from making a second trip: rocky portages a half mile straight up, so steep the stern of the canoe thumped the ground at every step. I had done them. That was my sense of my body and what it could do. That was why I had been in a fury at my son for taking the canoe: *I could do that,* I *would not* let it beat me. I had been twenty, that was how I knew myself. And now?

I got myself up, sitting, swallowed a handful of raisins, guiltily wolfed the chocolate bar intended for our after-lunch dessert. We still had to get up the hill. I took the pack and followed Jim up through the trees, slowly, one step at a time. At the top, I helped him down with the canoe; no thought of trying to go on now. He would have to get back to the house, get Jacques to come for us with the car. I would wait. Jim went off toward the road. I sat on the pack, cooling down. The mosquitoes sang in my ears.

Jacques, when he drove up in the Volkswagen, my son beside him on the front seat, was cheery but disappointed. We had been, it seemed, the subjects of an experiment, and it had failed. One of his schemes for saving the rapids from development was to make them into a kind of tourist attraction, a sporting event: canoeists would be delivered to a point along the river and follow the historic route down to Fort Smith. Ah! They would, I observed, need more guidance than we had had if they were not to be killed. And as for the portage, blocked by logs, invisible after a lifetime of portage hunting . . . Yes, he agreed. Something would have to be done to mark that trail.

It was late when we got back, getting dark. We ate the remains of a meal kept warm in the oven, in the kitchen, by ourselves. The atmosphere had changed in other ways. Would we mind leaving our muddy boots outside? We could stay another night, but we would have to sleep on cots in the basement—the smell; all right, we had our sleeping bags. He would give us a lift down to the river in the morning, but we would have to be up by six; his work. All right again; we aimed for early starts.

While my son snored, I was up most of the night, drying clothes, resorting and closing the packs for the next stage. The last act was a long, careful letter to my wife, to mail in the morning, making light of the rapids, intended to reassure. I was dismayed at myself but not ashamed. Or: To have done all you can, all you know, is not dishonorable even if not enough. And: To have lived through it, even badly, is the final test. A line shaped itself in my mind: *We are not dead but live.* A very modest thankfulness.

We were prevented from embarking this morning by a very strong wind. . . .

CHAPTER 5

Great Slave,
Ungentle Giant

After getting over the portages around the rapids, Mackenzie and his party made camp early, at five-thirty by his watch, actually about three-thirty by the current system of reckoning in the area. The place was another that already bore a name: Point de Roche he called it, Rocky Point. Probably it was the place known today as Bell Rock, a point jutting out into the river from the west bank about six miles below the Rapids of the Drowned. During World War II, the U. S. Army built a trans-shipping base here, a discrete distance from Fort Smith and its Canadian sensitivities, a link in a back-door water-and-road route to Alaska that was intended to supply the northern peninsula in the event Japanese submarines cut the sea route. In time, the regulation barracks, warehouses, and workshops devolved to the Canadian government and, with fresh coats of paint, became an Indian settlement set apart from the mostly white administrative center of Fort Smith.

On a map, the lower half of the Slave River, from Fort Smith to Great Slave Lake, looks to be about the same length as the section above the rapids. The river winds, however, in a series of languorous loops, some of them eight or ten miles around; in other places, long, low islands divide the half-mile breadth of the river, constantly eroding and rebuilding with driftwood and silt, held together by a spine of willows. Some of the bends are named: Le Grand Détour, Pointe Ennuyeuse (Tedious Point). These are old names—canoeists' names, boatmen's: You navigate the river by eye, from point to point, seeking the straightest course, the strongest helping current, usually the outside of the loop, though the interrupting islands and the sheer scale of the river confuse the mechanics of its flow. With its many bends doubling back on itself, the river distance from Fort Smith to the mouth is about 175 miles.

Mackenzie took four days descending the lower river. Weather slowed him. Starting at dawn the first day, around four-thirty in this latitude and season, and paddling into early twilight, they made eighty miles, but the north wind was against them all the way, cold enough so that the Indians, at least, protected their aching hands with moose-hide mittens. By the next day the wind had built up to rain that stopped them repeatedly and finally drove them into camp soon after midday, and the next day blew so hard with rain and harsh wind that they could not move at all. The canvas tarps that covered their cargo were only moderately waterproof, the deerhide packs of food and trade goods not at all; when it rained, they had to go ashore, unload, and shelter themselves and the packs under the canoes. When Mackenzie finally reached the lake on June 9, he found it still solid with ice except for a narrow channel along the shore, where it had begun to melt.

Mackenzie's weather was the main reason for the bulkiness of our kit. We had packed two sets of clothes, light for the warm days we could expect in July, heavy—long wool underwear, old ski pants—for the cold that seemed likely on the lake and, toward the end of the season, in the Arctic; we had two sleeping bags each for the same reason: One would be comfortable on mild to cool nights, but inside the second bag should be good for temperatures down to ten degrees or zero. I half expected to be stopped by ice on the lake, as Mackenzie had been, and actually, I heard later, the guess had not been so far off; the ice on Great Slave Lake had not broken that year till June 5, the day we started out from Fort McMurray, and when it came it had been helped by dynamite. Breakup: It is a date the people of the North know and remember, a pivotal point in the rhythm of the seasons; life depends on it. But with our later start and slower travel and the long cycle of climate that seems gradually to have been warming the entire Northern Hemisphere since the sixteenth century, our weather at this point in our journey was milder than Mackenzie's. Ice was not going to be one of the problems.

The distance down the lower Slave proved to be my last big error of the trip. In my haste the night before we left home, I had not bothered to measure it. About the same as the upper river, I thought. On the itinerary I left with my wife I put it down as a hundred miles—three easy days; actually, it would take us five. We started out several days behind that theoretical schedule and ended a week late, after pushing hard. It was no longer purely theory. If we continued falling behind, we would run out of time at the far end of the trip—or with the storms of an early fall, the cold and fog blowing down from the Arctic Ocean, we would run out of weather in which it was possible to travel.

We began that first day paddling into the face of a strong north wind. (We had had so far *one day* with the wind behind us, in the morning coming into Fitzgerald—and had celebrated by strapping the spare paddles up, sailwise, to help us through a fast passage; we would not have another such day of beneficent south wind till well past the Arctic Circle.) The current, pouring off the last of the rapids, boiled in turbulence, tossing up waves big enough to inspire caution. Across the river I could see what looked like a lea shore where the going should be easier, but after the strenuous education we had had in the rapids I was unwilling to chance a crossing.

The afternoon was peppered with rain, which continued, off and on, for two more days but, unlike Mackenzie, did not stop us; the packs would shed rain, though eventually they would soak it up after hours of standing in the water collected in the bottom of the canoe; the things inside that mattered were packed in sealed plastic bags. The clouds came down to the level of the water. You looked through them, swirling in dizzying convolutions, indistinguishable from the river, and drew back; best keep the eyes ahead, water-level, steering from point to point. Later, it cleared and the sky, blue flecked with white of cloud, sailing high, became the most immense thing in existence. An endless lake, I had thought in the sunny days along the Athabasca. Now, under that enormous sky, with the land spreading flat and featureless on either side, it was like traveling across a sea.

The banks, low on the inside curves, ten or fifteen feet high on the outsides, were more savagely undercut than ever. In places, between the plunge and gurgle of each paddle stroke, we could hear the steady, arhythmic *chunk* . . . *chunk* of blobs of the half-thawed black-earth bank dropping into the river. In others, a whole segment of the upper bank had broken loose and slid down flat into the shallow, the slender birch and aspen and pines still standing, still alive; everywhere, a tangle of bared roots hung loose in the air at the edge of the bank, groping for the water below. Rounding a bend, we startled a black-bear cub who tumbled down the bank, then scrabbled to get up again and at last turned to stare at us in wonder while I pulled out the camera to record his struggle. The current was stronger now. Crossing the river to hunt for a camp site—even a spot dry and level enough to pull out and sit down for lunch—required forethought, a wide, upstream arc to reach the intended spot; in a straight-line bearing, the current would carry us a hundred yards past where we aimed and leave us to struggle back again—or give up and go on to the next possibility. The monotony of the steady, unbroken, all-day paddling was beginning to wear me. Like the *voyageurs*, we now gave ourselves a regular break every hour, the length of one of my cigarettes, to inspect the map, take a couple of pictures, simply lie back along the gunwales and let the stretched muscles of back and arms and shoulders go slack. In the late afternoons, tiring, we passed a bag of raisins back and forth to keep going till we could camp, cook dinner.

In the silence of paddling between these minutes of rest, I found my mind much occupied with food, I would fill out the carefully rationed freeze-dried stew with chunks of bacon, tonight perhaps a double portion of vegetables and a big slab of hot bannock baked in the frying pan, slathered with butter and jam; yes, and in the morning a big bowl of oatmeal thickened with raisins, fat slices of bacon, and would we have pancakes or eggs or maybe both? I had figured the freeze-dried stuff would be inadequate, but for the time and distance there was nothing else: There would come a time, it might take a month, when we would begin to wear down, be hungry; we had reached it. We did not try to fish. The murky river looked unpromising. Time pressed —never enough, in the push to eat in the morning, pack up, get off; the evenings ran late, beginning with a search for a camp site—landing, looking, going on—that might take an hour, an hour and a half. Above all, though, this hunger was not for fish, it was *meat* I craved, and we had none and no way of getting it.

It was an experience I must be sharing with Mackenzie's canoemen. Worn by the fifteen or sixteen hours a day of paddling, resisting the cold, they would be thinking about meat: Would the hunters bring in some geese, ducks, per-

haps a swan? Or, praise God, a beaver, thirty or forty
pounds of honest red meat, with its marvelous tail, which
looks like leather but is actually a delicacy, exquisite? Or,
with an extreme of luck, a whole caribou, with its butter-
tender steaks and fat rump? About fish, they were fastidi-
ous. Whitefish, big, fat, delicate-flavored and firm, boneless,
was acceptable; bony pike, the commonest, was no matter
for rejoicing; others they resisted or ate only with grumbling
muted in Mackenzie's notes. Like them, between periods of
contemplating food, I sang, but in silence: stale old songs
whose words I could remember, mostly waltzes in rhythm to
the paddle strokes, over and over till that too grew weari-
some. Early on, I realized that it would be feasible to think
about food but not to talk about it. If that once began, we
would talk of nothing else.

The skin on my hands by now was dry and translucent,
burned the color of walnut by the days of sun. The fingers
were thick and stiff, layered with calluses, fissured with
cracks that at the thumbtips were becoming painful. I
patched them with bandages. On the bright days, we wore
gloves but had only the cotton ones I carry in the cooking
pack for handling hot pans—damp, with the wind blowing
through them, they were as if refrigerated; after half an
hour of paddling, my hands went to sleep, I could no longer
feel them and had to stop, change sides, work the fingers to
revive sensation. Adequate waterproof gloves seemed to be
the one serious gap in our equipment; working up to the
trip, we had canoed through the mild Pennsylvania winter,
the nearest we could come to the Arctic summer weather we
would sooner or later face, and had not needed gloves. Further instruction. I had never made a canoe trip where the
gradual toughening and conditioning process failed to keep
pace; now, although the vital muscles in my back and shoulders were not stiffening, they began each day tired. I woke
in the morning with a dull ache deep within one elbow
joint.

Even more than the Athabasca or the upper Slave, the river was deserted of people. Making our way around one huge bend, we saw in the distance a fishing camp, three cabins, a small dock, that looked occupied, but there was no one around. Occasionally we passed a trapper's cabin, long since abandoned, the roof falling in. One place that had been a village had been flooded and destroyed, heaps of lumber marking where the houses had been pulled down; it had been rebuilt on higher ground a couple of miles down the river—a cluster of new barrackslike government-stand-ard houses, gaily painted—and that too had been flooded, given up. Because there was no other open ground to pitch the tent, we mostly camped at such places, but reluctantly. Mosquitoes were thickest there, drawn by the lingering human presence, even twenty years gone. In the damp mud along the banks, there were fresh bear tracks, for the same reason, sometimes mixed with others that looked human, with the high arch that has never been confined by boots. I took precautions with the food. Everything with a strong smell—the sides of bacon, the lunchtime sausage, the open cans of oleo, the chocolate—we confined to the fiberglass pack box and kept well away from the tent overnight. We finished dinner each night by repacking everything else, try-ing to save a little time in the mornings.

At one point we camped among ghosts of another kind: an abandoned lumber mill. A big cookhouse and dining hall, a machine shop, a dozen cabins, most with screens on the windows, the roofs still weathertight, but the flood had come up the twenty-foot bank, burst open the doors, coated everything with mud. In the manager's house there was a neat, built-in desk in one corner of the front room, with in-voices and bills scattered around, some dated as recently as 1957. I could see him sitting there, working by the light of a bare overhead bulb powered by a thumping generator, the winter dark and cold rubbing against the windowpanes, and I pitied the bastard, trying to scratch a living out of this place. The trees anywhere in sight of the camp were too spindly to be worth cutting; any real timber would be miles inland along the side streams, dragged to the mill across the snow in winter. A wide boat ramp had been cut into the bank, where the barges and their tug could be winched above the ice in winter. We found the tug itself a couple of miles downstream: thirty or forty feet long and heavily built of wood, probably on the river, in the twenties (the first steel ships and barges did not come till the late thirties) and beautifully named, the *Porphyry*. It had been driven into the bank, the bow broken, but otherwise intact; someone had gotten the boilers and engine out and left them, half sunk in the mud. The lost ship must have been the final stroke; end of camp, end of hope.

We camped that night on top of a heap of damp sawdust, scavenging weathered boards for a fire; and then worried that the sawdust would catch, smolder, spread. It was chilly enough in the night so that for the first time I used the outer sleeping bag—and paid the penalty for that luxury by sleeping till seven-thirty the next morning, unable to pull myself out of the delicious envelope of warmth; only discomfort that woke me in the cold of dawn would get me out early enough so as not to lose half the morning.

The river's course was a puzzle I did not begin to understand till we reached the delta. In some places the bends enclose points of land four or five miles long and no more than a mile across at the base. The banks are an unstable mix of clay and sand, covered with black leafmold; except for a rare beach of stones and gravel, there seemed to be no rock to hold this soft alluvium together. Yet the compass bearings and distances Mackenzie recorded match the present. The river had not changed. Even the islands—swept clean each spring, pushing downstream and eroding at their upstream ends, crumbling, reforming—seemed to be still about where he found them. Why had not the power of the current straightened out those bends, removed those islands, in the nearly two centuries since Mackenzie came this way? It was a commonplace of every big river I knew, most famously the Mississippi (before the Army Corps of Engineers turned its attention to flood control): The river course might change from year to year by a mile or more, cutting off or flooding whole farms, uncovering others.

As on the Athabasca River, we followed the westernmost of half a dozen named channels through the delta of the Slave, aiming to come out onto the lake as near as possible to the next settlement, Fort Resolution. We had found no one to tell us about the route. I half expected to find the channels blocked again by logjams; Great Slave Lake is even bigger than Lake Athabasca, colder, stormier—open water was to be avoided. We reached the delta in the afternoon of a mild, sunny day. Near the beginning of the channel there was another lumber camp—flooded and abandoned too, but only this spring. We landed and spent an hour exploring, taking pictures. I was hungry to be among other people again, and this was a sign; we were getting close.

There were other welcoming signs: the end of a dirt track that must lead overland to the town, with a couple of boats pulled up on the bank; what looked like a boatyard, it too abandoned, but with a dozen rotting hulks scattered across a meadow, a kind of burying ground of the river traffic. In one or two places, as if to answer my questions about how the river worked, high water had delicately lifted the outer skin of earth from the banks to reveal the underlying structure: a core of huge, ancient logs aligned with the current, impregnated with water and silt, with brush packed tightly above, all cemented together by annual deposits of mud. I began to see. The rotting banks and falling trees upstream—and upstream would be all the way up, finally, to the source of the Athabasca in the Rockies—were part of a continuous process. The worst years might strip the banks back twenty feet but never enough to alter their basic contours; the next

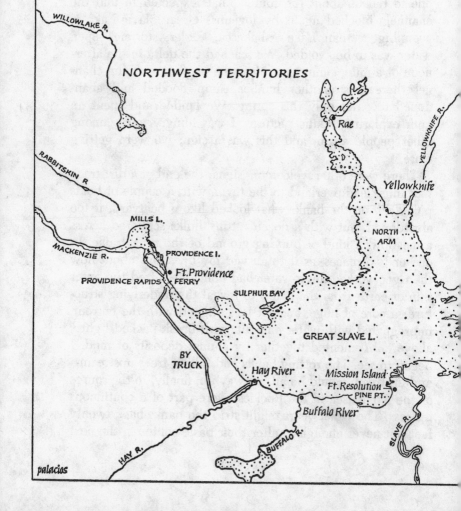

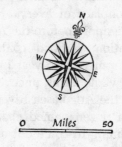

NORTHWEST TERRITORIES

WILLOWLAKE R.

RABBITSKIN R.

MILLS L.

MACKENZIE R.

PROVIDENCE I.

PROVIDENCE RAPIDS

Ft.Providence
FERRY

SULPHUR BAY

Rae

Yellowknife

NORTH
ARM

GREAT SLAVE L.

BY
TRUCK

Hay River

Mission Island
Ft.Resolution
PINE PT.

Buffalo River

HAY R.

BUFFALO R.

SLAVE R.

YELLOWKNIFE R.

0   Miles   50

N
W   E
S

palacios

flow of mud and drift logs rebuilt them to the limits the current would permit. It was a single connected system, earth, water, trees, the grasses; and it was in balance.

The trees were big now, sheltering, warming, the channel narrow and without current; along the banks were the first reeds we had seen since the start of the trip, untouched by the flood, the ice. It was as if for an hour or two we had been transported magically home, we were no longer at a midpoint in a seventeen hundred-mile journey but out for a lazy afternoon's excursion on a gentle, much-cultivated Pennsylvania stream, entirely human in scale, and at day's end we would load the canoe on the car again and sleep that night in our own beds.

We came out finally in a shallow bay, dead calm, sheltered by islands; there were logs scattered here and there, aground, miles out, but no jams. We paddled across to the base of Mission Island, actually a long point, and made camp on a rocky beach. Big logs, weathering white in the sun, were packed fifty feet out from shore but solid, no hazard. From where we camped a trail led inland to Fort Resolution, probably only a couple of miles off, though the distance we still had to paddle in the morning was closer to ten. Off there somewhere too was the town airport. From time to time we could hear but not see a small plane taking off, landing, and that too, strangely, was a pleasure: human things. We had reached the lake.

Great Slave Lake lies along an axis that runs for about three hundred miles from northeast to southwest. Its shape is like the profile of an immense bird in flight. Its raised wings are the North Arm, stretching a hundred miles up toward another huge lake, Great Bear. Its tail is a narrowing bay reaching east 150 miles, high and rocky, ruffled thick with islands. Its head and beak at the west end form the beginning of the great river Mackenzie was seeking. The main body of the lake is about 150 miles long, 70 miles across at

the widest point. The whole covers an area of more than
11,000 square miles, thousands greater than either of the
two smallest Great Lakes, Erie and Ontario.

To cross this formidable body of water, Mackenzie chose
a surprising route: east from the mouth of the Slave River,
north from island to island, then far up the North Arm,
across it, and around the north shore of the lake to its outlet.
The distance that way is at least a hundred miles greater
than the more direct route to the river, along the south side.
He never explained why he preferred the longer route except to mention in passing that the fishing was supposed to
be better than on the south. There are also a number of natural harbors in the east and north, none in the south, and,
given the prevailing north wind, the north shore is probably
more sheltered, if you can stay close in. Most likely, however, Mackenzie was simply following a known route as far
as it led.

Two years earlier, the English Chief, Ageena, had traded
as far as the North Arm—he had debts of furs to collect
from the Indians there, most of them owed, in turn, to the
traders at Fort Chipewyan. The north shore was the summering ground of a remote tribe whose language was nevertheless closely related to Chipewyan. Its various names—
Redknife, Yellowknife, or simply Copper—all point to the
same cultural fact: the deposits of copper that they dug in
the north of their territory along the Coppermine River,
where it empties into the Arctic Ocean. The copper was "native"—relatively pure, soft enough so that it could be cold-
formed into knives and other tools without the need for
smelting. (Characteristically, it was a craft they abandoned
from the moment they began to trade their beaver pelts for
steel knives and awls and axes produced in the factories of
Manchester and Birmingham; within a generation of
Mackenzie's first encounter with this people, another
explorer visited their home country to the north and found
the trails to the copper deposits overgrown, the mines for-

9. Virginia Norwegian, a Slavey Indian girl in the village of Jean Marie River on the Mackenzie, with the cornflower that, she thought, had earned my interest in taking her picture …

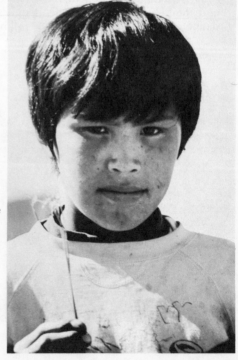

10. … and Virginia's brother Richard, with the same flower, and for the same purpose.

11. *Mister* Louis Norwegian, the Slavey chief of Jean Marie River, whose will and competence have been his people's survival, with his youngest grand-daughter and a whole bouquet of cornflowers picked for the sake of a picture.

12. Looking south, up the Mackenzie, through the long summer-evening day-light from the high bank at Rabbitskin.

13. After the immensities of the upper Mackenzie, near the river's Camsell Bend we catch sight of the first range of mountains, the Nahannis, not high but wild, dotted with snow through most of the brief summer.

14. Cooking breakfast beside the clear water of the North Nahanni, a side stream of the Mackenzie, which by now has turned brown with mud pouring in from the Liard a hundred miles south.

15. The archaeology of the North is still in its beginnings. Here, an archaeologist's marker at the first European site to be fully excavated: Fort Alexander, a trading post on the Willowlake River briefly occupied by the Hudson's Bay Company (1817-21).

16. Oil drums and crated machinery casually barge-dumped on the beach below Wrigley, on the east bank of the Mackenzie near the slowly advancing Mackenzie Highway.

gotten.) One of the side purposes of Mackenzie's expedition
was the opening of trade with this new tribe. The French
clerk, Laurent Leroux, was to stay the summer for the trade
and, if it prospered, find a site for a permanent post somewhere along the north shore of the lake.

Mackenzie and his party paddled along the lake shore
about twenty-five miles northeast from the river mouth to a
point where an outpost of Fort Chipewyan had been built a
few years earlier, probably by the same clerk whose accident had given the Rapids of the Drowned its name. Close
to the shore, the ice had melted enough to open a narrow,
shallow channel, passable for the canoes; beyond, it was still
solid and unbroken, as far as eye could see. They waited
there for five days, held by the ice. The men set the nets in a
small open bay beside the camp; slept; paddled out to a tiny
island to gather eggs—swan, goose, duck—and shoot a couple of birds. The Indians went inland, hunting moose, strays
from the migrating caribou herds, but with no luck. When
the sky cleared, Mackenzie took observations, climbed a low
hill to scan the ice for an opening. For two days, it rained
steadily. Wind-driven, the ice began to melt, open up. On
the evening of June 14, with the rain lifting, they were able
to load the canoes and risk a fast paddle through the driftice
to the nearest of the islands, just within eyeshot eight miles
off the point. Again it was stop-and-go. The wind blew hard
from the north, closing the ice around the island; turned
around long enough to open a brief passage to the next dot
of land on the horizon. Rain poured; the winds blew in
gales, stronger even than these canoes and their men could
paddle against. In this manner, from island to island, in the
intervals of opening water as wind and rain permitted, they
took another week to reach the north shore of the lake, a
distance of no more than fifty miles at this point, if they had
been able to travel it straight.

They continued far up the North Arm of the lake, to a
point where it is narrow enough to cross (the mouth, like

the bell of a trumpet, widens out to thirty-five miles from
point to point) and here found an encampment of the Redknife Indians. A day and a half for trading and speechmak-
ing; Mackenzie bought a big new canoe to replace the small
one the Indian woman had lost down the rapids, hired a
man, who said he'd been to the west end of the lake years
back, to guide them to the beginning of the great river. He
and Leroux shifted their loads around, more pemmican for
the long voyage, goods for the clerk, who would camp here
for the summer to trade. Mackenzie, with his three canoes,
departed to a salute from the guns of the *voyageurs* who
were staying behind.

The weather had not yet done with them. The ice, which
seemed to have cleared, pouring toward the outlet in the
great river, stopped them again before they could get out of
the North Arm and back onto the main body of the lake.
Heavy winds, then thick fog where a warming afternoon
clashed with the remaining ice, twice forced them off the
water. As they crossed the last of the deep bays, a storm
blew up and drove them to shore—there was nothing they
could do, even in the big North canoe, but run before the
waves, bailing constantly with the brass cookpot, until they
reached the shallows and the shelter of reeds at the head of
the bay, where they made a swampy, inhospitable camp. It
was not finally till June 29 that Mackenzie and his canoes
reached the outlet of the lake, the beginning of the river. It
had taken them three and a half weeks from the mouth of
the Slave. From here on, the season would drive them like a
lash.

At the mouth of the Slave River, we diverged from
Mackenzie's route. Partly, I was simply still not sure what it
was, but several times it had taken him across eight or ten
miles of open water, more, given the lake's reputation for
sudden and violent storms, than we could risk in our smaller
canoe. Avoiding those long traverses would add yet another
fifty or hundred miles to our passage through the lake, and

we too were time-driven; although we were following him,
our trip had an integrity of its own, its own conditions and
compulsions. Beyond that, at the settlement of Fort Resolution west of the delta, there was a man I wanted to meet—
a priest twenty years in the country, an authority, Jacques
Van Pelt had said, on the Indians and on the waters
Mackenzie had traveled. From the river mouth we would
head west along the exposed south shore of the lake.

With an early start, we had rounded the point and
reached the settlement by noon. The wind was beginning to
blow from the northwest, choppy, not rough; high, thin
cloud shuttered the sky, half bright. We hauled the canoe
up on the beach beside a couple of freight canoes. A hundred yards back, an elderly Indian carpenter was rebuilding
a burned house.

Father Minez lived in the basement of the aging three-
story convent, residence of the sisters who taught in the new
school fifty yards down the road. A sign on the rough plank
door said not to knock, walk in: three dark, sparsely
furnished rooms, in one of them a television set with an air
of always being on, three or four beautiful Indian children
sitting in a row of chairs in front, watching a Yogi the Bear
cartoon with silent attention—in French, by satellite from
Montreal. A man appeared, small and energetic, with quick,
awkward movements, a big curving pipe clamped between
stained, uneven teeth, black clerical trousers, a black
sweater like a sailor's: Father Minez, the French name half-
Anglicized, me-*nezz*. I told him what we were trying to do,
mentioned Jacques. Mackenzie? No, he knows nothing of
such things, but we can come and talk if we like, he has a
little time. I ask about leaving the canoe, and like everyone
he warns us against the children—not malicious but wildly
curious; we can ask one of the older boys to watch our
things.

Jim and I ate sandwiches and were back in an hour, I self-consciously lugging the camera pack. The cameras, I explain, setting the pack down. I do not really believe what we are told about the children, and yet the thought of small, ignorant fingers toying with the cameras makes me uncomfortable. So, the priest nods, you bring what is most precious to you. Almost a rebuke, but tolerant, wise in men's ways: *Lay not up for yourselves treasures on earth.*

The priest sat behind his desk; we faced him, talking across it. From time to time one of the children came in to ask a carefully phrased question: Why does the moon rise? Where do the birds go in the winter? He answered very gently and with equal care: I think you must ask your mother about that. Your mother will know. *Suffer the little children.* With us, however, he was severe as a schoolmaster. Why was I relying on a *printed* version of Mackenzie's journal, not the manuscript? (I had admitted to having a facsimile of the first edition in one of the packs.) He had spent some time once in the Vatican Library working on manuscripts, he knew how editors and printers could falsify, mislead—not to be trusted. And why anyway did we attach such importance to Mackenzie? Discovery! The Indians had known always that the great river was there. He pointed to a chart he had put up on a wall of the study, one of the products, probably, of his researches in Rome: the successive waves of European diseases that had destroyed the tribes. But Mackenzie, I insisted, had been *a just man,* honorable in his dealings and on the whole for the good; the real destruction had been the killing off of the game, a work of the Indians, beginning in the sixteenth century. Father Minez gave me a skeptical look.

I tried to get him to talk about his people, but it was like our conversations with the Indians; he would answer questions, briefly and politely, but he would not talk. We had noticed several impressive projects in the settlement: the new school (the rough board walls of many of the cabins were painted with proud declarations of achievement, "Graduate

74!"); an outdoor swimming pool with a bathhouse and laundromat attached, signs urging the benefits of cleanliness, a young woman volunteer from Ontario to teach the children swimming; a co-operative craft shop to sell the women's moccasins, mukluks, and mittens; a handsome old people's home that the men were in the midst of building across from the church. These things suggested intelligent and effective leadership—his? No, no, these were the people's ideas; he merely did what they wanted. He had admitted knowing their language ("not well"—it would be like his English, energetic, emphatic, strongly accented); half the Sunday Mass was in Chipewyan. I wondered then what he knew of their traditions—in the eastern Arctic the Baffin Island Eskimos preserve an accurate oral account of their first violent contact with European explorers. Perhaps here . . . No, they had no traditions; another disruption caused by the whites. And the written language? There was to be a parliamentary election in a few weeks, posters were around for the territorial candidates, in English and a strange syllabic writing devised by missionaries in the 1850s, based on a French shorthand. A few old people knew it, there had been experiments in the school, teaching the children their language, abandoned for lack of teachers; a missionary group in Alberta had created a phonetic alphabet for Chipewyan that he thought might be useful one day, they were translating the Bible. But this was still a preliterate people. They did not think in terms of written communication. When a man needed to know something, he went to another and squatted down with him face to face. *That* was communication!

I tried finally to get the priest to talk of what we had been seeing on the rivers—the abandonment of the cabins, which meant giving up not simply a place to live but a rooted tradition, the movement into the settlements and from there to the cities in the South—but again he was uninformative. And so: Enough of this patient questioning.

We said our thanks and good-byes, received the
northland blessing: "Good luck!" Jim shouldered the pack,
his turn. We headed back to the canoe.

It was midafternoon when we pushed off. The wind was
blowing harder now, steadily from the west. I aimed the
canoe for the farthest point I could see, the shortest straight-
line distance ten miles across Resolution Bay. The waves
were as always bigger, more menacing, once we were out in
them, than they had looked from shore. We moved slowly.
Nervous of all we had heard of storms on the lake, I shifted
course, angled the canoe across the waves in a long arc that
carried us close in to the shore of the bay. By five o'clock the
west wind had blown a storm over us, the sky black, lightning spitting in the distance. We were at the edge of reedy
shallows now, swampy muskeg behind, thickly grown with
willow, pines beyond. Narrow channels cut through the
reeds—the mouth of a stream back in there somewhere, if
we could get up it there would be shelter, solid ground to
pitch the tent. The sky was black as night, the lightning
coming closer in a rumble of thunder. Hurry! We poled in
through the reeds but could not find the stream. At the edge
of a mass of drift logs pushed up against the shore, a break
in the reeds must be the end of a muskrat run coming from
land in there among the thickets; in the spring the people
here went "ratting" for this commonest and cheapest of furs.
We drove the canoe in, pulled the packs out, and balanced
them among the logs. There was a plot of grassy earth, soft
as a wet sponge, held together by this year's growth of
willow, just space enough for the tent. I pulled out the ax,
chopped feverishly at the soggy earth to clear the willow
sprouts. I remembered Father Minez asking about the trip.
Poor camping, I had said—the flood; I wondered how the
Indians managed. Ah! he had answered sardonically, an Indian! An Indian can always find a spot to pitch his tent!

We got the tent up in the first spattering of rain, were

crowded inside with all the packs by the time it came down hard, in a rush of wind; we were learning. I wadded sleeping bags under my shoulders, lay back, dozed, woke again, dozed, tired, sure, but disheartened, stopped before we could even get across the bay; crawl into sleep, the refuge. Jesus! A little of the Canadian Club that I had rushed to buy in Fort Smith helped. We heated a can of stew on the little stove, working again, and passed it back and forth. A handful of raisins, half a bar of chocolate: dessert. And *sleep!*

I woke slowly in the morning, cold, hands aching and half numb, clumsy and slow trying to lace the boots. Cloudy overhead still but dead calm out on the lake, hardly a ripple. We ate hurriedly and pushed off.

The two rivers had been immense, inhuman, but the lake was huge in scale beyond anything in our experience, an ocean. All day we drove the canoe in a straight line from point to point along a line of low islands, far out, that seemed to follow us like a fleet of battleships: each point so distant the eye could barely separate it from the flat horizon of infinite water, hardly changed after hours of paddling. And all day—ten miles off, fifteen, twenty, finally through glasses—the white spire of the church at Fort Resolution glimmered across the water behind us, a beacon, beckoning, accusing. I regretted it, another Sunday had come, day of calm, and it would have been lovely to camp the night there, begin the day with a Chipewyan Mass; but we could not wait. We ate lunch drifting in the canoe, two or three miles out, the shore flattened and darkened by distance. I studied the sky, wondering how suddenly these sudden storms could come, how much time, if one did, we'd have to get to shore—or one of those islands off there, nearer, marooned? But the weather seemed to be clearing. We would chance the straight course, make time while we could. By late afternoon I was giddy with the constant, eventless paddling, the cramped sitting, the low points on this almost featureless shore that seemed to take a lifetime to reach and pass. A little archipelago of rocks thrusting above the water brought relief: a big gull colony, hundreds of gulls swooping and screaming, the chicks little gray-speckled puffs just out of their eggs, scattering into the water, their only defense, as we landed and tied the canoe up. We lingered, taking pictures, limbering stiff legs, went on; the final point was still hours off.

We camped late that night, on a wide, rocky, limestone beach: Pine Point. Somewhere inland was the zinc mining operation that has the reputation of being the biggest money-maker in the Northwest Territories—or, at any rate, until the oil comes in on the Athabasca and the Arctic coast; the reason for the highway north from Alberta, the railroad, both built in the forties. We were past the islands now. West and north there was nothing ahead but the boundless, gently stirring surface of the lake. Buoying up from the discouragement of the last night, we ate a slow and ample dinner. A little distance off the point, a pair of Arctic loons bobbed and ducked as they went about their business of fishing, heedless of us; smaller and darker than the common loon, with a high, whistling cry quite unlike the eery idiot's laugh of their cousins to the south. It seemed a welcoming sign. Afterward, we paddled out into a glowing sunset, close to midnight, to try some casting—promising, I thought, patches of reeds clumped around outcroppings of rock where pike would feed, but this time we got no fish; the whole point behind our camp had burned off in the past year or two, skinning the pines, leaving them dead and standing, with purple clumps of fireweed coming up between. It was dark when we pulled the canoe out, put the rods and lures away, but I was full of hope. Tomorrow would be good.

The morning began innocently. The good weather seemed to be settling. But we paddled around the point and into a storm. Our camp had deceived us, the only lea, apparently, on the whole coast. A west wind blew hard against

us, parallel to the shore. Big booming combers rolled in from
the north, far out on the lake, wide-spaced but three or four
feet high. Heading into the wind, we rolled in the trough of
the waves; turning fast to avoid shipping water, we took the
wind broadside, it was driving us out into the lake; another
fast turn between waves and we were plowing toward the
rocky shallows along the shore. We kept this up all morning
and made perhaps a mile down the point. Ahead was another small point that looked like shelter, an objective, anything to get out of this crossfire of wind and waves, but we
were barely moving; we could not reach it. I gave up, swung
the canoe hard toward the shore, and we rode the surf in to
the beach, jumped out waist deep to save the canoe. I stood
in the water holding it while Jim unloaded the two heaviest
packs, collected drift logs to serve as rollers. We drew the
canoe up above the waves half loaded. "Not much of a
camp," I said. We could wait here for it to calm down—
maybe by evening.

Above the rocky waterline, the beach was lined with big
logs laid down parallel to the water, half buried in sand, as
if the past year's storms had stripped this shore to its bones.
In places the exposed wood was charred down to the level
of the protecting sand: the flaring heat of the fire that had
swept the point, igniting the old logs fifty or a hundred feet
down the beach. Not much to do but wait, it could not last,
I said again, encouraging. We got down among some logs,
out of the wind; ate lunch, added to our journals. The wind
whined above our heads. The waves pounded at the shore;
it looked well armored by rocks, the immovable water-
logged hulks of trees behind. A few sea birds—big gulls, the
smaller, angular terns—came around the point the way we
had come, laboring against the gale, struggling opposite us
out on the water and then like us let go and were swept
back as if shot from guns.

Waiting. Later in the afternoon, on a level patch of sand a
few yards back from the water, we put up the tent. Shelter

for now from a wind that was beginning to chill, to tire; we would go on. My mind had become oddly passive, a receiver of sensations from moment to moment, not thinking. Now a message entered it: *a house built on sand.* Yes. If we were going to stay we should clear a spot on the high ground among the burned trees, well back from the water. Shelter, something to lash the tent to. It was too much. I braced the tent stakes with logs. We got inside, out of the wind.

Toward evening the wind grew stronger, spitting rain like buckshot. We went out, struggled to put the rain fly up, a huge, billowing sheet of blue nylon, like trying to raise a sail in a hurricane; more logs to brace the corners, weighted now at each end with smooth red-granite boulders scrabbled up out of the sand. We would be staying after all. I turned the canoe over where we had brought it up at noon; the waves were breaking only a few feet below it, but it was on a sandy rise above the water level, shielded by rocks and driftwood; safe enough. In an interval of the rain we cooked dinner; in the wind, the wood flared in the fire like paper. Again we brought all the packs into the tent. It was no longer chilly but cold; we left the tent open at both ends, aligned with the wind—maybe if the wind blew *through*, the tent would hold. I layered myself in spare clothes, shivering, and climbed into the two sleeping bags. The tent filled like a balloon. The wind whip-snapped the fly ceaselessly, without mercy.

When I was little, the first night or two of those Quetico canoe trips, I went to sleep to the sound of lapping water, and my sleep was uncomfortable with a recurring dream: The sound was the sound of waves washing against the canoe, I was no longer safe in the tent but lying in the bottom of the canoe, far out on the lake, drifting, alone. My father always carried the canoe high up from the water. I teased him about his caution. A storm, he said patiently; a storm could come up in the night.

I went to sleep listening to the waves, the sound folded

into the sound of the wind. Had they reached the canoe? Washing up under it, slapping against the sides, lifting, floating? *Get the canoe up.* Cold out there; wet, dark. *Get the canoe up.* No, too much. I was tired, I had to sleep.

I woke from the warmth of a happy dream, a story of myself going back to a wrong turn in a not wise life for a second chance, reliving it and this time right. Something in the dark shape of the tent seemed to have changed, the drumming of the fabric was less rhythmic. Rain, harder, soaking the sand. I got out of the sleeping bags and went outside. A corner of the tent and fly had pulled loose. I found a new log to put through the loops. Another tore loose, flapping wildly in the wind. I grabbed it, shouting to my son for help.

We did not sleep much more that night. I lay listening to the sounds of the tent, wondering how much longer before the whole thing went. As stakes pulled loose and were lost, useless anyway in the wet sand, we went out to replace them with logs, rocks, more and more, piled on top of each other. Toward dawn, as the long dusk changed to twilight, I glanced toward the water and could not see the canoe. Jesus! It was gone! Then I saw it, a red blob, far down the beach toward the point. I sprinted, waded out into the water, pulled it in, carried it out. The waves had driven up the beach, almost tidal, flipped it over and floated it off; only the painter, trailing and caught now between two logs, had saved it.

I followed my son back to the tent, shamed. Inexcusable, I said. *I knew better.* My father never would have left the canoe like that *in a storm!* But I had done it. Christ!

The blow continued all this second day, interspersed with scattershot rain. All this was new: In a lifetime of canoeing, I had never before been windbound. We dressed several layers deep in the warmest clothes we had, clothes brought chiefly for the unknown weather of the Arctic. In intervals of sun, I patched the canoe where pounding on the rocks had cut gashes in its vinyl skin. I hiked along the beach, studying its underlying structure laid bare by the winter, the bright red sweet peas and deeper spikes of fireweed flashing into bloom along the margin of the forest fire. Mostly we stayed in the tent, reading, playing chess with Jim's magnetic pocket set; cleaning and rewaterproofing boots, sharpening knives; sleeping. We debated going on by night, when it might be calm. It was more than I was yet ready for. We compromised. We would sleep early, get an early start; even if the storm blew up again we should have at least till noon.

The next day was bright and warming: long, slow swells like water sloshing in a tub, but the storm seemed past. We coasted from point to point. For lunch, we pulled out on a sheltered limestone beach layered with fossils, an outcrop of the same geology we had met on the Athabasca, and lingered in the delightful warmth and sun. Too long; by the time we went on, the waves were getting big again. We tried to work our way across the next small bay, cut for the shore and whatever lea its indentations offered, and ran down to the bottom, the waves driving in off the lake as if through a funnel, stopped finally and sheltered again by reeds. A muddy, moose-trampled beach, big drift logs, weathered white; sure, we could camp here but better to go on, we would eat, taking up the time, waiting on the weather. Toward eight, the sky darkening, I told myself the bay was calming, and we reloaded, pushed out, and zigzagged out through the chop to the next point. Sulphur Point, the map called it, the name signaled by a momentary whiff as we struggled with the waves. Again too much, the problem that had contained us for the past three days, head-on wind driving along the trough of inbound waves that were about the limit of what the canoe would take. I skidded the canoe around and, just past the point, we skied it toward a steep, narrow, rocky beach, jumped in the water, and passed the packs up to safety.

There was just about room to sit. I lay back on a big log and pulled off boots, socks, pants to dry. The limestone had come apart in neat slabs like paving stones. Jim leaned them together to make a baronial fireplace by the water's edge, collected six- and eight-foot logs for an enormous fire, and, getting interested, his designer's instincts awakened, built fire and fireplace bigger and bigger. We lay back in front of it, toasting, looking out across the stormy, darkening lake. The fire flared upward, a curtain of flames; the limestone glowed and splintered in the heat.

There was no longer a choice. We would have to try the strategy we'd been talking about, wait out the end of the storm and go on by night; like Mackenzie, we would measure the limits of the northern dark by the only means that mattered. I lay back, dozed; roused myself to hang a can of beans over the fire to heat, sustenance for what was to come; morosely smoked the last of my cigarettes—we should have been at the next settlement by now, Hay River, where I'd expected to get more.

Toward eleven, the sky became streaked with sunset reds and scarlets; not sunset precisely—the sun did not go down, it slanted in a long arc toward the north and slipped finally below the rim of water far out on the lake; not for long, you could see, the curve would delicately reverse and bring it out again a little to the northeast. As the sun dipped, the colors changed: no longer the deep, final reds of sunset but watery pastels, pinks, and pale blues, taking on the first look of sunrise. We waited till after one to be sure of what was happening: Dawn *was* coming, light enough to steer by; the lake was quieting. We hiked along the beach, hunting a place to load without another soaking, and chose a massive log anchored out into the water.

The waves had subsided to long, rising swells, lifting the canoe up and over, caressing, forgiving, maternal. Again we chanced a far-out straight-line course, point to point; far off, I could just about discern the land I steered for, a solider darkness against the dark western sky. In front of me, Jim paddled steadily and, as the night wore on, slowed and slumped forward, dozing off in midstroke, and I shouted to him to keep awake. I would keep going; I felt the exhilaration that always rises to difficulties that can be faced with mere labor, mere endurance, a feeling that goes very far back, to the severity or gentle encouragement of doting parents: *I will not, by God, let it stop me.*

The darkness was chilling; only the steady labor of paddling warmed us. I kept glancing back over my shoulder for the sun, longing for it, the warmth and light. At each point thrusting out into the lake, as our straight course brought us in toward land, we went ashore, gathered sticks, made a fire, and curled around it like dogs, dozing till the wood burned down and the cold roused us again: Time to go on. The sun did not finally nudge its way past the horizon again till four-twenty, no longer dawning but full daylight now, in a rush. Toward six we pulled in beside a sleeping Indian fishing camp to cook breakfast, swarmed with mosquitoes.

We should have at least till noon before the sun, warming, called fresh winds off the waters. Comfort: That far we would get. But not much past eleven, as we reached the beginning of a last big bay, the cloudless phosphorescent light glowing across the water, the wind began to blow again, the waves to build. Again my mind seemed to be working with an odd detachment, no longer precisely mine to think with, to direct, control. Messages flashed, and now there were answers, only half disbelieved. *You promised us, God damn it, till noon. It's not time!* It was unfair; I was outraged. And: *Aw, come on, I was only kidding! Why d'ya hafta get so mad about everything?* It was the whining accent of a bad stand-up comic, wanting to be liked and not succeeding; a big overgrown lummox of playful stupidity, not meaning harm, really, but imbecilic and too strong beyond imagining for the pair of human gnats crawling across its breast. The lake, the spirit of the lake; the Great Slave. My mind answered primly, taking the advantage: *You have no right to play games with our safety. With our lives. Do you understand? No right!*

End of dialogue; the rough seas for a time quieted and we crossed the bottom of the bay to the base of Fish Point, the last between us and the town, still fifteen miles off. The shore here was no longer rocky but brim full, riffled along the edge in canoe-size slips where the earth drained and muskrats came down to fish; in the clear water, swarms of minnows clustered around our paddle blades. Muskeg and peat bog stretched flat to a line of trees a hundred yards back that marked the beginning of solid ground, carpeted with the bright, unnatural green of sprouting horsetail like miniature pines. Along the bank and here and there across the muskeg, as if planted in a great park for calculated effect, clumps of willow shrubs drooped in graceful curves, their tips puffed with catkins: spring; the late north spring, compressed into these few days at the end of June.

The bank was draining but looked wet still, terrible for mosquitoes, but we would have to camp here; we could go no farther. We tied up to a willow clump, unloaded, and spent the rest of the afternoon cooking and eating a long and elaborate brunch; out of lunchtime cheese and dried eggs I contrived an omelette that seemed magnificent. The mosquitoes were untroubling after all, and I realized why. Under the willows, the air swarmed with dragonflies flying in their sharp-turning geometric patterns, and occasionally one lighted with a mosquito or one of the big, stupid deer flies in its jaws; in the silence you could hear the jaws, chewing.

We crawled into the tent; slept; woke to eat again; and slept.

In the morning we were off in the cool of the dawn. This much, anyway, we had learned. Again it was a bright and merciful morning calm, and the lake, miles out, was no longer boundless. Far off, at the edge of sight, was the point where the Hay River came out from the land, we had only to get there and up the river to the town; beyond it was the low, dark line of the lake's northwest shore, coming into view across the water, separating from the point. A couple of times we rested, drifting with the waves. Through the glasses now I could make out a couple of buildings, then a pair of dredges anchored out beyond the river mouth. A motorboat pulled out from the shore and swung in a wide curve toward the river. We were among people again, God be thanked.

We were still a mile or two off when the lake gave us a last reminder of its indifference and its power. Noon again, this time not playful. The swells began to lift, the rising wind blowing the crests white. I lengthened the course, angling toward the safety of the shore. Wait here till night? Carry along the beach till we could get into the shelter of the river? *We will not be stopped!* The canoe crept on, riding the waves, the crosschop from the spreading river current. We had rounded the point. We were in the river now, out of the wind, digging in against the current. Arrival: Another destination opened out before us. I turned to look back. The lake, still glittering under brilliant spring light, was boiling up in the final lash of the storm. Half an hour, another hour: But that was behind us. We had made it.

The river now turns to the westward, becoming gradually narrower. . . . The current is very strong. . . . A stiff breeze . . . drove us on at a great rate. . . .

CHAPTER 6

In Pursuit of Mackenzie

"Anybody who can paddle all the way to the delta," Don Tetrault was saying, "has earned every mile of it!" He offered me a Lucky Strike, imported and expensive here, and leaned back behind the spacious walnut desk, shrewd eyes in a slightly fleshy face set off by a bushy Edwardian mustache. *Captain* Tetrault: fifteen years a Mackenzie pilot with the Canadian Coast Guard, plotting the river channels for the tug-and-barge traffic, replacing the buoys and the targetlike channel markers on the banks in accordance with the river's whims; and for three years now the head of a company operating a tiny summer cruise ship, the *Norweta*, up and down the Mackenzie between Hay River and the coast. That was why I had hunted him up. I'd heard of the ship, thought it might solve our one big problem—getting back up the river again—but we'd missed, even if I'd had the money for the fare: only twenty passengers on each weekly run, Don explained, and the ship was already booked solid to the end of the season. Starting to make money, evidently. I'd arrived to find him moving into offices in a new shopping center in the middle of the new town of

Hay River: cartons piled on the thick beige carpet, most of the furniture and equipment still in transit; pastel walls; and the thick feeling of confined air—the day was warm, the windows small and sealed, and neither the freon gas for the air conditioner nor the men to service it had arrived from Edmonton. Having dismissed the possibility of getting back by ship, we talked about the river, the delta, the North, our trip.

While we talked, my mind stayed on the problem: getting back, an obsession. Flying, we'd have to abandon the canoe; for ourselves and the packs, it would be expensive. Hay River, the home port of the barge lines, became doubly important. Something, I thought, could be arranged when we got here: a couple of spare bunks on a tug southbound from the delta, at the least, a vacant corner of a barge deck where we could unroll our sleeping bags. But the government-subsidized bureaucracy that runs the barges was averse to arrangements: They no longer took passengers—something about insurance and unionized work rules—but had I talked to Captain Tetrault about his ship? The return up the river remained an unknown. We were at the edge of a void.

The morning of our arrival, hungry for a cafe meal after the early start, we had paddled a mile up the Hay River to the place where our map showed the town. There were great open areas that had the look of shipyards, tugs and barges moored along the banks, but all was eerily deserted; lunchtime. We steered for one of the boats. Aft in the galley a pudgy cook was fixing himself a meal. The *main* part of the town? I delicately inquired. You mean the *new* town, he corrected me, with the waspish satisfaction that is the style of cooks everywhere. Five miles up the river. Strong current, lots of *rocks*—you'll have to watch it. The town had moved.

We worked our way a little farther up the river. I noticed a man standing beside a float plane tied up at a dock, and we went ashore for further directions. Within an hour we had stored the canoe, called a taxi for the haul into town, and were checking in at a motel in a thriving new town that, except for the dark-skinned men loitering by the doorway, might have been a suburb of Edmonton seven hundred miles south down the gravel track known as the Mackenzie Highway—or of any other North American city.

Hay River's history is the history, in little, of the settlements dotted through the Mackenzie Valley; its present is the urban future of the North that seems to be the unstated goal of Canadian government policy. Around 1860 an Indian village began to appear on maps at the mouth of the river's east channel, but probably it was much older, at least as a summer gathering place for fishing. A Hudson's Bay post was built a few years later to trade for furs; missions followed, eventually a detachment of Mounties, representing government and law. At the beginning of World War II, a new town was built opposite the Indian settlement, in the place shown on our map, a big alluvial island cut off from the mainland by the river's two channels. As in most other places in the North, the U. S. Army Corps of Engineers turned up a couple of years later to demonstrate that, pockets of permafrost notwithstanding, roads and an airport runway could indeed be built. In 1949, the Mackenzie Highway arrived, run north from the wartime road to Alaska; in 1964, with the discovery of lead and zinc at Pine Point sixty-five miles east along the lake, a railroad line followed the highway. At about the same time, after a particularly damaging spring flood, the government began building a new town safely up the river on the mainland, a process that, with newly opened stores and offices like Don Tetrault's, was nearing completion the day we arrived ten years later: not only the neat rows of suburban houses, the motels and gas stations, but the skeleton of a future city in the town hall, library, hospital, the RCMP command post and jail, the government liquor store, the fortress-modern monolith of a school made of purple poured concrete, and the thirteen-story concrete apartment building, black, that towers over the town.

With the coming of the road, the town began to grow to its present official three thousand (unofficially perhaps a thousand more), evenly divided between whites and Indians. Of the latter, about a third have formal tribal connections; the rest are Métis for census purposes, one or other mixture of blood. Except for voting rights in the tribal councils (and whatever new settlement finally regularizes the exploitation of the tribal lands), the distinction no longer has much meaning. The Indians, drawn to the towns by several forms of official beneficence, have become indistinguishable from the Métis.

Like any town where nearly everything is new-built or building, Hay River has a look of prosperity. More than in most places of the North the appearance has a basis in reality: minerals that only ten years ago sparked what is said to be the greatest rush in the country's history and, in all likelihood, barely hint at the riches that eventually will be dug out of The Territory (it is not a prospect that a cautious national government likes to talk about); a fishing industry whose government-run processing plant annually freezes four million pounds of whitefish and lake trout taken out of Great Slave; round-the-clock shipyards where most of the valley's tugs and barges are built from steel plate manufactured in Vancouver and hauled the 1,500 miles north; port facilities (including a new synchrolift, one of three in the country, capable of lifting a two-hundred-foot ship out of the water as bodily as a toy boat in a bathtub) for the 150 barges and two dozen tugs, some of them 170-foot oceangoing giants but all shallow-built for the rapids and low-water season of the Mackenzie, for which Hay River is the home base. Yet the appearance is deceptive. Local boosters, waxing lyrical over the gas and oil strikes in the Mackenzie Valley and on the Arctic coast of Canada and Alaska, talk about doubling the shipping tonnage to handle the building of the pipelines that, one way or another, will follow; and in the next breath grumble at the inefficiency and operating losses of the barge lines that have to be made good by subsidies. The veneer of prosperity in Hay River and the other half-urban centers of the Northwest Territories is a luxury paid for in Ottawa, to the extent of $320 million per year—roughly $8,000 for each of the 40,000 people who inhabit the Northwest Territories; what comes out again in the form of actual production—ore, including gold, and oil, gas, fish, lumber—amounts to only about one sixth of that total.

Except for our travel-stained packs piled in the corner, the room where we landed might have been lifted from any salesman's hotel: gold all-over carpeting, a pair of double beds, soundproof masonry walls, even a television set. For two nights, we would be back among urban niceties where I still, I ruefully noted, felt more at home than on the rivers and lakes; so be it, town-bred after all. We headed downstairs to the barroom, carved out of the permafrost and decorated with leaping stuffed fish, a snarling lynx, a bobcat in the act of capturing a snowshoe rabbit, three winter-white ptarmigan but—dark-oak-paneled walls and buxom pink-and-gold barmaids manning the taps—with the air of an English pub. Over ninety-cent bottles of Canadian lager, brewed in the South, Edmonton or Calgary, we talked with two commercial fishermen, on the beach for now, protesting the low prices of the government marketing board, men who had been thirty or forty years in The Territory working at one thing and another, now with their own boats. I wanted to know what they thought of the past week's weather, half expecting that for them, boatmen, fishermen, it had been no more than a little choppy; but no, they certified it, that was a real storm we had been through. They talked about the lake, rocky, shallow, and dangerous along the south shore, not a harbor anywhere; the east end, which we had missed, was beautiful, high cliffs of pink granite, many islands, good

fishing for them as it had been for Mackenzie. I described
some of the plants we'd noticed that were new to us. Yes,
they knew them too, but the names? The names they knew
no more than we did.

Jim and I ordered more beer. Later, back in the room,
there would be long, steaming showers, separating a month
of grime that, covering the tan, had turned hands and faces
Indian dark. Later still, in the windowless dining lounge in
the interior of the motel building, there would be an ample
and quite respectable dinner, the menu signed by the chef;
we ate in silence, hungrily, hunched over the table, wiping
the plates and speaking only to ask the waitress for more
beer, more rolls and butter. English licensing hours: the
lounge served drinks from noon to two and six to ten, and
only with a meal. In the meantime there was a load of food
to buy; and two problems to solve, the one of getting back
from the delta that took me fruitlessly to the barge line
headquarters and to Don Tetrault's new office, and another,
equally complicated, of getting to the west end of the lake
and the beginning of the great river.

Back in Fort Smith, Jacques had talked skeptically about
canoeing the last hundred miles of the lake. Why bother
when we could do it by road? There would be trucks to give
us a lift along the spur of the Mackenzie Highway that leads
around the lake to Yellowknife, the territorial capital, on the
North Arm, and branches downriver 160 miles to the next
town, Fort Simpson; there would always be someone going
that way. It was the final reason we had come this way and
now, two weeks behindhand, it was no longer a choice; another week lost to a storm and we would not make it to the
end of the river—or so I told myself. But the problem was
interesting in itself.

I spent the afternoon in the motel room telephoning. No
trucks going that way; someone offered to share a chartered
plane, but it was more money than I could afford, even to
make up a lost week of canoe time. There were, however,

several people, new immigrants with British accents, who had light trucks to rent, at stiff rates and on condition that we make our own arrangements for getting them back. Eventually we had a deal; and I had found a refugee from Ontario, summer fishing guide and winter trucker, who would take the day to go with us to the end of the lake and drive the truck back.

And how long would we take, Don had asked, to get to the delta? If we could connect with the cruise ship at, say, Aklavik, on the west side of the delta, he could at least offer a ride across to Inuvik, sitting up overnight in the lounge. Maybe I could write something about it. I considered. We could get there in three weeks, I thought, but we'd allow four—places to explore, people to meet. And of course the weather, I cautiously added. "You'll have earned every mile of it!"

We were up early to load the packs onto the pickup, lash the canoe. We crowded into the cab, the three of us. The road, steep cambered as the others that lead north, cuts inland, then, toward the place where the lake narrows into the Mackenzie, returns to the water and a ferry crossing to the road to Yellowknife. In low spots where rain overnight had washed out the thin coating of gravel, the truck skittered as if on glare ice, despite the year-round snow tires. I drove cautiously, keeping down the middle. A couple of cars passed, bound east and south. Mal, the guide, regaled us with fishing stories: enormous walleyes and northerns, lake trout that you could take all summer up on the surface of this frigid lake, but getting scarce now. He was a big, wide man with the shape and music-hall face of an Oliver Hardy, the same small, square mustache bristling under his nose, but soured out of shape by bad teeth (a new set had been fitted but would not be delivered from the Edmonton lab for months). Fifteen years now in the North, long enough to

be no longer comfortable "outside"; on the occasional vacation trip to one of the cities to the south, he grew nervous of
the crowds, the oversize buildings, and flew home before the
time was up. Before that, there had been several years with
the Canadian contingent in Korea; now occasionally, part of
his job, it fell to him to backhand a fighting-drunk Indian
into submissiveness and loft him out of the bar at the motel,
but—"Violence, I hate violence. Up here you've got to help
each other"—as he was doing.

The hundred miles took us all the morning. There was a
gas station in sight of the ferry, the first since Hay River,
and I pulled in to tank up for the return trip. A woman in
jeans and carpet slippers lumped across the rutted mud from
the cafe to man the pump, plump and fortyish, blond and
curly-headed, with a Thames-side accent that had crossed
the Atlantic intact. Where were we headed? Down the
river? "Ow, I shouldn't like that, out in the bush. Too many
mosquitoes. Course, you can build fires, they say, and the
smoke will keep them off, that helps." Yes, I agreed. That
helps. All around us mosquitoes swarmed and whined,
pricking at hands and face.

The ferry landing where we would load the canoe was a
heap of boulders shoved out into the river and plastered
over with bulldozed earth and gravel, wide enough for the
three or four cars that would fit the little boat's flat deck. I
pulled in front of a waiting truck to get near the water, and
we climbed down to unstrap the canoe. The truck driver got
out, a thin, crushed little man, and let fly with an inventive
burst of obscenities delivered in a despairing monotone. I
had other things on my mind, it took me a minute to get the
gist of what he was saying, and—"I beg your pardon?" I
asked, meaning that I hadn't made out what he was saying.
The little man continued, not repeating himself. Mal took a
step toward him and very gently explained that we were not
taking his place on the ferry, just loading a canoe. We let
the canoe down into the water and I started passing the
packs to my son. The driver waited by his truck, watchful.

17. Ken Johnson, one of the men responsible for cutting the road that will connect the Mackenzie Valley's Arctic frontier with the cities of the South.

18. A few miles downriver from Wrigley, a water-carved cleft in a rocky hill, Roche Qui Trempe à l'Eau—one of the few of Mackenzie's camp sites that can be identified with certainty.

19. On a wide curve of Mackenzie beach near Fort Norman, slabs of mud-covered ice dropped by the spring floods, still melting in mid-July.

20. Windbound on a narrow beach below Norman Wells, we waited out another blow, leaning against the canoe to doze, while dinner cooks.

21. "Two rivers opposite," Mackenzie had noted, the Redstone and the Saline, another point on his route that can be identified with confidence.

22. Julie Lenny, an Indian craftswoman, in the door of her shop at Fort Norman. She holds a pair of moosehide *mukluks* (winter overshoes) and a doll dressed in the pigtails, leggings, and tunic of the past.

23. At CANOL, built by the U. S. Army during World War II, an Indian boy swings from an electric conduit while his parents dismantle the abandoned workshop for the lumber—still, after a quarter century, fresh and unweathered in the clean northern climate.

The river here in its beginning is a mile and a quarter across. Another couple of miles and it narrows inside a big island to a five-mile stretch contradictorily named the Providence Rapids. Mackenzie, coming through here, had described a strong current but no rapids, but after our scare on the Slave River the name had made me nervous enough the night before to hunt up someone who knew enough of the river to tell me what course to follow, and I'd spent an hour talking with a helpful Mountie. No, not really a rapids, he'd assured me, nothing to worry about except maybe in low water at the end of the summer, just keep to the right bank, the north. He was not the fair, open-faced Scots-English type we'd met so far but a rare Québécois, small, dark, neat, and quick, like the gigolo in a French bedroom comedy of the thirties. Canoeists? Canoeists were a pain in the ass, getting lost, having to be hunted for. They were already checking the hotels when we got to Hay River four days late; next they would make the rounds of the fishing boats, then go out in one of the fast RCMP boats, send out a plane. A pain in the ass! I wondered if everyone had as much trouble as we did getting the Indians to talk. What was it about us, exactly? "The trouble with you is, you look like a sociologist." Sociologists: crazy people from Ottawa, always filling up questionnaires, asking the same crazy questions. Did your mother sleep with your grandfather? Did your father sleep with your sister? The Indians wanted to be polite but did not understand. Why should people want to know such things? I considered: the horn-rimmed glasses, the month's beard, the outlander's clothes, for the moment freshly washed; a funny-looking pair, yes. Perhaps, I suggested, the trouble was simply that there weren't enough Indians to go around. Now, if each learned ethnographer, with his government grant and his social policy to devise, could be provided with an Indian of his own . . .

The canoe was loaded now. I checked the trim, nervously

puffed a cigarette, waiting for the ferry to start across and get out of the way. I studied the crossing; the current was strong enough to pull the ferry in a long arc, downstream. I tried to clap Mal on the shoulders, but he was too big around to reach. Time: farewell and good luck. With a long push of the paddles we swept out into the current.

Keep to the right bank. With an eye to the ferry, which had already gone over and was starting back, we crossed the river. The current here ran deep and fast under steep, high banks, only a little turbulent out in the middle, five or six miles an hour. We dug in hard and in a rush of exhilaration made the ten miles to the first of the river settlements, Fort Providence, in an hour: a marvelous sensation, birdlike, flying, weightless, like skiing through deep powder in high mountains. It was only the outer and most tangible of a whole series of feelings that lifted us now: to have reached at last, after a month's traveling, Mackenzie's river and the real start of the trip; but, equally, to have put behind us the guilty luxury of our day in town, back in our element, with no arrangements to make, no human complications, and none to depend on but ourselves. Behind these feelings was another I kept to myself: that we were now within less than a day of Mackenzie; with effort and luck and the grace of the river, we could catch him.

It was the last day of June. Mackenzie with his canoes had come down this channel from the lake 185 years earlier almost to the day, and with the same exhilaration we were feeling. After the three weeks' tedium of his lake passage—dodging the floating rafts of breaking ice, often stopped by gales and downpour, running down deep bays that led no-where, till the heavy seas drove the canoes in among reeds and muddy shallows—he had reached the great river after all. It existed. It flowed west, as predicted: the passage through the mountains. The wind blew strong from the east. They raised the clumsy square sail on his big canoe and ran before the wind. His journal here was filled with excited notes on the strength of the current, promising ease and a swift passage. At one point another day down the river, sounding its depth, he lodged his lead on the bottom and lost it, "the current running so strong that we could not clear it with eight paddles and the strength of the line."

Below the first of the houses that must be Fort Providence, I stem-turned the canoe upriver into the current and headed into a small dock. We tied up and climbed the hundred-foot bank. There was a man I wanted to talk to here, another priest, supposed to know the river and its people. Except for a couple of children playing in the dusty street, the place was deserted: Canada's National Day was coming, another of the official long weekends that dot the summer calendar; the people were off down the river in their boats, camping; in the distance we could see the white dots of their canvas wall tents along the shore. I roused an Englishman locked in the living quarters behind his store, and got directions. The man we were looking for lived at the other end of the village, a mile. I thought about it: too much; I did not feel like walking it. We went back to the canoe and paddled. It was an odd feeling I had noticed in Hay River, a resistance, but we had not tested it much there with walking: sea legs, weak, all muscle in the arms and shoulders. It was a feeling the French canoemen often expressed but never talked about, lacking the language. I understood. They would run the canoes, loaded, half loaded, down rapids at the edge of being passable and not rarely spill a treasure of trade goods for future archaeologists, sometimes their lives. Not for the sake of pride, of skill: They were *canoemen,* they *hated* walking. So also the portages, when they had no choice: double- and triple-loaded with the ninety-pound *pièces,* and not the slow, stable, swinging stride of the heavily loaded packer but a shuffling, hobbled trot; anything to get it over with, get back in the canoe.

Father Pichet was not at home. Mass done, he'd taken his car and like everyone else gone off for the day.

From Fort Providence the river's course is another fifteen miles, more west than north, to a great elbow called Mills Lake, ten miles across. There it swings west and south for sixty miles, then gradually, in a succession of slow loops, northwest again seventy miles to meet its chief tributary, the Liard, a French word meaning "aspen" that the Indians still pronounce in the old way.

We pushed on as far as a small round island on the edge of Mills Lake. Along the way, in the distance, we passed a white family of weekenders making camp. The children, seeing us, started to wave, and their parents shouted across the water: How far you going? All the way! I answered between paddle strokes. They could not hear: How far? Inuvik? Yes! And last their valediction: Come back! Yes, come back. We would try.

The island, lapped by fast current all around, looked likely for fishing, and after dinner, in the long sunset, we walked it, casting out from the shore where the current trolled the lures down the river. Jim had the luck of a big northern, which we filleted and kept for breakfast. After dark, feeling happy with myself, I sat up late by the candle lantern in the tent, writing and reading; went out for a last look, and for the first time since Lake Athabasca saw the moon rising through haze to the west, tiny and round, pale as a grape; and went back to find that the candle had guttered down and melted a hole through the nylon floor of the tent. I spent another hour patching it, embarrassed, while my son slept.

Below Mills Lake, Mackenzie distanced us, and we were never again close. His weather was cold, sometimes thick with fog, there were slabs of dirty ice along the banks, left by the retreating spring flood. One afternoon a squall drove them off the river early. Other days, keeping on till dark, midnight or later by our time, they covered close to a hundred miles. In three days, marveling at the strength of the current, he was camped below the mouth of the Liard, which took us five; we did not keep up.

It took us most of the next day to cross Mills Lake. We started early, with the wind beginning to blow. By noon it was coming hard across the open water from the north, raw and harsh. We worked in close to the shore, zigzagging with fast turns in the trough of the waves, finally poling through shallows where thick reeds and willows broke the white-caps. We camped early on wet ground cleared by the spring ice, worn out and much discouraged; the river was not going to be much help. I raged at myself, the much-protected son of lovingly nurtured parents, beguiled by small hopes. My language, I noticed, had become foul enough to silence the liberated vocabulary Jim had brought home from college; with my sons I had always been careful, but now I could not help myself.

The weather continued against us—cold enough at mid-day when we stopped for lunch so that I built a fire for warmth—and made the third day on the river slow and painful. It improved, the sun returned, the river, swinging north, narrowed to a stronger current, and we made fifty miles, a good day for us, though mediocre for Mackenzie. We camped that night on a high, grassy bank no more than a fast morning's run from Fort Simpson, bright sun till after midnight gilding the long reach of river in both directions: Rabbitskin, the name of a stream cutting through the bank here but also a place, signified by three ruined cabins that had housed an Indian band till the chief died and those who remained retreated to the town. Pike scuttled through the reeds as we landed. A good portent: We would eat fish for breakfast.

Where the Liard and the Mackenzie join, they have carved the bank in a sharp, high point like the prow of a battleship, which the *voyageurs* named Gros Cap. The Mackenzie is here a mile and a half across, the Liard at its mouth, though broken up by low islands and mud flats, about the same, doubling the flow. Below the joining, the two rivers flow north side by side for a hundred miles un-mingled, the Liard on the left bank coffee-colored with the mud it carries, the Mackenzie on the right clear and shining as a mountain brook. Coming around an island in mid-stream, you see the town, Fort Simpson, first across three miles of open river: a row of low, white-painted, blue-roofed buildings on a hundred-foot bluff, with a sharp church spire sticking up in the middle like a dart in a target; the spring we arrived, the flood had reached almost to the top of the bank. Somewhere near the confluence of the two rivers, Mackenzie's North-West Company by 1804 had a profitable fur post operating; the present site and the name were con-ferred after the merger by a Scots grandee of the Hudson's Bay Company, Sir George Simpson.

We crossed to the town and paddled a mile up the Liard, hunting a place to camp; no more hotels now. Half a mile inland, the town had carved a tourist campground among the spindly pines. We landed, hiked in to look. Again, my legs protested; for the night we had, it was not worth carry-ing the packs and canoe. We lazily returned to the river, paddled a little farther up to get above the town's effluvia, and cleared a patch of willow on the mud-flat beach. It would do.

Fort Simpson is a frontier town, in the mode of the North in the 1970s: The Mackenzie Highway defines the frontier. Parts of the road have been built farther north along the river—twenty miles here, fifty farther on, like the cut-off segments of an immense worm—as far as Inuvik a hundred miles above the Arctic Circle, but in the unhurried manner of this land it will be ten years or more before all are con-nected and the road is complete (that is observation—the official schedule is more optimistic). For now, the road ends here, and here is repeated the same destructive grinding together of two peoples, white and Indian, that has occurred at every meeting since the first white fishermen landed on the Nova Scotia coast to swap beads and hardware for furs. One may feel grief but not, in justice, apportion blame. They were incommensurate from the beginning. They are so still.

The Indians here and all along the upper half of the Mackenzie are the Slave, linguistic cousins of the Chipewyans, darker-skinned but also less Mongol in their looks. Even colloquially softened, as it is, to "Slavey," the name is harsh to an American ear made sensitive by centuries of racial and ethnic hatred, but to the people who bear it, it is simply their name, as Liard is the name of a river and Gros Cap the name of a point, without other meaning; or so far. As a tribe, they are doubly dispossessed. The name translates one given in the eighteenth century by the less numerous but more aggressive Cree, pushing west from Lake Winnipeg into the Athabasca country, then north along the Slave River and west around Great Slave Lake. It meant inferiority, not servitude; slavery in the latter sense was unknown among the tribes of the Canadian Northwest, whose warfare was long-distance raids against the Eskimos a thousand miles north on the coast, where they rarely bothered with prisoners. And the Cree superiority was real: From their earlier contact with the traders, they had European goods, guns above all; they fought to protect and expand their advantage as middlemen. The Slaves were driven from their homeland, the river and lake that still bear their name, and settled on the Mackenzie, a minority among minorities, and now outnumbered by the strangers pressing in to wherever the road ends.

Of the eight hundred people at Fort Simpson, fewer than half are Indian—Slave. Altogether in the valley the tribe numbers perhaps twenty-five hundred members who actually speak Slavey, another thousand who understand it. For all, after a generation of schooling, English is the language of reading and writing and, in the lilting sing-song of a second tongue, of everyday speech; the tribal council conducts its meetings in English, and among these leaders are those who, for the world they will live in, see no purpose in preserving their own language for their children. It may well, therefore, disappear without ever having achieved a written form. For a century there has existed a clumsy syllabic version, but few know it (it appears in an occasional government pamphlet explaining, in simplest terms, what to do when the Mountie arrests you, how you should apply for welfare). It is only in the past ten years that a serious effort has been made to convert the language to writing, by an evangelical group seeking a means of translating the Bible. One of the two men supported in this project, Vic Monus, a Hungarian-Canadian, lives in Fort Simpson. It is a life work, begun at the beginning, with mastery of linguistics, then several years in an untouched tribal settlement, transcribing into phonetics the language as he heard it, constantly questioning, and working what he heard into a Roman alphabet much modified by accent marks. Besides the translation, which is his living, he is allowed to volunteer an hour or two a week in the local school, teaching a few children to speak and write their language, but he is not much encouraged. With the pragmatic assurance of the tribal chiefs, men like Father Minez, half a lifetime in the North, deny that there is anything in the language worth writing, but they are not linguists. The reality is rich in tribal myth and tradition, the exact poetry of the names for things and places of a people whose perceptions of the world are more aesthetic than practical; the oral history of a race, its identity, if it can be preserved.

The whites are the young graduates who man the territorial government offices and the school, the Hudson's Bay store, well placed in the new bungalows a hundred yards back from the river that give the place the air of a town like any other; and a volatile mix of driven men, in retreat from something or in pursuit. The helicopter jockey who hauls drums of water and chemicals downriver to the periodic forest fires (and steaks and wine to geologists hunting oil and metals from camps in the bush) is an ex-Marine who learned his flying in Vietnam. The slender blond youth with a gold ring in one earlobe who drives a pickup up and down the dirt road from the flying field faces a manslaughter charge in one of the settled provinces—driving and drinking —and cannot well go back. The thirtyish Australian woman behind one of the two bars has escaped a typewriter in a Sydney office, no prospect, boyfriend, husband, family to hold her. There is a sprinkling of American boys, avoiding draft. Women are scarce. The work here is done by men on the loose, but they are not the saloon brawlers of the legendary American West, they have been tamed by education and fantasy; for every out-of-date news magazine, paperback, or week-old Edmonton newspaper on sale at The Bay, there are dozens of four-color slicks packed with breasts, buttocks, and, this year, pubic hair.

There is no city-bred skill that the frontier North has in abundance, to see it is to sense the lack and feel the corresponding tug of money to be made: drive a cab or truck, open a garage or store, bar, restaurant, hotel; start a charter-plane service or a short-run barge line to rival the subsidized giants in Hay River. New immigrants with no other ties are steered gently north. A Pakistani engineer, darker than the local Indians, supervises the latest resurveying of the lagging Mackenzie Highway route. Chinese families from Hong Kong run restaurants—chop suey or steak and potatoes—dotted along the roads north as far as they lead. (At one on the road to McMurray where we stopped for coffee, my mind ran on the two oriental-looking girls behind the counter, speculating on what tribe they belonged to, what the real history of the Bering Strait migration had been, how they would fit, in looks and language, if they were somehow transported back to the Asian heartland—until Jim sensibly asked what they were talking between themselves and learned that it was—Mandarin! So much for theory.) A highway builder soured by big corporations where he was only a notch in a production schedule has come North to be his own master and make human contact with his work crews. Land is a paradox: limitless and all but untouched; but also—to buy, freehold, prospect, or mine—scarce and expensive. An Indian who has actual title to a piece of ground becomes the focus of elaborate stratagems. As in De Maupassant's tales of land-hungry peasants, alcohol is still the one that works best: Keep them drinking for a week, a month, and they'll sell. Landless again and with a little cash, they wander the dusty streets, doze the afternoons in the friendlier of the two cafes.

With the tent up and the packs cautiously out of sight inside, we scrambled up the muddy bank from our camp, lugging the clumsy camera pack in hope of some pictures, and started back toward the town. There was a hotel. We would not stay, but we could blow ourselves to dinner. I was feeling starved again for solid meat.

Toward the middle of town and for a couple of blocks on either side of the hotel, the dusty main street was lined with board sidewalks. In a muddy yard beside an aging white-painted house, a man was hosing down a battered station wagon. California license plate. With the welcoming warmth that Americans sometimes feel for their countrymen alone in a foreign place, Jim and I stopped to talk. Like characters in a Dostoevski novel, the whites in this northland introduce themselves by telling their life history. This casual intimacy is bred of the country. Cast together in a million miles of wilderness, isolated, you instinctively take care to know and be known; survival depends on the kind of man you are and have to deal with.

Bob Henry's story was wilder than most. As a kid in the thirties he had flown through the country with Wiley Post in a light plane. He was sixtyish now, gray-headed, tough, muscular, hard-drinking, humorous, volubly energetic. Early in June, soon after breakup, he had come back with a partner, had hired the house for the summer, and gone to work on a scheme that had been ripening for forty years: to suck gold up from the river bottom, using portable dredges mounted on a small outboard boat. And the scheme had worked! Six pounds they'd collected in the first couple of weeks, twenty thousand dollars' worth on the current market and on the rise. Then one day going up the Liard they had started through a rapids, unmarked on the map, and the boat had dumped. His partner was lost. Bob had made it to shore and spent three days crawling back through the mud to Fort Simpson, at one point running up against one of the huge black bears. Indians had found the boat and fished from the river mouth a headless corpse they thought was his partner. But no! That was not the man: never found. They talked of strong spirits, *manitou*, guarding the river and its gold; far up, there is a place called Headless Valley, named for earlier prospectors whose bodies were found but never their heads. "God-damned superstitious Indians! They think their medicine men praying was why the astronauts got to the moon!" But it was a bad river for sure. He was taking a break, waiting for another partner promised to come up from California; keeping an eye out for what was going on in town, for strangers like us coming down the river, down the road from the south. His feeling for the place was proprietary and cherishing: This was *his* town now, and the collection of freaks who inhabited it.

"Get away from there, you little vermin!" Bob shouted at a couple of Indian children playing around the yard. The kids ran. "Nothing to do but booze all summer and breed all winter! Like the God-damned mosquitoes." He pulled a clipping from his wallet, the story from the local weekly about his partner's death, picked up by a dozen American papers. Maybe we'd like a story about ourselves? Not, I thought, worth drowning for, but "That would be fine," I said. O.K., he'd introduce us to the editor. Or how about a lift to the territorial liquor store? We climbed in and rode the two blocks. Party tonight: Promising to be around, we headed for the hotel and dinner.

The hotelkeeper was an Englishman—tweed jacket, mock-regimental tie, round puffy face and sagging eyes of late middle age—of the type that once peopled the semide-tached Tudor stucco villas beside railway lines in close-in London suburbs: with the calculated insolence of that inter-mediate class perpetually pressing upward against the threat of sliding down; "going out to Canada," as he would call it, would have been the means of a social leap, an es-cape, but he was a little late for such a change. Now, throned behind the desk in the lobby of his forty-two-room hostelry at the end of the frontier road, he lived on terms of disesteem with the Indians and roughneck whites who were his clientele. They threw rocks through the lighted sign out front, mudballs against the walls; he put up signs in the lobby forbidding loitering and kept the men's room locked. When you asked to wash your hands, he came ponderously out from behind the desk, key in hand, to unlock the door and stood waiting to lock it again when you finished. When Bob Henry turned up from California, Mr. Kidd tried to persuade him to take the bar in hand, the square win-dowless room behind the dining room in the interior of the hotel that was called the cocktail lounge. "Jesus Christ!" Bob told him, "I *spill* more liquor in a day than you sell in your God-damned bar in a week." Or so he told it; it became one of his stories.

The restaurant was Chinese: a manager and cook with the energetic smooth-faced assurance that would one day own the lot; and a couple of spindly boys, still learning the lan-guage, who waited on tables and evidently did not enjoy serving the white barbarians. Jim venturously tried the chop suey. Famished for meat, I ordered a wafer-thin steak with "vegetable," a half-dozen watery canned peas. We stuffed ourselves with bread and beer.

Afterward, in the intoxication of the northern summer light, we wandered the town and did not hike back to camp till after midnight. We slept late. It was close to noon before we had packed up and paddled back down the river to town to mail letters and film and replenish our food for the next jump. Bob Henry was up and cruising the main street in his car. Where the hell had we been? Looked for us but couldn't find our camp—the party had gone on till six o'clock at René's camp up the river. René: a trapper who'd wintered in northern British Columbia and come down for the summer, fabulously strong but drinking too much, nothing else to do and getting worried about it. No one knew his last name; Tarzan, people were calling him, that was the look of him, from Quebec but a half-breed (probably—trapping in The Territory had been reserved to "natives" since the twenties, and he would need a touch of Indian to sell his furs). The party was regrouping at the Eskimo, the other bar, at the other end of town from John Kidd's cheerless hotel. We climbed in.

In the half light of the Eskimo Cafe a dozen men had collected themselves around small tables shoved together, filling the room, the remnants of the party: young truck drivers drifted north from British Columbia and Alberta; four men from Minneapolis—young professionals, neat and small, each with a pipe and the beginning of beard grown on the drive out—who were flying that afternoon in two chartered float planes to the headwaters of the South Nahanni for a two-week canoe trip down that arduous mountain river; too busy with their maps to talk. Their faces wrinkled with collective distaste when Bob tried to kid them about a girl at the party last night. Everyone was ordering hamburgers and beer. The dentist, however, was calling insistently for a glass of milk. No one challenged him. This was the new frontier.

I sat down next to René: a big man neither young nor old, wide, bony shoulders thrusting through a striped T-shirt, heavy forearms, angular, long, dark face framed by a wedge of shoulder-length hair fluffed out from his neck like the stylized tresses of a pharaoh. An elderly Indian, addled by drink, sat down and put his face between us, trying to tell me something. "Listen, my friend," René said quietly, "we are trying to talk." The brown face and swimming eyes leaned toward me: "I love you," the Indian was muzzily saying. It was important to him to say it. "Don't hurt him, René," I said. "I love you," the Indian said, "I *love* you!" René picked him up and propped him at a table along the wall of the room.

For the Canadian Centenary in 1967 René had joined one of the crews that paddled sections of the transcontinental canoe routes of the *voyageurs;* probably it was what got him out of whatever Quebec village he'd been born in. I tried to get him to tell me about it. We talked about the mosquitoes. He had a cure, he told me with great seriousness: a teaspoon of lemon juice in the morning coffee. The lemon came through the pores and kept them off. I studied his bare arms and wondered.

The party was starting to move. The Minnesotans were getting anxious to load their gear into the planes and be off. René was going back to his camp. With Bob, Jim and I followed him back.

The camp was another mile up the Liard from where we had camped last night, on high, cleared ground back from the water, but reachable by car from the road south. It was meticulously built, everything new, like a demonstration of how such things are done: a new pickup truck, shiny Hudson's Bay axes, a chain saw; stove-size logs, exactly cut, were stacked beside the cooking place. The furs that year were paying again, and well. In the spring since coming down, René had built two cabins side by side, one solid and chinked for cold weather, the other open at the sides; the mosquitoes could not bother him much. Two dog sleds and a high-runnered sleigh leaned against the winter cabin; an elegant fiberglass canoe lay bottom up near the water. The dogs set up an excited yipping as we drove up, and again it was like a lesson in trapper's proficiency. There were two teams. The two lead dogs, big as wolves, were chained to stakes at one end of the line, the sixteen smaller team dogs spaced out behind them, each with a collar. The stakes were four-inch logs driven into the ground; for each dog he had knocked together a neat house, with a can of water set into the earth in front. The afternoon was hot. Flies tormented the dogs, sucking at their eyes. René was filling their water cans from a bucket. The dogs were frantic with excitement, leaping against the sharp snap of their chains. A treat: He was going to take them down to the river for a swim. He went from dog to dog, unchaining them. The small dogs swarmed around him, yipping and jumping. Not the lead dogs? No, set them loose and they would lead their teams off into the bush, a pack. A swooping, final gesture of the hands: gone!

Another truck came down the track, and the girl of last night Bob had been kidding about got out and drifted purposefully toward René and the milling leaderless dog pack: Birgit, a twenty-year-old Swede like the materilization of an adolescent fantasy; lithe and slim and barefoot, the short, boyish hair bleached almost white around her tanned face, firm young nipples popping through the flimsy T-shirt. Hitchhiking *around the world,* Bob had said. He had picked her up on the road on her way into town, gave her a bed in his rented house. She had offered to sleep with him the first night, fair exchange. He had refused: Not on your sweet ass, sweetheart, with all these kids around to screw and me old enough to be your God-damned grandfather. Pouting, she had joined his repertory of tales.

René was taking the canoe out to swim the dogs. Did she know how to paddle a canoe? A *little,* Birgit meltingly admitted, in a charming accent. In Sweden . . . "Then I will *teach* you!" He got her into the bow, handed her a paddle, and pushed off, the dogs swarming and splashing in the shallows around them.

The afternoon was slipping by, and Jim and I had miles to

go: time to get going in our own canoe. Turning back toward Bob's car, I waved, but René and the girl, intent on instruction, did not wave back.

I was beginning to be nervous about our loaded canoe, moored for hours now at the RCMP dock below the high riverbank: everything we possessed. Bob drove us back. From the top of the bank we could see a couple of kids prowling toward the canoe, tentative, innocent, curious. "Get *away* from there, you little bastards!" Bob shouted down at them. The children looked startled, backed off. We scrambled down the bank.

"Come on back this way when you get there," Bob was urging. "Give you a couple of beds, plenty of room in that dump. Have a party."

Sure, I said, we might do that. There were a dozen ways of getting back from the coast, none more likely than the rest, and Fort Simpson was one of the possibilities: a short-run barge that far, then take to the road. Why not? And, thanks, we said. Then we were off and moving, eyes on the new course. The current does not give you time for looking back.

The beach was covered with coals, and the English chief gathered some of the softest he could find, as a black dye. . . .

CHAPTER 7

Of Men, Oil, and the River

Below the Liard River, the Mackenzie continues west-north-west for another seventy-five miles, then, at Camsell Bend, where it collides with the first of a series of mountain ranges, swings north and from there runs generally north or northwest till it empties into the Arctic Ocean—another thousand miles, or nearly so. Until the end, Mackenzie recorded these directions with the westerly bias of his compass and his hopes for a passage through to the Pacific; the river's two banks were north and south, not east and west as they show on a modern map.

They passed the mouth of the Liard at a distance and did not cross the river for a close look. It was known by name and approximate location from the gossip Peter Pond had collected from Indians trading at Fort Chipewyan, perhaps also from Ageena's travels in the great valley, for hunting or warfare: the River of the Mountain. You do not see the mountains until you have traveled several days up it, but that Indian name is true and, ironically, if you were resolved to reach the Pacific by canoe, it pointed to the most likely route anywhere on the continent. In the rush of summer,

Mackenzie could not permit himself the time from travel to explore farther; that day in particular, it was already late, the men could think only of camp and food. It was not till the next day a few miles downstream, in a raw morning fog, that Mackenzie's canoemen crossed to the west bank—seeking, as always, the strongest current, the shortest paddling distance, point of land to bend of river—and he noticed how the river had changed: "The water, from being very limpid and clear, was become dark and muddy. This alteration must have proceeded," he surmised, "from the influx of some river to the Southward. . . ." The change was from the muddy Liard, carrying a brown, soft sediment that you see at each stroke swirling against the paddle blade, uniform into the sunless depths of the river. It is harmless, without taste or smell. If the look of it bothers you, you avoid it by camping on the river's east bank, where for a hundred miles the pure water of the Mackenzie flows unmingled with the muddy Liard; or you fill your water pots and let them stand till the mud settles out. Later, when the two waters are joined and the whole river has turned murky, you paddle up the clear side streams to camp, draw water for cooking or drinking—but only for the look of it.

The weather, which had been mild when they entered the river, turned cold, the kind of harsh, steady chill that makes hands ache gripping the paddles, that you need fresh meat to withstand. The Indian hunters had little luck. Swans and geese and ducks nest on lakes back from the river on both sides and north of the Arctic Circle in the channels of the delta that cut the river mouth into thousands of low, alluvial islands. Beaver and muskrat and moose keep to the smaller streams. The caribou—it was early July by now—had completed their spring migration down the valley and scattered onto their treeless summer grazing grounds far to the north. Those strays that chanced to the banks of the great river were heavily hunted, then as now, and scarce. Along the cobble-paved beaches of the river there were still great blocks of ice, coated with mud from the spring flood like the sawdust-insulated ice in an ice house. At Camsell Bend, when they got their first sight of the mountains, there were still patches of old snow glistening in the sun on the barren peaks: *Manetoe aseniah,* the Indians sagely called them, spirit stones. *Manetoe:* the word for whatever possesses supernatural power, majesty, awesomeness, from the all-father of the universe to a merely whimsical ghost, surviving in place names spread across the northern half of the continent, in many variants and several languages.

On two days in this mountainbound part of the river, the cold north wind blew hard enough, turning to rain, to drive Mackenzie and his canoes off the water. Nevertheless, they traveled at a killing rate, a hundred miles or more a day when not stopped by weather. In his notes, he marveled at the strength of the current, driving them along. "It was, at length, in an actual ebullition," he wrote, using and misspelling the learned word, and then explained: "The current produced an hissing noise like a kettle of water in a moderate state of boiling." The Indians, he noted, "complained of the perseverance with which we pushed forward, and that they were not accustomed to such fatigue." The voice would have been Ageena's, speaking for his own dependents, insisting on his dignity and not quite sure of himself against the powerful white chief—but also, one suspects, with a shading of Indian mockery, deeply hidden. Mackenzie at the end of one of these fourteen- or fifteen-hour days still had energy to sit up all night to record the hour of sunset and sunrise (darkness that night, July 5, lasted exactly four hours). At another point, where they camped at the foot of a low mountain "which in some parts rose perpendicular from the river," he set out immediately, without waiting for the meat to stew, to climb it—not for the pleasure of the view but to learn the lie of the country and the river course. (At the top, after an hour and a half of hard walking through the thick-grown scrubby pine and birch, he did not stay long, "from the swarms of mosquitoes, which attacked us on all sides.") It is one of the few of Mackenzie's camp sites one can be sure of, 185 years later. The low mountain bears a poetic and descriptive French name, Roche Qui Trempe à l'Eau (rock steeping in the water).

By the fifth of July, Mackenzie was camped below another river more or less known and expected, the Bear, which flows out from Great Bear Lake, its water still, as he described it, "clear, and . . . of the greenish hue of the sea." Against the resistance of bad weather, he had covered the three hundred miles from the Liard in a little more than four days where Jim and I took ten. For us now it was mid-July, the weather mostly kindly—immense blue skies puffed with soft white clouds bespeaking infinities of peace; the intervals of bright warmth had lengthened out, and the buildup of north wind cold and storm, when it came, was brief. After Mackenzie's enthusiasm, the current was again a small disappointment, it pulled us along at forty and fifty miles a day, but always exacting conscious, dogged effort; we would still, as Don Tetrault had predicted, earn every mile of the way.

In a couple of places, where the river narrowed through tight channels around rocky islands, there were small rapids that we approached with the precaution we had been taught on the Slave. At only one point, at that season and water level, did the surface swirl in innumerable small eddies, as Mackenzie had described it, like water on the boil; mostly, the eddies were slow and huge and languorous, like the coilings of a snake, lazily gripping the canoe and angling it first right, then left, in their counterclockwise motion, and you summoned a further squeeze of energy to dig in harder and hold the course. The river was full of sounds. Invisible springlets rattled through the rocky beaches along the banks. Where the Liard and Mackenzie at last mingled, the water hissed with sand and sediment borne along by the current, and in the silence between paddle strokes you heard its silken sibilance caressing the sides and bottom of the canoe.

Despite the heat, there were still a few traces of winter such as Mackenzie had noticed: on a point where a sharp bend of the river had formed a long, wide beach, a row of cubular ice slabs, black-coated with mud and rotting in the sun, each big as an Indian shack; up a stream that cut through a cliff at a north-facing angle, a mass of compacted snow, permanently shadowed in the cut of rock, clean and brilliant blue-white. Birds and animals were scarce: An occasional swan startled into flight as we rounded a point, a pair of young bald eagles, dingy gray-brown mottled with white, still a season short of their plumed white caps. On one such half-thawed beach where we stopped for lunch, we lazed in the sun, stretched out on a big drift log. I opened my eyes to see a large black animal coming toward us along the edge of the woods, two hundred yards away: a young bear, I thought, from the color and size, the rolling hobbyhorse gait, and I started toward the canoe to get a camera. The animal kept on coming, unmindful of us. The breeze was from the north—he could not get our scent. Maybe, I suggested then, we'd better gather up the food pack and get out in the canoe for our picture taking till we could see what this animal had in mind. I untied the painter and began to shove off. At that moment, now only fifty yards off, the animal finally saw us and with a start turned and loped off into the trees and I realized what it was: an enormous wolf, pure black and twice the size of the rare gray survivors of the timber wolf packs I'd come across years back in northern Minnesota.

After the flatland immensities of the upper river, the beginning of the mountains at Camsell Bend was energizing as a change of season; like the first coming of spring, with its renewal of warmth and growth and hope. Just past the bend, we paddled a couple of miles up the North Nahanni

River to camp, wide and shallow, the clear water running fast over a bed of sand and gravel, with a flat flood plain stretching for a mile on either side and then the mountains, green-brown and autumnal, shining on the heights with patches of wet clay and rock that looked like Mackenzie's *manetoe aseniah*. I seemed to recognize the place, it was welcoming, familiar, and relieving, and I remembered: a swift, gravelly stream where we had camped once in New Hampshire, the White Mountains all around us. These mountains, the Camsells, were like the Presidential Range, a succession of linked peaks, scree and bare rock at the top, lightly wooded on the shoulders; you could spend days up there, hiking the peaks, coming down at night to the tree line for shelter and water, for the simple joy of it. The mountains are not in fact high as our maps marked them, thirty-five hundred or four thousand feet, but the effect is grand. We were by now above sixty-two degrees north, only four degrees short of the Arctic Circle. That, it occurred to me, is why north in our minds is always *up*: the northland is an immense mountain laid out flat, and we, assisted by Mackenzie's river, were climbing it.

We were both of us tiring by now. Each day we started out fresh and determined, but by late afternoon Jim in the bow was paddling slower and slower, dozing between strokes; when we stopped for a restbreak, drifting with the current, he lay back on the packs, hat shielding his face, and went solidly to sleep, snoring. By seven o'clock, when we were ready to give up for the day, I had barely the energy to unload the canoe, gather wood, and build a fire. In the minutes while dinner cooked, I lay flat and slept. Resolution dissolved. During the day, we talked about setting the net as soon as we landed that night, to vary the freeze-dried dinner with slabs of pike, but never did it; the effort when the time came was always just beyond the possible.

A hundred and ten miles down from Fort Simpson, we paddled up the Willowlake River, meaning to take the next day off as our one voluntary break in the trip. The weather was bright and warm and looked as if it would hold. The river was clear and looked promising for fish; laundry had been accumulating since Slave Lake and would take a morning to do. A mile or two up the river was the remains of an earthwork ramp, the crossing of a winter road, and behind it a fifty-acre clearing where a work camp had been set up the year before, building a section of the new highway. We put the tent in the clearing and spread our packs out on the beach. Around the edge of the clearing there were piles of abandoned skids that excited Jim's building instincts, and in the morning, while I heated water and washed dirty socks and underwear, he pulled them apart and reassembled them as tables.

There was another camp, with a couple of canoes moored in the water, just in sight on a bend up the river from us, and in the afternoon, with the laundry drying on lines, we paddled over, fishing along the way. It was a lucky curiosity. The camp, it turned out, belonged to Bob Janes, a young archaeologist from Calgary, with his wife, a photographer, and three Indian helpers. In the extended community of the river system, I had heard of him and his work as far back as Fort Smith but had expected to find him farther down the Mackenzie. The work that summer was the excavation of a Hudson's Bay trading post, Fort Alexander, built in 1817 to compete with the North-West Company and abandoned four years later when the two companies merged; ancient on the time scale of white men in the North and the first such site to be comprehensively explored. The digging had some urgency—it was on the planned route of the highway and scheduled to vanish, one year or another, under a bridge. The fort itself—the foundations of several cabins, with a free-stone hearth uncovered at one end of the biggest—was less interesting than the way Bob had found it. From the recollections of elderly Indian trappers and archives in Ottawa, he had known about where to look. Then, flying over,

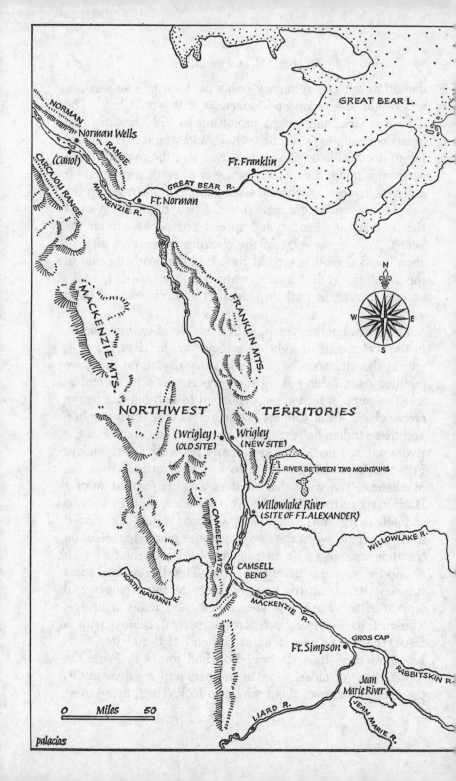

GREAT BEAR L.

NORMAN RANGE

Norman Wells

(Canol)

CARCAJOU RANGE

MACKENZIE R.

Ft. Franklin

GREAT BEAR R.

Ft. Norman

FRANKLIN MTS.

MACKENZIE MTS.

NORTHWEST   TERRITORIES

(Wrigley)
(OLD SITE)

Wrigley
(NEW SITE)

RIVER BETWEEN TWO MOUNTAINS

Willowlake River
(SITE OF FT. ALEXANDER)

WILLOWLAKE R.

CAMSELL MTS.

CAMSELL
BEND

NORTH NAHANNI R.

MACKENZIE R.

GROS CAP

Ft. Simpson

RABBITSKIN R.

Jean
Marie River

JEAN MARIE R.

LIARD R.

0   Miles   50

N
W   E
S

palacios

24. A teepee frame (for smoking meat) marks a trapper's winter camp at the mouth of the Tsintu River a few miles above Fort Good Hope. In the foreground, a broken and abandoned sled.

5. A mystery at the Tsintu River apper's camp: a formless heap of fur, e remains of a sled dog still chained to is post.

26. The Ramparts, two-hundred-foot cliffs between which the river runs fast and deep to Fort Good Hope and the Arctic Circle. The Indians warned Mackenzie of a great rapids here, but it proved harmless, then and now.

27. A new earth-fill jetty at Little Chicago, an abandoned trading post beyond the Arctic Circle and now the center from which men and machines hunt for oil and build the gas line south and the Mackenzie Highway north.

28. A stainless-steel monument to an American boy, overlooking the Sans Sault Rapids in which he was drowned.

29. In the doorway of her cabin at the mouth of the Travaillant River, an elderly Loucheaux trapper's wife preserves, in her dress and style and memories, the past.

he had been able to spot it instantly: Around the fort, the traders had cleared the natural subarctic climax growth of pine and spruce, and when they left, birch and aspen had grown up instead. Now, 150 years later, that had not changed. (Mackenzie had noted and puzzled over the same oddity on burned-over land along the river.) Far more than in the forests farther south, this seemingly harsh land, with its fierce winters and short, explosive summers, exists in delicate ecological balance; once altered, its coming back is a matter not of decades or a human lifetime, as it would be farther south, but of centuries—if ever.

Fifty miles farther downstream, government policy had moved the Indian settlement of Wrigley, 150 people, across the river, though our government maps were innocent of the change; that was where the airport had been built, where the road, eventually, would come. The old town was a dozen decaying cabins, spaced along an old clearing on the west bank, with, at one end, the snug, solid, whitewashed cabin that had been the RCMP post. There was a new log dock in front of it, a light helicopter snuggled among the trees nearby: prospectors. We crossed the river to introduce ourselves.

It was midafternoon. Sunning himself in front of the Mounties' cabin was a young man with a sharply trimmed full beard, a Prince Valiant haircut. The cook, he explained, fresh out of chefs' school in Calgary; the geologists were out in the bush on their daily hunt for lead and zinc. Would we like to come in? There was cold pop in a bottled-gas fridge —the British slang—one of the scientists had rigged up. His speech was north-country British—his father, from Rocky Mountain House west of Edmonton—quickened by the Canadian prairies and laced with many compounds of *bugger*: obscene in the strict sense, not profane, God being spared; around his neck was a small gold cross, gift of the young wife he called at appointed times on the radiotelephone in the cabin.

There was room inside for the dining table where the men ate, his bed. The old camp rule, *keep the cook happy;* the prospectors slept in tents. On counters there were fresh-baked pies and bread, a roast of beef; fresh meat and vegetables, wine and beer, came in several times a week from Fort Simpson on the plane that carried out the rock samples for analysis. Perhaps we'd like a cup of coffee? a piece of pie? We accepted and sat down at the table.

I cut a slice of cherry pie, poured condensed milk into the steaming coffee. The team would be going out in a few days now, but in the course of the summer Peterson had gotten to know the Indians across the river in the new town of Wrigley. The men dropped in with after-shave lotion on their breath, shyly sampling vanilla and other cooking essences—there was no liquor to be had on the river for a hundred miles in either direction (a lack occasionally made good by a flight in a chartered plane, brought back loaded up with whiskey); when a bear became too interested in the growing garbage pit behind the cabin, several Indians came over, shot it, and roasted it on the beach. The women—beautiful, he thought—came in groups, curious about cookery. I invited myself to a second slab of pie, then a third. It was not easy to keep my mind on the conversation. In the rafters, mice scampered—at night, they sounded like a roller derby overhead, Peterson complained—and at moments a small brown-and-gray face peered at us from a corner, observing. Nasty little buggers, the cook thought; couldn't stand them for bugger-all, if a mouse got into a new pie, he *threw it out.* Inwardly, I mourned the waste. Perhaps we'd like some beef? We accepted several slices between thick slabs of new bread, then guiltily a second sandwich and a third. Through all this, Peterson, lean and muscular, did not eat. Cook's instinct, it seemed, pleasure in others' appetites. Our compliments were of the sincerest kind.

It was three hours before we were in the canoe again and moving. The wind was starting to blow from the north. By the time we had recrossed the river, it was too rough to go on. We cut in to a steep, rocky beach and pitched the tent above in a meadowlike clearing on the slope of Roche Qui Trempe à l'Eau: wet and cold and deeply shadowed from the mountains behind, with thick grass growing on a bed of ice just below the surface, stunted wild roses, flowering pink, around the edges. Off to one side there were signs of trappers in winters past, perhaps an earlier team of geologists, cut wood that in that climate might take fifty years, a century, to rot; ten miles up the river to the south, the end of the Camsell Range rose before us like the gates of heaven. More than possibly it was Mackenzie's men who had made the first clearing here for their tents in 1789, and in the nature of the country, the last flicker of a retreating ice age preserved by the height and slope and angle of the sun as in a museum, the trees had not come back. It was from here that Mackenzie, unfed but driven by the passion of discovery, had set out to climb the mosquito-swarming mountain to view the course ahead.

We permitted ourselves another meal and slept early, intending a fast start in the morning and a long day. I woke at dawn, cold, with a light rain pattering on the tent like dew in the high mountains. Clouds had come down almost to the base of the Camsells. In the clearing, the tent was in shelter, but down on the beach the wind was blowing hard, tossing the river in big whitecaps. In midstream, a tug passed, heaving an empty barge downstream, and the barge lunged heavily in the surf, waves breaking over the square bow and pouring along the deck. We ate in haste, but by the time we'd packed up, the storm was worse and the light rain was falling again. We hiked a quarter mile along the beach to a small point where it was possible to see down the river, looking for a lea shore, but the river here ran straight and unsheltered, tossing with white-topped waves as far as eye could carry. Windbound again, I concluded, reasonably. Oh, we could *do* it, sure, but we wouldn't get very far, and it would be exhausting: Maybe by afternoon it would let up enough to make it worth going on. We went back to the tent, another, less rational part of my mind sputtering with silent taunts: *fair-weather sailor! Never let the weather stop you, oh, sure!*

The rain came off and on most of the day. We stayed in the tent, reading and playing cards, sleeping, coming out periodically to build up the fire and eat. I changed into long underwear, heavy pants, thick sweater and jacket over my wool shirt, all the cold-weather clothes I had, and was almost warm. We should, I realized, be using the time to climb the mountain as Mackenzie had done, and I went so far as to study possible routes, talk it over with Jim, but the effort was more than either of us felt like making. All right, enough of that. You do what it's possible to do. Enough.

Coming down the river, Mackenzie had seen many signs of the local Indians: a fresh-killed goose with an arrow through it; several camps, some from that spring, where he deduced that the trees had been cut with stone axes. It was an important point, both for Mackenzie the trader, opening a new territory, and for future historians of the Mackenzie Valley tribes: These people had acquired no European goods, either direct from other traders or from Indian intermediaries like the Cree and Chipewyans; their traditional life was as yet undisturbed. There was a more immediate reason for finding Indians summering on the river. Mackenzie was still carrying (and feeding) the Copper Indian he had hired on Great Slave, although the man knew nothing of the river. He needed a new guide. There had been tales of impassable rapids somewhere along the river, which in any case the canoemen expected, that was part of their experience on every other river of the North. Beyond that, he wanted information on the river's ultimate destination—where did it lead and how far? And, if not through Alaska to the Pacific, was there another route?

It was not till near the Bear River, 460 miles down from

Great Slave Lake, that Mackenzie found his first occupied camp, five families set up for the summer fishing about where the Fort Norman trading post and settlement has stood since 1810. As the strange canoes sped across the water, the Indians ran around in terror; strangers coming down the river meant only a raiding party from a neighboring tribe, intent on glory—women, possessions, death. The women slung their babies on their backs, Eskimo-fashion, and made off into the woods. Ageena went ashore first, speaking peace, but the men, surprised and trapped, could not understand what he said. Mackenzie landed and ordered his men to unload the big canoe and set up the tents as a sign of peaceable intentions. It was midmorning.

When the Indians realized they were not about to be slaughtered, they discovered that they could after all understand what Ageena was saying to them. In token of peace, Mackenzie distributed presents and offered pipes and rum, their first experience of either—they were well north of the area where tobacco could be grown or had in trade—which they accepted, he surmised, "rather from fear than inclination." Speeches followed. With a copper kettle, an ax, and a knife, Mackenzie hired one of the men as a guide. The women came out of hiding, joined their men in a ring around the fire, and began to dance: thanksgiving, celebration, entertainment; a hunting dance, with animal cries entreating the spirits' blessing.

Recovering their self-assurance, the Indians told fabulous tales of the river ahead that Ageena translated and embellished: horrid monsters, two impassable falls, immense distances—it would take several winters to reach the sea, old age would overtake them before they returned. Besides, the English Chief concluded, the hunting farther north was poor, they were certain to die of hunger if nothing worse befell them; it was absolutely time to start back to Lake Athabasca before the season grew later. Mackenzie spent several hours arguing his Indians into going on.

All this while, Mackenzie seems to have been making

careful notes on the band's artifacts: clothing elegantly decorated with dyed porcupine quills and moose hair; tools and
weapons; their method of striking fire; nets made from
willow fibers spun into cords; big gourd-shaped jugs woven
from *watape*, split spruce root, in which water for cooking
was boiled with hot stones; snares of green caribou hide cut
in narrow strips and braided together, a technique the people of this area have not yet entirely forgotten. Some of their
knives were made from jagged chunks of meteoritic iron
that they would have had in trade from the coastal Eskimos
—like the Indians everywhere on the continent before the
coming of the whites, their hunting range was immense, and
trade was part of the pattern of subsistence. He was much
struck by their birchbark canoes, small, low, and light, just
big enough for one hunter, with which a paddle twice the
size of the *voyageurs'* was used. It is a type the people call a
rat canoe—for muskratting in the spring—the only traditional boat still built in the area, though now canvas has
replaced bark over the light frame; the big paddle suits the
powerful currents of the Mackenzie and its tributaries.

Although Mackenzie's description suggests a people
remarkably adapted to the country they lived in, he found
them strikingly unhealthy: thin, misshapen, and ugly, their
bodies lightly muscled and coated with filth, their legs thick,
clumsy, covered with scabs. The smear of dirt may have
been a defense against mosquitoes and flies, still trouble-
some here in early July, the scabs an effect of parasites
transmitted in caribou flesh. Possibly their diet, overreliant
on caribou, which is short on fat, was permanently deficient,
or perhaps it was simply that Mackenzie met them in a bad
year. Everywhere, the tribes' general health, their vigor,
character, and culture, varied greatly with the available
food.

By late afternoon, Mackenzie had learned all he could
and ordered the tents taken down, the canoe loaded. The
guide now decided that he did not want to serve them after

all. When the strangers made it clear they would compel him to go, he took solemn leave of his wife and two children, cutting a lock from his hair for each, which he divided into three parts and placed on their heads with invocation and prayer. The canoes pushed off and moved on down the river to the night's camp, below the Bear River.

Mackenzie's first contact with the Indian tribes of the valley was the beginning of a process that has continued in a straight line down to the present. Canada's federal government, working usually through the territorial government and supplying the cash and the administrators, is the successor of the traders. Its policies are tricked out in the toplofty guff that in Ottawa or Toronto passes for moral superiority to the traders' simplehearted pursuit of profit and the mutual advantage of commerce, but to an observer with a modest sense of the history behind them, they do not seem fundamentally different. The Indians are still the passive objects of these worthy intentions, sometimes their obstacle.

Within twenty years of Mackenzie's voyage of discovery, trading posts, like Fort Simpson and Fort Norman, had been established at most of the places he touched at and described. For the frugal fur companies, these locations were as natural as they had been for the Indians, sources of food —abundant whitefish to be netted in the sidestreams, moose and beaver, caribou in their migrations—and of usable wood. As they had everywhere else on the continent, the Indians, increasingly dependent on what they could buy with their furs (or, at stiff discounts, on what the traders would advance against the next season's catch)—guns, powder and shot, clothing, food, efficient and destructive new iron and steel traps—gathered around these posts. The Hudson Bay drainage basin and more vaguely the land beyond it to the west and north, claimed by right of discovery, had been the British Crown's endowment to the Hudson's Bay Company. In 1870, pursuing the policy that had given Canada the sta-

tus of a dominion, the British bought this land back from
the Hudson's Bay Company and conferred it on the confed-
eration: most of the Northwest Territories together with
large chunks of the future western provinces.

These legal maneuverings had, of course, no effect on the
actual life of the North. Trade continued on the established
pattern. A half dozen or a dozen missionaries followed the
traders, building churches near the trading posts and sometimes providing schooling. The Indians and Eskimos, few
and thinly scattered, caught the white men's diseases in successive waves. In 1919, however, an oil company made a
strike on the bank of the Mackenzie not far down from Fort
Norman. (Mackenzie had noticed on the beaches blobs of a
gummy coallike substance that the Indians valued as a dye;
he found it by its smoke and smell—like tailings in an old
mine tip, it tends to catch fire and burn spontaneously.
Traveling down the river today by dark, you can see the
scintillations of these fires, still burning, and by day the dull
orange ash of burned-out deposits.)

In consequence, the Canadian government showed a fresh
interest in its rights in the Northwest Territories, and in
1921 it gathered into the settlements about two thousand
of the remaining thirty-four hundred Indians from three
tribes, with their chiefs and counselors, to sign a treaty. By
this treaty, the tribes surrendered all claim to the Northwest
Territories. In return, the Indians received a modest sum of
money and a supply of equipment, with the promise of a
smaller annual stipend and distribution of twine for nets
and ammunition, to the value of three dollars per head; one
square mile of land per family to be set aside as a reserve,
subject to future laws, regulations, settlement, and development (the reserves are still on the maps but have never had
much practical meaning—640 acres is about one twentieth
of the land a family needs here to live by hunting and trapping); and, finally, the Indians were assured that they
would be allowed to go on fishing, trapping, and hunting,

again subject to whatever controls the law might devise. The Indians supposed that they were being assured of schools for their children, medical services, some provision for those too old to hunt, but the government refrained from mentioning these matters in the treaty. Of the seven chiefs and twelve headmen of bands who represented the tribes, seven were able to sign their names, three using the old syllabic writing devised by the missionaries; the rest set their marks on the paper.

From the standpoint of Anglo-Saxon law, it was a neat tidying up of a situation that had been annoyingly vague. Treaty Day is still scrupulously observed: A team of Mounties tours the settlements in the course of the summer, distributing the annuities to the descendants of the original signers (twenty-five dollars per chief, fifteen dollars per headman, five dollars for each head of family). These people are therefore known as Treaty Indians, in distinction from those of whatever mix who lack that tribal connection.

Since World War II, federal policy has been to gather the Indians into the larger settlements. Its purpose, unacknowledged or at any rate unpublicized, is to "integrate them into Canadian society," a bureaucrat's expression that means transforming them into wage earners, working regular hours like everyone else, separated from the land and from the kind of livelihood it provided. The means have been health services—nurses in the settlements, doctors and hospitals in a few of the biggest places; for a while, boarding schools, which left the children after their nine months a year of town living unwilling to return to the land and at the same time drew their parents after them to the places where there were schools (the system is now limited to a few high schools, but the cost per child of education in the Northwest Territories is still nearly three times what it is in the rest of Canada); and cheap housing, either low-rent apartments or houses subsidized by government loans (an Indian who chooses to build a camp out in the bush for the sake of the trapping—a feasible project in the recent boom in fur prices after years of depression—gets no help from the government.)

Today, there are about twice as many Indians in the Northwest Territories as the government was able to find in 1921 for the purpose of the treaty. Roughly half the population is classified as native—Indian, Eskimo, or Métis—but for 27 per cent of this group English is either the mother tongue or the primary language, used at home and in day-to-day life. Apart from mystical notions of race, it is a question in what sense a man who speaks and writes only English, lives in town in a government-subsidized bungalow, works at an hourly job and is ignorant of hunting, trapping, and fishing and all they imply of adaptation to the land, can still be regarded as an Indian. It is a question the Indians themselves are only just beginning to ask.

Having left the land and followed the encouragements into the towns, the natives have discovered that there is not yet enough productive work in the Northwest Territories to support them. A benevolent welfare program takes up the slack, in the form of direct payments, summer jobs fighting forest fires or cutting lumber, loans to encourage commercial fishing, hunting, guiding, and outfitting. Hence, the question of what will become of the Indians is inseparable from that of how the land is to be developed and made productive, both from their standpoint and that of the government.

A very modest oil production began in 1933 at what came to be called Norman Wells, sixty miles downriver from Fort Norman. It was not seriously developed till World War II, when the ubiquitous U. S. Army Engineers demonstrated that, given the men and money, it was possible to build roads, bridges, airfields, and pipelines anywhere in the North (the project, known as CANOL, was part of the plan to defend Alaska in the event the Japanese got closer to the peninsula than the Aleutians); today, the oil wells and refinery supply the whole of the lower Mackenzie Valley and, at the present rate of consumption, will continue to do so for another fifty years. During and after the war, a flurry of uranium prospecting and mining on the big lakes fueled the first atomic bombs. Although overshadowed by the strikes in Alaska, in the early 1970s oil was found in the Mackenzie delta, along the Arctic coast, and around the islands farther north. In 1974 came a gas strike big enough to provoke talk of hundreds of millions of dollars a year in earnings and a major pipeline running south along the river, with or without the co-operation of the Alaskan producers.

The Canadian government has been extraordinarily reticent about the prospects, but the oil and mineral companies seem to have no doubts. Everywhere in that summer of 1974 there were teams of prospectors like the ones whose food we feasted on at old Wrigley, the orange surveyors' tapes marking off claims inland from the riverbanks. A dozen oil camps had been set up along the lower half of the river, dumps of equipment, trucks, winterized trailers, supplies, waiting for the freeze that makes the country navigable for trucks and tractors—and for the latest hint of policy from Ottawa and the great world beyond. And the road inches north, and the pipeline, although publicly still a matter for deliberation, indecision, and international bargaining, was already begun.

The oil discoveries stirred the natives to organize themselves: local hunters' associations; territorial organizations of Eskimos, Indians, Métis—or at any rate a directorate for each whose salaries and programs are paid for by foundations or by the federal government. The Indian Brotherhood, actually an organization of chiefs, has been provided with a private radio system, not much used; native-language broadcasts on the government stations and a flow of mimeographed pamphlets in words-of-one-syllable English attempt to explain the effects of development, the meaning of ominous terms like "intimidation (putting down)" and "inadequacy of welfare budgets (not enough)" and "arguments pro and con (good and bad)." The federal government has been willing at least to hold local hearings, require studies, before approving new drilling. The issues are almost too local to be visible, except to the few hundreds of trappers directly touched by them: whether the seismic blasts geologists use to locate oil pools will hinder the white Arctic fox from breeding; whether their scouting planes and helicopters will drive off the polar bears; whether the vulnerable environment can ever recover from an oil spill; whether the trap lines running back from the rivers can survive the pipelines, roads, and bridges that will follow. (The government has no objection to looking for answers, if there are any—provided the oil companies will put up the several million dollars it will take to find out.)

Behind these local and specific issues is the more general one that at least some of the native organizations have managed to express: the natives' rights in the land that is both their livelihood and their identity; hence, whether the treaty by which it was ceded to the national government was valid in the first place, or, if valid, whether it can now be renegotiated. (The Eskimos, whose territory includes the oil lands most likely for immediate development, were never party to a treaty; for the Mackenzie Indians, as for those everywhere else on the continent, land was a resource for collective tribal use rather than exclusive legal ownership; land, in most tribes, could no more be "owned" than air or water.) The Mackenzie people have already seen something of land settlement on the moneyed American model and will resist it—if indeed the government ever actually proposes it. A good many of the delta Eskimos are Alaskan migrants who in the summer of 1974 had received sizable cash payments for their rights in the North Slope oil lands—with spectacular consequences in the consumption of alcohol and liquored-up murders by young Eskimos. The ultimate goal, therefore, is not that kind of once-and-for-all cash settlement but one that will both preserve the land for its traditional use by whoever chooses it and at the same time allow it to be developed with profit for the natives. This double goal seems in fact no more possible now than when the first European fisherman traded the first Indian a knife for a beaver pelt. As governments go, this one is benign, sensitive; for the natives, the situation is not absolutely hopeless. Yet in the scale of human affairs, the interests of twenty thousand Indians and Eskimos—even if they knew them precisely and could express them with a single voice—do not weigh very heavily against the interests of the twenty-two million other Canadians. And that, finally, is the issue.

In the meantime, the history of this land goes on happening, and the Prime Ministers and the presidents of native associations can comment on it, perhaps even realize truly what is happening, but are powerless to control it; it is a force, like the river itself, beyond human reckoning. But traveling down this heartline artery of the Northland with the reflective slowness of a canoe, putting in where you find people, you catch glimpses. These images remain.

At the settlement of Jean Marie River forty-five miles up from Fort Simpson, we paddle over for a visit. It is a warm day of pure white clouds, the sky glowing with a high blue. A boy and a girl are waiting on the bank and help us land on a grounded log, the boy taking the painter and tying it; the people here still face the river, as they always have, and children know to help with the comings and goings of boats. Richard and Virginia, brother and sister, the girl perhaps eleven or twelve, the boy a couple of years older, both slender, dark, and deft, beautiful; Slavey. Virginia is overflowing with curious questions, her brother conscious of a man's dignity and more reserved: Where are we from, where going, and what are our names, my wife's name, my children's names, and what are their ages? I mention Philadelphia and start to explain but they have an idea where it is—from school. I know the chief here by name, Louis Norwegian: *Mister* Norwegian, one says; he is the chief. As we go to find him, mindful of all our warnings against the Indian children, I ask Richard to watch the canoe and he is puzzled; here, it is a needless precaution.

We find Mr. Norwegian in front of his cabin overlooking the river, making door frames and window frames with a big table saw. Most of the dozen or so cabins are new, built of logs neatly squared and fitted on the inside, cut at the sawmill up the Jean Marie that, with furs, provides the village's cash income. There are also a gasoline-powered electric plant (which he had the idea for years back and now runs), an elementary school with a teacher sent in each winter. We exchange cigarettes and crouch down in the sun to talk, resting. He is perhaps sixty, bespectacled, gray-haired, a few white stubs of whiskers sprouting on his chin that he missed shaving in the morning; not tall but broad-shouldered and strongly muscled, dark, like all his people. He wears a wristwatch with a gold band and a Masonic ring. What do *you* call the stream, I ask, refraining from saying "your language," suggesting that his accented English does not seem native. For a minute or two he thinks about it, then says the Slavey word and translates it—a metaphor, "water that explodes," meaning the rocky source where the stream begins. I wonder at the hesitation: forgetting his own language without gaining another? (No, Vic Monus, the linguist, told me, civility: The question had several answers, depending on what I meant by it; he was thinking through the possible meanings I might have.)

I ask if I may take some pictures and go to the canoe to get a camera. As I climb the bank again, Virginia is telling me a story about another white man who came down the river in the spring. She does not say *white man:* Her world is not divided into white and Indian. "A man," she says, and for a moment hesitates, considering *me* and my sensitivities, "—*a man like you.*" The bank is covered with bright blue cornflowers, and she picks one. What does she call it, I venture. "A *flower*"—and I tell her its name and ask if I may take her picture with it. A moment after, Richard is holding the flower, and I take his picture too; he has not asked. Later, while we talk, other children keep coming by with flowers, and finally the chief's youngest granddaughter, tiny and barely walking, triumphant with a double handful of cornflowers; and each time, with my camera, I comply.

Mr. Norwegian has brought out a handful of color prints from a trip he took in the spring, a chiefs' meeting at a town down the river we will be seeing in a couple of weeks. They are not very successful pictures but he talks about the composition, light, color—a few gestures of the hands—and I see what he was after; and something else. He is not a mere subject of pictures but a maker; and therefore an equal, the point firmly but delicately made.

The new road through to Fort Simpson—the effective frontier—is twenty miles or more inland and with luck will never come here. From the smallest child up, the people's respect for themselves is so considerable it does not have to be asserted, certainly not to a couple of touring strangers. They have learned this, it seems, from this one strong man who is their chief.

At the new town of Wrigley 150 miles below Fort Simpson, the road has not yet come but it is a matter of dispute. The trappers want it far enough off, 20 or 30 miles, so as not to disturb their trap lines; others, closer, or through the town. The surveyors, engineers, interviewers have come, held meetings, asked their questions, and moved on. The road is building farther down where there are no people to argue over it, and the government has time for the two hundred Indians here to make up their minds. Meanwhile, it pays for new rows of sawmill-log cabins, arc lights over the one dirt street. The new town faces the airfield and the eventual road; from the river it is invisible at the top of a hundred-foot bank, hidden by trees. On the beach below, drums of gasoline and oil, big machines in crates, have been dumped and not yet hauled up.

We arrive about noon and climb the bank. Another warm day. The town seems deserted. In the street, a woman with a carton of groceries identifies us, jerks a thumb toward the south end of town, and informs us that The Bay is closed. We have not come, I think, five thousand miles to visit the Hudson's Bay Company store, but at home a son's birthday is approaching, I want to write to him, and we walk down to find it. The door is locked. A sign says it will be open in an hour and a half.

We walk back. There is an office building for the town administrator appointed by the territorial government, also locked. A notice in English and Slavey syllabics says that he is the licensed dealer in furs. His house is next door, log-built like the rest but bigger, with a car and a new pickup standing beside it, two guns on racks across the rear window of the cab. A rich man: As in the big American cities in the immigrant days, working for the government is the first step. We knock. A young man with shoulder-length hair answers and we try to talk to him through the closed screen door. Inside, there is country music, turned up loud. He does not talk, he answers questions, officially, yes and no; turns to change the record. There was a dump of fresh-cut logs halfway up the bank we climbed, deserted. What, I ask, getting desperate, do the people here do for a living? *They work for the government.* Heavy irony. The door closes.

Back at the store, the door is still locked. We sit down on the steps to wait it out. A small boy joins us. His curiosity too is intense. He takes Jim's knife from the sheath on his belt. *What kind of a knife is that? Will you guys give me that knife? Will you buy me a knife like that?* Jim takes the knife back. The boy reaches for my knife. I take his hand. *Will you give me some money? Will you buy me something?* Jim is wearing a sweatshirt with the name of his college printed on it. *What does that say?* Jim tells him to read it. He cannot. Jim spells it out.

The hour for opening has passed. The storekeeper lives in a trailer next to the store. I go and knock. He opens a bugproof slot in the door: not time! The slot slams shut. Fifteen minutes later we are still waiting on the steps, but the storekeeper has gotten in through the back and is looking out furtively at us through the front door. Finally he unlocks. My clerk, he explains, always late. Down the street a teen-age Indian girl is striding toward the store; she presently will stand at the cash register punching the charges. The storekeeper retreats to an office at the back and as I follow gets behind a counter and seats himself busily at a desk. By now I have forgotten the letter to my son and am making a speech before the multitudinous servants of the Hudson's Bay Company assembled in the amphitheaters of heaven: *I have not come, gentlemen, five thousand miles to be* . . . But I am checked by pity. He is a big, soft young man grown neurotically fat from his first year of living in the North, alone, the only white in this place. A Canadian, not a Scot. The hostility of it is driving him out of his mind.

The afternoon we leave Fort Simpson, the terminus of the Mackenzie Highway, we have the luck of meeting the local priest, who spends most of his time at one or other of the smaller communities along the river. A gentle graying Belgian with an air of cultivation that seems better suited to a comfortable suburban parish than to the rigors of the Northland, but he has grown old in the North: twenty-four years—people remember these anniversaries as if they were the benchmarks of a prison term; "I will die here."

The Indians here, he is saying in a tired voice, are sick, disoriented, a minority in a town dominated by virile white newcomers who have the jobs, but the government supports them, provides the new houses. And alcohol? In the random issues of the Edmonton newspaper that have found their way up here, there are always prominent stories about drunken, murderous Indians—usually in the North but increasingly in the slums of the big cities—and the unavailing efforts of the tribal councils to prohibit the sale of liquor to their people, which the government refuses; a civil right. Ah, yes, drink for them is truly an evil. Then, his voice for a moment emphatic: But *welfare* is the greatest evil.

The Mackenzie Highway project for that summer was a twenty-mile section of gravel road between the archaeological dig on Willowlake River and the next stream north, River Between Two Mountains. We landed below the work camp to meet the project supervisor, Ken Johnson, a tanned, sandy-haired, beak-nosed man with the bearing and the hunching, heavy shoulders of a brawler. We climbed into a truck with him and in half an hour drove the length of completed road that had taken us most of a morning's paddle on the river; nearly finished now, though a wet spring, when the trucks and graders could not move, had slowed them— winter, with the earth frozen hard and the big machines running twenty-four hours a day, was the real time for work. A lifetime of road building had taken him south for a while to an executive job with a big American construction firm, which he had quit: too impersonal, too little initiative. It is a real difference between the two countries, or at any rate between Canada's West and North and the United States as a whole, and it does no honor to the kind of people Americans have become. It is the woman marking prices in a Winnipeg supermarket who stops what she's doing to lead you through the store to find some item you've asked about, takes it off the shelf, and hands it to you. It is the clerk who when asked directions comes from behind the cash register, takes you out onto the sidewalk, and points the way. Hardly what we call efficient, of course, but personal and humane.

The men running the machines were Eskimos and Indians recruited throughout the North—"from dog team to earth mover," Ken told us several times. Each was flown in for a month's work and paid one thousand dollars, with room and board in the camp; building the road was secondary to training them to work with the machines, maintain them, repair them, a policy written into his firm's government contract but also, for him, a matter of much conviction. The Indians when they arrived set their hearts on the biggest, most dangerous machines—a test of personal courage—and were firmly started on a light service truck, making the rounds, working up. For now, there is not much for them to do but learn, but when the roads and pipelines, the mines and factories and cities, do finally come to the North, they will be built by natives trained by men like Ken Johnson.

A few days later, Bill Knopp, the superintendent of the oil pumping and refining operation at Norman Wells, made much the same point, though here hiring and training natives seemed to be more a matter of his temperament than of Imperial Oil policy. In the cool, spacious living room of the superintendent's house, set apart on a point overlooking the ceaseless convolutions of the river, we sipped gin and tonics and talked. Getting toward midnight: still bright sun outside by now, mid-July, and hot, the dust boiling up from the unpaved roads in golden swirls. Earlier, he had driven us around the installation: the uniform houses of a company town in neat rows, with post office, store (fresh meat and vegetables flown in once a week), church, library, recreation hall, a baseball field in the center; and, dominating all, the silvery blue storage tanks, heavily insulated against the underlying permafrost, and the white towers of the refinery. And everywhere sprouted the low, red-painted tubing of the oil wells, some of them flaring with burning gas there was no means of storing. Here and there were still a few khaki-colored oil tanks, worn-out Jeeps, fragments of machinery salvaged from the wartime CANOL project across the river.

When Bill had arrived, there were still only a couple of natives among the sixty or so employees. A few others had been tried but had not lasted: They kept odd hours, or after months of apparently cheerful work silently vanished and were not heard from again. Something resistant to corporate notions of time, efficiency, authority: Well, why not? In the summers, there would be families out on the land somewhere, needing a man's help to get in the fish and meat, dry and smoke it for the winter. Adjust to that, make it a policy: Give them the time, fly them out and back; only ask permission, so the work can be shifted around and go on, replacements found. Asking: That came hardest, unmanning; but he was working at it, they were beginning to get the idea. It is one more variable in the equation that the government, the native organizations, and the oil producers are attempting to solve.

It was beginning to be dark by the time Bill drove us back to our camp. We had pitched the tent well up the beach, near where several Indian families had camped, in sight of the refinery and a big new government dock that was being bulldozed out into the river with earth fill. The weather was changing again, the wind beginning to blow. I opened an emergency can of stew for a late supper and heated it on the stove, out of the wind in the tent. In the darkness while we ate, two Indian women came over to the tent: "Would you guys help us with our canoe?" They had just arrived in a big freighter with a motor. The waves were pounding it on the rocks at the water's edge. We collected driftwood rollers and pulled the canoe up dry above the waves. It was too late, I was tired, but I rolled up finally in my sleeping bag feeling for once oddly pleased with myself. "You guys": We were no longer completely separate from this country and its people.

*I discovered a strong rippling current, or rapid, which
ran close under a steep precipice. . . .*

CHAPTER 8

Homage to Trappers

Below Fort Norman, the river flows more west than north
for 120 miles. Its course is shaped by outreaching arms of
two mountain systems named for the valley's earliest
explorers: on the east bank, the Norman Range of the
Franklin Mountains; on the west and twenty miles back
from the river, the Carcajou Range of the Mackenzie Mountains. (*Carcajou:* one of several medium-size animals, most
often the wolverine; an Algonquian word borrowed into
French, brought here and applied by French-speaking
canoemen.) The two ranges come together and end in low
mountains close by the river, East Mountain and West
Mountain, and here the river breaks through and plunges
north again. The place where this geological change occurs
is called the Sans Sault Rapids, the one serious and concentrated section of fast water in the thousand miles of the
Mackenzie. At this point, the maps show three rock ledges
spread across the river, which narrows between the final
mountains to a breadth of about a mile and a half, and
stretching downstream for something over half a mile: the
rapids.

A map can alert a canoeist to possible danger but not tell

him how to face it. Coming down the river, we had heard of
occasional drownings in the Sans Sault; a tug a couple of
years back that had lodged on the shelving rock and had to
be broken up with dynamite to get it off. No one seemed to
know anything of the rapids from a canoe or a small boat. It
was not till we reached Fort Norman that we found anyone
who could tell us what we needed to know: the course.

We camped on the beach at the foot of a sandy, grassy
bluff below the old Hudson's Bay warehouses, painted
white, with red roofs and trim, in a style now replaced by
steel prefab stores in bright pastels. We loafed through the
morning, eating breakfast, writing letters, packing up,
replenishing our food at The Bay when it opened. Toward
noon we hiked to one end of the town to meet a trapper
who that summer had received an outfitter's license and a
loan to set up a fishing and canoeing service, using his winter
cabin, on a lake midway between the river and Great Bear
Lake, as a base. The government-subsidized bungalow was
full of people: daughters and their husbands, children.
Alfred Lenny was just waking up and came out of the bedroom yawning and coughing, lighting the first cigarette of
the day. A compendium of the human history of the North:
the clipped, laconic speech of the Scots; the slender, narrow-
faced good looks and bristly black mustache of the French,
the deeply tanned coloring of the Slaves. I got out our maps.
Sure, he had canoed the rapids; rough on the right, easier to
the left of the middle, depending a bit on the water. If it
looked bad, there was a clear channel along the left bank,
but rocky in very low water.

A real canoeist, for once. I put the maps away and we
talked about canoeing. In 1967, celebrating the centennial
of Canadian federation, he had been one of the half dozen
chosen for a television re-enactment of Mackenzie's voyage;
it had given him a start. Now he had new fiberglass canoes
at his cabin over on the lake, hopes for taking canoeing par-
ties on a circuit from there to the Bear River and down, or

across to Great Bear Lake; one day maybe he could build canoes here. In the winter, with the good prices for furs, he still trapped but had given up the dog team for a snowmobile. (Like all machines in the North, they are often broken down, with no one to fix them; as in the early days of the automobile, older Indians tell you mirthful tales of the ski machines giving out in midwinter, far out on the trap line—and mushing out with their teams to haul them back. *Get a dog!*)

In their old cabin next to the house, his wife Julie had started a craft shop, gathering the work of the local women. I asked about it and she sat down expectantly, ready to talk. Her husband spoke for her and she kept silent. When I asked to see some of the things, he gave permission and we went next door: smoke-tanned moose-hide mukluks and mittens decorated with beadwork in abstract flower patterns, small buckskin bags like the ones Mackenzie had noticed every Indian used for carrying tinder, flint and steel; greenskin cords like those he had admired; bundles of caribou tendon, stiff and translucent as nylon; ceremonial moccasins bleached to creamy-white softness with weeks of cold water and soap. She apologized tremulously for the few things she had—the tourists from the little pleasure boat, the *Norweta*, we had heard of at Hay River but still not seen ("a floating box!" Alfred Lenny had said with contempt—to know the North, the tourists should come onto the land); and summer was a time for the women to be with their men, their children back from the government schools—in the long nights of winter, there was time enough for work.

Sophisticated people: They had discovered that native goods made with native materials—a pair of mukluks stitched with caribou tendon rather than Singer-sewn—might be valuable, both in money and in themselves. Her husband had talked about the local canoes, the moose-hide boats used to bring the meat back from the winter hunt, down the furious mountain streams west of the river. No one, he thought, built them any more, but he knew how; techniques he had relearned in middle age, as his wife had taught herself to tan and sew the hides and now was teaching the other women of the village.

From the day he left Great Slave Lake, Mackenzie had been expecting rapids. He does not say what he knew of them or how, but probably it was part of the lore collected by Peter Pond, and it was in the nature of the country—there was no waterway Mackenzie had traveled, from there east to Montreal, that was unbroken by these man-killers. He and his men traveled in tense alert for the muffled thunder sound of water breaking over shelving rock that would mean rapids ahead; often, where streams poured in and springs rumbled down the paving-stone banks, they seemed to hear what they had been nervously expecting. A few miles down from the Liard River, they landed on an island and buried two buckskin packs of pemmican, both to lighten the big canoe against rough water and to assure emergency food if, as seemed possible, they lost everything else (Ageena was coldly skeptical—he "entertained no expectation of returning that season, when the hidden provisions would be spoiled"). Where the river divides around a rocky island below Willowlake River, forming a short rapids in the right channel, it seemed that the test had finally come, but the current smoothed out again and still they did not reach the great fall. When he stopped to question the Indians camped near the Bear River about the river ahead, they told him fearful tales of "monsters of such horrid shapes and destructive powers as could only exist in their wild imaginations"; and of "two impassable falls . . . the first of which was about thirty days' march from us."

From there, in one sixteen-hour day, they traveled to within a mile or two of the Sans Sault Rapids and camped that night at the foot of East Mountain. The distance was 110 miles (79 by Mackenzie's cautious reckoning), their

30. Point Separation, where the Mackenzie divides and spreads north through its immense delta. Here, for once, the wind was at our back, and we rigged our spare paddles like sails to speed our journey north.

31. A cutoff bend of the delta's East Channel, near Inuvik. We paddled in, not triumphantly but with gratitude . . .

32. . . . to pitch our tent on the rocky edge of the channel and eat, within walking distance of our goal, Inuvik, the new town from which the Canadian Arctic is governed.

33. Inuvik: the modern city begun in the 1960s, its houses and apartment buildings linked by above-ground water and sewage pipes in utilidors (foreground) so they won't thaw the frozen ground on which everything is built.

34. Grant Mackenzie, skipper of the summer pleasure boat *Norweta* and bearer of a famous name, though he claims no kinship to the explorer.

35. Two girls from Aklavik, mixing all the breeds of the North. They had worked all summer cutting up fish at Holmes Creek to earn money for a trip to the metropolis of Edmonton, twelve hundred miles due south.

36. A golden afternoon beyond the tree line: canoe and river a few miles in from the mouth of the East Channel, from the height of the Caribou Hills.

greatest of the voyage; the current in this section is the strongest on the river, though it does not seem it—the river here is in places as much as three miles across but much broken up by islands big enough to seem another shore line. Camped as they were, they still could not hear the rapids— the sound was blocked by a shoulder of the mountain angling out into the river. Again, with one of the Indian hunters, Mackenzie set out to climb but got only halfway before they "were almost suffocated by the clouds of mosquitoes, and were obliged to return." There was time, however, for him to see that this was the end of the mountains; that a good-sized river flowed in from the west; and that on the near side the great river broke in "a strong rippling current, or rapid, which ran close under a steep precipice."

After our late night at Norman Wells, talking with Bill Knopp about the oil operation, Jim and I slept long. By daylight, the beach where we were camped, with its several other tents and its odds and ends of human and industrial discard, was unattractive; we decided to cross the river and cook breakfast at the wartime oil base at CANOL. The day was bright. In the late-morning warmth, the wind, which had started up the night before, was blowing hard from the southeast; the river looked rough, but no worse than we'd been through in the weeks past. Once we were out in it, too far to turn back, I began to wonder if we could do it. Tearing among islands in midchannel, wind and current combined in two sets of waves three and four feet high: one set moving downstream, aligned with the riverbank, the other coming straight at us, across the river; as I swerved to avoid one big wave, another slapped us amidships and slopped over the gunwales. The wind roared in my ears, lathering the wave crests white. We paddled hard. I kept my eyes on each oncoming wave, hunching the bow into it as if avoiding a lash. Ahead, below an island, it looked as if there was a lea, but reaching it—a hundred yards, seventy-five, fifty, still not into it!—seemed interminable. When we were half-way across, one of the big power boats came out from the beach, the man at the wheel shouting something; I could not hear him through the roar of wind and water. He came in closer, it looked as if the wash from the boat, a third set of waves to steer for, was about to swamp us; drowned with the best of intentions. I wanted to wave him off but could not take time from paddling; let up for a stroke and the waves would swing us into the trough—and over. "Are you all right?" Yes, I shouted back, but he could not hear. "Are you O.K.?" Yes, yes, we're all right—and, furious, left the rest unsaid. He gunned the motor, satisfied, and veered off back toward the town with a final rolling swell of his wake.

The approach to the old Army base was surrounded by shallows and mud-coated sand flats. The canoe ran aground. We waded it, climbed in to paddle, waded, then carried everything across the sodden sands to solid ground, the sandy road leading back to the camp. The wind blew hard, spinning the canoe as Jim tried to carry it, dancing along the edge of the sand flat. In the sunken road, with a thicket of willows on either side, we could get out of the wind for a slow and ample brunch. A six-foot abandoned tire from a wartime earth mover gave us the luxury of a table. The weather for the first time was warm enough to sour the leftover dried-milk mixture from the night before, turning it solid; we mixed what was left with flour, called it sour-milk pancakes, and pronounced them delicious.

We hiked up the road to the camp. It made an odd kind of ruin, thirty years old and here an antiquity, but compounded of elements familiar in my own life: a rusting water tank; a Quonset hut; a repair shop with the grease and oil still fresh on the plank floor, odds and ends of spare parts in neat wooden bins; drums of foot-long bolts that must have trussed the hundred bridges on the pipeline road from here to Alaska; gleaming white porcelain toilets and urinals stacked beside a camp street choked with grass. In the mess hall, bags of flour spilled across the floor beside cast-iron wood stoves of a design that must have been standard since the Civil War. In a corner of the wood shop where winter snow had not yet broken through the roof, stacks of window frames looked as fresh as if milled that spring. Here and there, stenciled signs proclaimed that everything we saw was the property of the United States Army, not to be molested under penalty of law; like the curse in the doorway of a pharaoh's tomb.

An Indian family was dismantling one of the sheds for the lumber. The man and his son had stripped the tarpaper and were pulling off the long roofing planks, carefully handing them down to the women. Inside, a small dark boy swung from a dangling electrical conduit, grinning. The wood was clear and soft as if new-cut, unweathered, after thirty years, and almost green; easy work. The climate is a paradox: both cold and dry, almost a desert. Nothing that lives—plant, tree, animal, man—grows easily or fast; neither does it quickly age, weather, rot.

We left the Indians to their work and went back to where we had dumped our packs. The afternoon was getting on; time to move. After the struggle of getting here, it was not going to be easy getting out again. Upstream from the road end were the shallows, the powerful and unpredictable current, aimless channels, and over all the south wind still roaring; below, the sand flats stretched for miles, a few drainage streams wandering among them, leading nowhere. We decided to portage across to the main channel of the river. It was close to a mile, our first of the trip: soft, clinging sand, oozing with mud; in places where it had dried, the wind howled it up in sand devils like a miniature Sahara. We labored across it with the packs. I plodded back to get the canoe. As I got it up, the wind caught it broadside, steering it. I fought it, raging and cursing, halfway across and had to set the canoe down, no strength left to fight. I rested, tried again, and staggered another hundred yards; gave up and waited till Jim came back empty from the river and we finished the carry between us. It was late afternoon by now.

We pushed on another five miles down the river, looking for a place to swim and found it on an island: a wide, flat, gravel beach, cut at the shore line by the current to a sharp drop; perfect. Swimming had been on my mind now for several days. In a letter we'd picked up at Fort Norman, my wife had asked about it. Was the water too cold? I'd once or twice made the effort of washing but had never swum. My mind had filled with all the reasons: the mud-clogged banks of the Athabasca and the Slave; bad weather, storms; haste and fatigue. Excuses; I felt embarrassed. We landed, got the tent up, dug towels from a pack, and spread our clothes on a long drift log beside the water. The water felt icy but after a minute bracing as a massage, warming. I climbed out and lay back against the log, drying in the sun and wind while Jim swam with his fast, efficient crawl, drifted on the current, swam again. It was twilight before we had eaten, washed up, and gotten into the tent; late.

In the night, as if to remind us of the rough water ahead, the weather began to turn around again, the south wind once more defeated by the north. Up the river there were sheets of rain, lightning, but the wind held it off. It turned cold, and in the warmth of our sleeping bags we slept late the next morning, started slow. By lunchtime the wind was blowing hard against us, churning the river up, roaring in the trees and along the water as it had the day before. I headed to the left of a big island, the straight and short channel on the map, but the current caught and swept us around to the right, taking us where it would. As we struggled against it, my fiberglass paddle started to come apart, first the grip, then a big split where the blade joined the shaft; a light drizzle began to fall. Against the wind whistling up the channel we were barely moving now, and I cut in toward a narrow sandy beach on the inner bank of the island. All right, wait it out; we were getting used to that.

The blow lasted through the next day, the on-and-off rain, depressing; the season was getting ahead of us. It *needn't* stop us, I told myself—but the effort. We stayed in the tent, reading, playing cards, sleeping. I thought about fishing, a change, a duty, but worried about getting back to the camp against the current. In the intervals of rain I patched the broken paddle, touched up a gash in the canoe; waded out to fill the pots with fresh water, but by now, no matter how long it settled, the water remained murky above the slick of sediment collected on the bottom of the pot. The day passed; rest.

After the day of idleness, we were up early the next morning. The river was calm, with cold mist billowing across the surface. The light, scattered rain of the past few days had had an immoderate effect. We had pitched the tent as far back from the water as we could get, perhaps ten feet, against a wall of willow at the top of the beach; now the water had almost reached the tent, loosening the outlying stakes—a vertical rise measured in inches but amounting to as many feet on our gently sloping beach.

With the early start and less hostile weather, we were able to cover the last fifty miles to the rapids and camped on another low beach a mile above, opposite East Mountain, where Mackenzie had climbed to get his first look at the "strong rippling current." From that angle, the sound of the rapids was just within earshot, faint and distant. I had worried a little about reaching it in midafternoon, making the run when we were tired, without carefully looking it over first. As we came near, a scatter shot of rain across the water decided for us, and we headed into the nearest level beach. We had traveled slowly after lunch, keeping cautiously to the left bank, listening for the first sound of the rapids. For ten miles up the river, the banks were low cliffs of rusty rock (Mackenzie had noted iron ore in the area), sliced through in gently splashing waterfalls by many small springs; up one, deeply shadowed, there was a mass of pure, blue-white ice with the fall cutting through beside it, and on the cliff a neat sign painted by some humorist: "Please leave the water running," and a name.

In the morning, the river was still rising, undercutting the guyline tent stakes, washing up around the door of the tent, and we packed up in haste; along the shore, the river was thick with small driftwood floated off upstream beaches. Still humbled by our brush with the Pelican Rapids, I carefully stowed all the loose gear in packs, and for the second time on the trip we put on our life jackets. We moved off slowly, stopping often to try to connect what we could see with the map, study the course through binoculars, but there was not much we could make out: a dark line stretching across the river that would be the beginning of the rapids, whatever violence of water lay beyond hidden by the slope of the riverbed; here and there a tossing, white-topped standing wave. The river now encouraged deliberation. A little way down from our camp, on a high bank, there was a stainless steel pyramid in the shape of a tent, with grillwork across the door, surmounted by a cross: a monument. We tied up and climbed the bank for a look. A plaque, in English and Slavey syllabics, commemorated an American boy, Hugh Donald Lockhart Gordon, who had traveled the river alone in 1961 and drowned in the rapids; he had been twenty-one. The monument was placed on what was thought to be his last camp site, looking north down the river; inside was a blue metal box—what was left of him, pulled from the river weeks after? his ashes?

A little farther, beside the Mountain River, which Mackenzie had glimpsed from his hasty climb up East Mountain River, a road led up to a work camp, and again we tied the canoe and hiked up, hoping for a final word of advice about the rapids. A sign facing the river proclaimed it a test site for the gas line that would follow the valley down from the ocean, and shiny steel pipe ran miles back along the road, above-ground. The cleared land was covered with blueberry bushes, the first we had seen, the berries dusty blue and almost ripe. The camp was eerily deserted, as if the whole work force had departed in haste the day before and would be back tomorrow, or had been destroyed by a mysterious, celestial disease. Across from a workshop, trucks were parked, their windows half open. A power saw lay across a big wood beam, cut half through. From the tops of bright-red storage tanks and in the steel trailer bunk-houses and offices, all locked up tight, lights burned, and in the distance a gasoline generator thumped, on to charge the batteries, off, on again, automatically.

No more excuses now; nothing for it but to go. We climbed into the canoe, pushed off, and pointed straight down the river a little left of the middle. Still not much to see. In midstream a line of big rocks stuck up, the river seething around them, and I cautiously angled the canoe a little more to the left. Were we headed right? It was several days now since I'd talked with Alfred Lenny about the course. Had my mind reversed what he'd told us? It was possible. My eyes inventoried the packs, laid flat. The camera pack, probably, would float if it came to that—I still had not tested it—but nothing else; medicine and pictures, that was what we would have. Eventually, if we got out, we would probably recover the canoe somewhere, the paddles; in my pockets there were matches, a length of sawblade, twine, a sheet of plastic; my knife on my belt—survival. The thought of the dead boy went through my mind. It was the twenty-second of July, my birthday; as good a day as any.

Then we were in it, paddling hard to hold the course: rolling waves frothed with white, the exhilaration of speed. Droplets danced along the gunwales but did not come in. We could do it, the canoe would take this! We had been through worse.

We were down and through it, drifting in the roiling and

still fast current, looking back. After the weeks of anticipation, it had not been bad, and in the bravado of survival I
wished we had taken the more difficult right channel, for
the sake of doing it; it looked no worse. It is a feeling
shared, probably, with everyone since Mackenzie at this moment in the Sans Sault Rapids. He made note of it, prim and
pleased and skeptical, in a few lines of his journal. Starting
early in the morning, they had

> crossed to the opposite side of the river, in consequence of
> the rapid; but we might have spared ourselves this trouble,
> as there would have been no danger in continuing our
> course, without any circuitous deviation whatever. This cir-
> cumstance convinced us of the erroneous account given by
> the natives of the great and approaching dangers of our nav-
> igation, as this rapid was stated to be one of them. . . .

And hence the name *sault* (as in somersault), a leap, but
also a drop or fall: Sans Sault, *without a drop*.

We camped that night beside a stream with an oddly
oriental-sounding name, the Tsintu. We were entering the
territory of a new tribe, the Hare, so called because, in the
scarcity of caribou (and moose, beaver), the winter-white,
snowshoe hares of the Arctic have always been their distinctive source of food and clothing, though unreliably—the animals breed in a seven-year cycle, from abundance to famine
and back again; the tribe's language, still within the
Athabascan family, stands apart from the musical liquidity
of Chipewyan, broken up by clicks, by *dg-* and *tch-* sounds
("man," *dinee*, has here become *dinjee*). The Tsintu is cold,
fast—and distillation-clear, a relief after the storm-muddied
Mackenzie. The mouth of the Tsintu forms a wide, high,
rock-paved bank, clear of wood; a natural camp. A trapper a
winter or two back seemed to have departed in panicky
haste, leaving several odd signs of his stay: the wide four-
pole cone of the teepee frame where he had smoked his

meat; a damaged toboggan; the row of heavy pine stakes where his dog team had been chained. At one end of the line, the lead dog's stake was clearly recognizable, heavier than the rest, with clean-picked bones and blackened, coughed-up fur in a hollow in front, first choice from the hunt. Attached to one of the stakes was a grisly remnant of a dog, the chain still around the place where its neck had been. Nothing remained but a heap of soft fur, gray and black, emptied of flesh and bones. We puzzled over it: a desperate attack by a hungry wolf or bear? or punishment and example, beaten to death or left to starve?

To celebrate my birthday, we opened a package of freeze-dried strawberries, a jocular Christmas present from my wife anticipating the trip. They had been in the food pack now for nearly two months, awaiting a suitable occasion. (We found them delicious but as usual wished the quantity had been double or triple; hunger had become a permanent condition.)

Mackenzie at this place found a camp of twenty Indians gathered for the fishing up the Tsintu, with the high banks as a lookout for game. The people ran off into the woods, leaving an old man and woman too feeble to escape, too tired of life to care much about dying. The old man hobbled toward the explorers, distributing handfuls of hair torn from his head, entreating mercy for himself and the band. The Indians, watching through the trees high up the bank, came back, less fearful, and began telling stories of another terrible rapids a few miles farther down the river. When Mackenzie was ready to go on, four Indians in small rat canoes went ahead to show the course.

The rapids the Indians had described are formed by three-hundred-foot cliffs, known today as the Ramparts. The river, which had been nearly three miles across, here narrows to not much more than a quarter mile and runs thus for seven miles, opening out in a great northward bend. Until you are within a couple of hundred yards, you cannot see the entrance; the creamy, iron-mingled cliffs seem to form a continuous wall, and the river has simply ended, disappeared. Mackenzie noted the illusion with disquiet and fumbled to describe it: "The river appeared to be enclosed, as it were, with lofty, perpendicular rocks, which did not afford us a very agreeable prospect." No: Rapids walled in by a canyon are the worst a canoeist can face—in a capsize, there is no way of getting out. He landed, climbed the cliff, and walked along the top—but could see nothing of the wild water the Indians had foretold. Satisfied, he followed them on through and, still wondering at their tale, took the trouble to sound. The depth he got was fifty fathoms—three hundred feet, the underwater inverse of the cliffs, as any fisherman would guess. Halfway through, where a spring has carved away the stone in a flat, wide meadow well above the high-water mark, he stopped to parley with another Indian band camped there, who traded a supply of fish for a few trinkets. When he went on, the men followed in a flotilla of small canoes, fifteen now, besides the four that had joined at the Tsintu.

Jim and I nonetheless approached the Ramparts with a certain caution. Even with the river's immense depth, in higher, faster water the passage might have been less easy than Mackenzie experienced; we had no fresher information. Hence again it was with relief that we found it as he described it. We relaxed, drifting with the current, looking up at the cliffs as we passed: soft rock, like sandstone, water-marked twenty feet up from the present water level by spring floods. Winter ice and cold worked at it, crumbling it in big chunks into the river; at one point, a huge slab leaned out from the top of the cliff, letting the light through behind, as if about to fall.

At the end of the Ramparts, Mackenzie found yet another Indian camp at the mouth of a stream flowing in from the east bank, and there is a settlement there today. You see it first from within the cliffs, a white wooden church shining in the sunlight across the five miles of open water as the river angles to the left and north again; opposite the town, along the west bank, is a big island, spirit-guarded and so named still: Manitou. Mackenzie's North-West Company built a trading post here as early as 1805, giving it the optimistic, abstract name which, like Fort Resolution and Fort Providence, it still bears: Fort Good Hope. (The Hudson's Bay directors when they came North preferred to name their posts after themselves.) In 1859, the first solitary Catholic mission-priest ventured to the area as a peacemaker and before he died erected a cross beside his hut at the top of the bank as a sign of reconciliation; this was (and is) the heart of the Hare territory, but it was also a border, fought over by neighboring tribes, occasionally raided by Eskimos coming up the river from the coast in umiaks, the skin boats used for whaling (Mackenzie heard tales of recent deaths, of Eskimo ferocity and duplicity). The symbolic dividing line of the Arctic Circle is now not much over twenty miles downriver. A church named for the trading post—its dedication is Our Lady of Hope—began building about the time of the American Civil War, with lumber cut and squared up the Hare River; for seventy years or more it was the most northern Catholic mission on the continent, and it is the oldest still in use north and west of the Great Lakes. Inside on the board walls, using paints mixed with fish oils, the builders designed florid frames, intertwining vines heavy with fruit and flowers, which later missioners filled with scenes from the Bible and miraculous local appearances of the Virgin, the last not completed till a century later. The church is an object of local pride and protectiveness; unlike most others along the river, it can be left unlocked. It is surrounded by old graves, Indian and Métis, bearing Indian names. In a style that is older among the Indians of the Northwest than missionary Christianity, each is surrounded by a neat, low fence; the permafrost here is only a foot or so below the surface, impenetrable as stone.

The church had been largely built by a succession of lay

brothers of the missionary order. One, an Irishman who had spent sixty years at it and grown into remote old age, never going home, was remembered for his skill in training dogs for the teams: The trappers brought their pups to him to learn to haul. Nuns had replaced the brothers now; the priest, handy at carpentry, had moved out of the mission house and rebuilt a garage next door to live in. As we started down the road to the beach and our canoe, the nun who had shown us around the church called to us. We went in. On the floor of the living room, three small boys—day care for absent or working mothers—were playing with blocks, chattering in Hare: two of them dark and obviously Indian, the third with the pink skin and ash-white hair of a Scandinavian child but not less native, apparently, than they. The house was surrounded with a neat green border flourishing in the long summer daylight: leaf lettuce, which I had admired. Now the nun had picked and washed a bag of it, which she wanted us to take. No, really—what would we do with a bag of lettuce? She insisted; we thanked her and accepted.

The day, which had been dull and raw since morning, was closing down, darkening; cold mist and cloud lay along the water, dizzying, horizonless. It had begun to rain now, light and steady, as if it would go on. The north wind was blowing again, not hard yet but beating the current up into a rough chop that made slow going. We moved off down the river, looking for a place to camp, and as the rain came on heavier settled on a narrow, sloping beach a few miles below Manitou Island. In a muddy crevice made by spring runoff, I managed to get a fire going, but it was too wet and cold outside to cook. We crowded the packs into the tent and started a can of emergency stew heating on the stove. That lettuce. What could we do with it? We tried a few leaves on a plate, dressed with salt, pepper, and sugar, a splash of bottled lemon juice, then another plateful and another until it was gone. Delicious! It seemed that greens were another of the things our bodies were famished for.

The storm lasted through the night. It was not the random summer storm we had learned to live with by now, an interval between warm days, but a fundamental change of weather, the first warning flicker of the Arctic fall, heavy with cold and rain and thick, soaking mists. It was not yet August. The warm days might come again, but from now on we would be driven by the approaching season.

In the morning I woke up chilled. The rain was still wringing from the clouds, steady but not heavy, at times letting up and then starting in again. The whole river boiled with whitecaps; we would have to wait it out. Lighting the fire had become an anxiety—finger joints aching with the cold, odd muscles jerking in my arms, barely the strength to hold a match no longer felt; I remembered a Jack London story about a greenhorn in an Alaskan winter trying to light a fire and failing, one match after another, until all were gone. It had seemed extravagant.

The fire roared under the steady drizzle but gave no warmth. We ate and got back in the tent, soaked. I put on all my heavy clothes in layers and was almost warm; and, finally, after much weighing of pros and cons, the last pair of socks still more or less clean and dry, and lay back to wait. The river was on the rise again. The driftwood was no longer small but heavy, twenty- and thirty-foot logs carried off from high up the banks, sometimes a whole tree, still green, complete with roots. It swarmed in midchannel, collected in log booms where the current eddied in curves of the river and above points of land, until the weight broke it loose and the boom came apart and moved on. There was not much wood left on our beach. When I went out to tend the fire, I picked chunks of driftwood out of the water and tossed them onto the flames, soft and heavy with the wet, to dry and light; and they burned.

By midafternoon, the water had filled the six feet between the river and the tent, had loosened the front guyline and was washing at the tent door; it lapped in a pool under the fire but did not put it out. It was like being on a sinking ship. I lay and watched the water and could not think what to do. There was no other spot on the beach to hold the tent. Our things were spread around the tent, drying; if we tried to move, all would be wet again, coated with mud, and in the wind we could lose the tent. Jim wanted to move before the water started coming in. We argued lethargically. He went out to hunt a spot, and I roused myself to lace on the stiff boots, struggle into the wet rain parka. We walked along the beach, slipping in the mud. Nothing. Resistance roused me a little. Mind beginning to work again, I noticed now, as if an angel had led my eye, a level spot at the top of the thirty-foot mud bank where, with some clearing of the brush, we might squeeze the tent in. We climbed and found a hunter's tent site from late winter or early spring, admirably neat, solid, and compact: cleared to exactly tent size, leveled with loose earth held together by heavy squared logs laid down like the foundation of a cabin; nearby, there was a rough frame, ax-shaped, for skinning and butchering meat, nailed between two trees. It was a labor you would undertake for a season's stay, perhaps for as little as a week or two in bad weather; not one I have had to practice more than once or twice in a lifetime. The tent, walled in by trees, would have been sheltered from storms and nearly invisible from the river, but from the doorway the hunter had a view, two or three miles in both directions, of any animal crossing the ice: the caribou herds in their spring migration north, ahead of breakup, which here would come in early May. He had had his wife with him, a small boy; among the debris were a pair of worn-out, child-size Keds, a whittled toy boat. Further instruction. I accepted, with gratitude.

We repacked and slithered up the bank with the packs, finally the tent. It was a close fit, like a bear in a Pullman birth, but enough. Warmed by the sheltering trees and out of reach of the cold mist drifting along the water, we cooked in the tent again, the last of our cans. This was our place now. Why go back to the beach?

The rain was letting up. Through the tent door, down the river to the north, we could see a few hopeful patches of pale blue parting the clouds.

Here the river widens, and flows through various chan-
nels, formed by islands. . . .

CHAPTER 9

Into the Delta

Midway between the Arctic Circle and the Beaufort Sea, the great river divides into a multiplicity of channels: the delta. It spreads like an immense hand, 120 miles long, 60 across at its many-mouthed debouchement into the northern ocean. A large map shows and names four or five main channels and as many connecting links cutting the delta up into islands. The reality is more complicated: hundreds of water-courses winding and interwinding, doubling back, through the half-thawed marshy alluvium left by the retreat of the latest ice age, constantly changing, pushing a little farther out into the sea, like a thrusting breast, with each violent spring's deposit of sand and topsoil. The only constraints on the spreading of the delta are geological: on the west, the snow-topped Richardson Mountains, a last northward reach of the Rockies; on the east, the naked Caribou Hills, which have the look of gigantic dunes left behind by a departed ancient ocean of unthinkable depth.

There are two towns within the delta, both with Eskimo names: Aklavik, halfway down, on the west, and on the opposite side, Inuvik, its mirror image. *Akla* names the subspecies of grizzly the people once hunted in the area, *vik* a settlement or place: "the place of the bear." It must always have been good for fish and meat, in summer a meeting place for Eskimos from the coast and the northernmost Indians of the Mackenzie, trading and feasting, sometimes murderously. In 1915, after decades of casual trade by whaling men and fur companies based as far south as Vancouver and San Francisco, a permanent trading post was built here, and the place became a town. In the mid-fifties, however, after repeated flooding, the Canadian government set about replacing Aklavik with a new town that was to be the administrative center for all the western Arctic: Inuvik. To themselves, the Eskimos are *Inuit*, a word that means both their own race and mankind in general; as with other peoples evolved in isolation, their language made no distinction. In the early sixties, when Inuvik was formally dedicated, a few Indians, Eskimos, and white traders were persuaded to move across the delta from Aklavik, but most stayed; their numbers were filled out by newcomers from the South—officials of a dozen agencies, teachers, oil men, barge operators, and businessmen—and "the place of man" became, at least in structure and intention, a city.

From the beginning, our plan had been to find our way through the channels to Aklavik, then cross the delta to Inuvik and from there, somehow, get out to the sea and back. The details, even after much studying of delta maps, were vague. As we got nearer, we would need advice on routes, but all we got was negative: impossible to find your way across the delta without a guide. Now, apart from that difficulty, which I doubted, time pressed. As we waited out another windbound day at the camp below Fort Good Hope, we were still close to three hundred miles from Aklavik, with sixty miles of delta to cross after that: a week, at the best, and July was nearly over. In the circumstances, connecting with Don Tetrault's cruise ship, the *Norweta*, seemed no longer an irresponsible little luxury but a necessity. Beat it to the last settlement on the river, Arctic Red

River, another 220 miles, and we could catch the promised ride to Aklavik, then through the delta to Inuvik. It became an obsession. Oddly, in the month on the river, we had not once seen the ship. It would have passed us at least four times in its weekly runs, but that must always have been at night or along the deep-water channels of the river, screened by islands, which we had avoided.

The storm wore itself out and we were able to move again; sunny now but chilly, the wind blowing, as always, from the north. The water had become the color of weak coffee laced with a little milk; a murk of fine sediment flowed across the paddle blades at each stroke; when the waves rose and the wind blew their tops to froth, they were browncaps, not white, almost invisible. The mud was homogenized; I left pots of water to settle overnight, then strained the water several times through towels—there would be a slick of mud in the bottom of the pots, discoloring the cloth, but the color of the water was unchanged. Thinking about the millennia of human and animal deposits stirred up off the river bottoms, I wondered what form the sickness would take, but nothing came of it. Harmless, apparently; good clean dirt and plenty of it—a perennial canoe-trip joke of my father's. Nevertheless, at each side stream we paddled up to collect clear water for drinking and cooking and aimed our nightly camps at these fresh tributaries.

The driftwood was thick in the strong currents we tried to follow, collecting in eddies, rafting out across the river at bends. I steered among it, zigzagging, but the logs, though big, seemed harmless, and those I could not avoid the canoe pressed down and rode over, with a muffled thumping along the bottom.

By noon on that first day of moving again we had crossed the Arctic Circle, and while we ate our cold lunch I took the time to make a fire, warming feet and hands. The cold was

simply the weather of a changing season: The reality of the
Arctic Circle is the tree line, which angles northwest from
midway up Hudson Bay at about sixty degrees north latitude, surrounding the big northern lakes and embracing the
banks of the Mackenzie to within sixty miles of the coast;
beyond the tree line is the heathlike tundra called the Barren Lands—not truly barren but rich with a plant life ob-
durate enough to survive and breed in the two-month summers that are both cool and arid, though the biggest trees
are no more than shrubs; and with the scattering of animals
and men as tenacious of living as they. Here, on the
Mackenzie, there were still trees, though nearing the limits
of growth: short pines, wide-spaced as if planted and narrow as cypresses, hugging their branches around them for
warmth; and very rarely now a solitary birch or aspen, sheltering among them.

Along this final section of the river, Mackenzie had called
at half a dozen Indian camps. They were of a new tribe,
differing in style and spirit from the Slave and Hare. As the
strange canoes approached, the men sent their women and
children into the woods but stood their ground on the
beach, shouting ferociously and brandishing their weapons,
and were only pacified with gifts and lengthy, diplomat-
ically phrased speeches. *Deguthee dinee*, the English Chief
called them, "quarreling people"; a tribe known today as
Loucheux or Loucheaux, both of which sound more like *liu-
shiou*. Clean and healthy, Mackenzie thought them, compared with the others, well-muscled; a difference, probably,
of diet—big and abundant whitefish in this part of the river
and its tributaries, plenty of caribou in spring and fall for
smoking, occasional moose (the people said they knew nothing of beaver, but the animals, though scarce, are found in
the area today). They looked on the Indians to the south as
"no better than old women and abominable liars"; exactly
the view, Mackenzie dryly noted, "we already entertained of

them." What they told him of the country ahead was accurate, for once, and firsthand: distance downriver to the sea, the shorter overland routes to either side of the delta, locations of Eskimo summer camps. They had been at war with the Eskimos a couple of years back, but at the moment there was peace, hence also trade: scraps of iron for knives; a short, two-piece, double-curved Eskimo bow with a very strong pull, the same type, unknown to other North American natives, with which the Mongol hordes had conquered much of Asia and Europe. Their clothing was similar to the Eskimos', high boots stitched to their trousers, long mittens reaching up the arms, caribou-hide parkas with long tails for ice hunting, loose-cut for the women who carried their babies inside. All were elaborately fringed and tassled, decorated with beadwork; Mackenzie offered them knives and other tools as gifts, but they preferred beads, especially blue ones (one man surprised him by trading back a knife for a handful of beads).

At each camp along the river, Mackenzie had hired a guide; each, when the strangers started to embark and he realized what he'd agreed to, became reluctant and went only after much persuasion and, often, bodily force applied by the phlegmatic canoemen. Each thereafter had made a nuisance of himself, telling gloomy tales of dangers ahead and running off at the first chance if not constantly guarded. Among one of the Loucheaux bands not far from the beginning of the delta, Mackenzie at length found a lively young man eager to make the journey and vain of his knowledge of Eskimo matters. As the big canoe pushed off, the man jumped in and started to sing what he said were Eskimo songs. Then, standing up in the canoe, he danced to his music, an Eskimo dance, he told them, and everyone, fearful of a foot going through the birch bark, was shouting at him: Be *quiet!* The young man complied but had other tricks: He pulled out his penis and, holding it in one hand, showed it around, telling the canoemen and their Indian wives the Eskimo word for it. (The incident is preserved in the early manuscript of Mackenzie's journal; his tactful publisher let him say merely that the Indian displayed "various indecencies, according to the customs of the Esquimaux, of which he boasted an intimate acquaintance.")

There are people today living at most of the places where Mackenzie found Indian bands, and for the same reasons: clean water and good fishing up the tributary streams, productive trap lines running inland, meat to be had along the riverbank. Most of these camps are single families, but in one or two places they have grown into settlements of half a dozen cabins not yet shown or named on the maps. The number of people actually living on the river is less than Mackenzie found. Most have stayed where government policy drew them over the past two generations, in one of the recognized river settlements or the newer delta towns; or have taken the next step, to the native slums of the cities to the south. Success in hunting and trapping is a talent, a gift. Not everyone has it.

At the Travaillant River, we paddled up to draw the clear, icy water. It was late afternoon and we were still seventy-five miles from Arctic Red River and the hoped-for connection with the *Norweta*. In the rush to get there, we were trying a new plan: stop late in the day, when we were tired, and eat, then go on while the light lasted.

There were nets across the stream, tangled by the high water since the storm. As we came out, a man standing on the bank waved and we landed: Julius Norbert, a small man, aging and gray-headed, sickly; the temperature was in the fifties, sunny, and felt warm, but he shivered in a down-stuffed nylon parka, coughing. He had been down on the beach pulling out drift logs to cut up for winter firewood. A rifle lay on the grass near the sawhorse. Had we seen any game as we came down the river? Nothing but fish all summer—he was getting hungry for *meat*.

Fifty miles up the river there is a place designated on the map as Little Chicago, an independent trading post in the thirties and forties but long since abandoned, in our summer an oil, gas, and road-building camp. There are several local explanations for the name: The trader had been remotely connected with Chicago; or, more picturesquely, the post had been the scene of several Chicago-style murders, the bodies surreptitiously buried. A few miles above Little Chicago there was a huge nesting colony of Canada geese on a low island thickly grown with willow; hundreds of the big birds wandering clumsy and flat-footed among the shrubs. Yes, Norbert said, he knew the place but was not much interested. What else? We had camped a few miles down from Little Chicago and in the morning there had been two strange animals down on the beach, drinking: wide-spreading plated antlers that looked at first like moose, but the color was wrong, a warm, dark brown, almost chocolate—caribou. They eyed us curiously for a moment and then without haste climbed the bank and moved off inland. Ah! Norbert said, meat! and wanted to know exactly where we had seen them and how far. We described the place: a triangular island close in to the east bank, the land burned clear by an old fire, years back. Yes! In the morning he would go there in his canoe, with his gun. *Hungry!*

I was thinking about food again myself. Would he mind if we cooked our dinner down here on the beach? Sure, why not? But maybe first we'd like to come up to his cabin? We followed him up the bank.

The cabin was made of unpainted tar-papered planks, winter-sealed inside with sheets of fiberboard, about eight by fifteen feet, with an enclosed porch built on in front against the cold: room inside for a table, a wood stove, a couple of chairs and an empty oil drum to sit on, a pair of beds one above the other like bunks. Behind was a log house, set on posts out of reach of dogs and, possibly, bears, where he stored smoked meat and fish, another ancient gun, a pair of long, narrow snowshoes he had made, webbed with caribou hide cut in strips—good for fast travel in light snow. A square framework next to the house was hung with whitefish, split and drying in the sun, beside it an old Hudson's Bay canvas tent where he smoked the fish. It would keep, like that. Some of it he crumbled into pemmican, mixed with fat, with berries for sweetness, when he could get them; quick food on the trail, in winter.

His wife was much older, in her seventies, a face structured of fine and symmetrical bones that must once have been beautiful, her thin white hair braided in a single queue down her neck, one of the styles Mackenzie had noticed among the Loucheaux women. Dim eyes peered out through plastic-framed glasses. Arthritis had crippled her legs, but her hands still worked at beading moccasins to sell to whatever tourists came down the river (the year before had been good, many travelers, but this year we were the first; would there be others?—but we knew of none). Her clothes were of a kind the younger women had now abandoned: narrow leggings with a long, loose-fitting, parkalike dress over them; for warmth, a worn cardigan, held together with safety pins.

We sat in the cabin and talked; Julius, Robert, James, Northland style. He "made conversation" like a white man. His wife broke in with gestures of impatience: talk-talk-talk, useless white man's talk. I got out our maps to ask about the channels to Aklavik, but it was forty years since he had been that way, he had forgotten. He pointed to the stream on our map, not Travaillant but Travailleur, in a soft, archaic pronunciation, *tra-vay-yuhr;* the map was wrong. He had spent years guiding at a fishing lodge on Great Bear Lake and had built his camp on the river only twelve years back, about the time the fur prices went up. Three times a year a seaplane came out from Inuvik, flew them in to sell the skins, buy food, but he seemed not to be thriving: a single small canoe, no boats or motors; he had given up the dog sled for snowshoes but kept the dogs, a small team, staked outside; in the winter they had run out of kerosene for the lamp and he had used a bowl of beaver fat with a floating wick for light. There had been rabbits by the hundreds when he first came out, in an afternoon he would shoot more than he could carry back, but they were scarce now; what had happened? The talk turned more to food. Meat—we must have much canned meat in our packs, he suggested; tourists always carried canned meat. No; I tried to explain about our freeze-dried stuff. It was getting time to cook and move on, and I asked if they'd like to try some of our food: Come down to the beach in half an hour and it would be ready.

As we started down to the beach, Julius offered us a whitefish from the smoke tent. Smoked the color of buckskin, oily, the flesh neatly segmented where the bones had been lifted out; while we made the fire and cooked, I picked chunks off the stiff, flat skin to eat, famished, and by the time dinner was ready it was finished. Julius came down alone, carrying two tin plates—his wife's legs; she could not manage the steep bank. All right. We carried the pots up to the cabin to eat. He had built up the fire in the stove, and the room was steaming hot. Inside my wool shirt, I felt the sweat in rivulets. No more talk now; we attended to the serious business of food.

It had gotten later than we meant. We said good-bye, gathered up the pots and plates, and went down to the beach to wash. While we packed up, Julius brought another whitefish and waved us off. We paddled on till nearly two, but slowly, tiring again. A succession of gulls mocked us down the river, hooting: their time of day, not ours. A gull would dive toward us, calling, veer off just out of reach, and land on the water ahead, waiting till we got near, then another and another; probably there were hatchlings swimming somewhere near, but we could not see them. Enraging: we pulled chunks of driftwood from the water to throw,

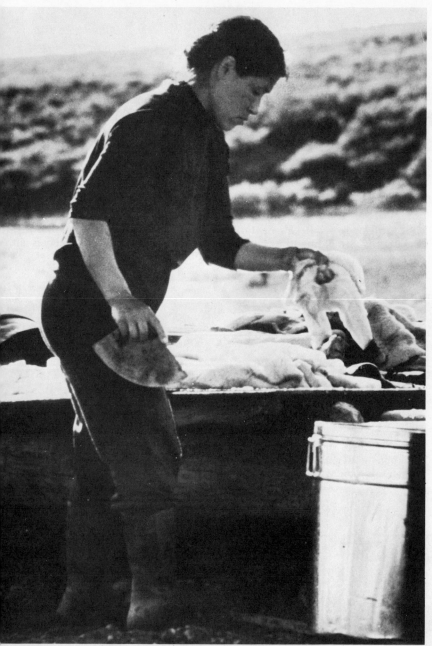

37. Using a steel version of the *ulo* (the traditional rounded woman's knife), an Eskimo woman cuts into strips the white blubber of a fresh-caught beluga whale.

38. Kittigazuit, where for centuries Eskimos gathered by the hundreds for summer whaling, now the camp of a single family from Inuvik, fenced with driftwood against the harsh Arctic winds blowing off the ice pack.

39. Whitefish Station, the beach a few miles east of Kittigazuit where the Eskimos now gather in summer: "whitefish"—the small, pure-white beluga whales, hunted with rifles from power boats.

40. Yellowknife: the original gold-boom town of the 1930s on a rocky point jutting into Yellowknife Bay, on the north side of Great Slave Lake ...

41. ... and now the capital of The Territory, a bustling, rebuilt city of seventy-five hundred, with hotels, government office buildings, and (at right, on the main street) a multistory shopping mall.

42. Anabasis: trucks mired by the mud of the Mackenzie Highway south of Hay River, their drivers attempting to pull each other through with chains.

43. A final emblem of the Eskimo North: the face, half human, half spirit, carved from a chunk of semipetrified whalebone picked up on an Arctic island off the Mackenzie delta.

but never quite managed to hit; for the one time on the trip, I wished for a gun.

There was still light when we camped, on a steep, narrow, muddy beach, but the sun was behind the high bank, *to the north;* cold.

Even with the long days we were not traveling fast enough. We went on the next night till after midnight but still were thirty miles short of Arctic Red River, and though we had seen nothing of the *Norweta* yet, I was no longer hopeful of catching it. The driftwood was bigger now and threatening. With the high water that followed the prolonged rain, the river boiled with unpredictable currents. In midstream, where the current should have been strong, it revolved in huge eddies blocked with logs; along the banks, the current ran backward sometimes harder than we could paddle, and we moved back and forth, dodging wood. At bends in the river, where several currents contended, whipped by the wind, there were billowing, brown-capped standing waves stretching clear across the river, temporary rapids half a mile long, and whole trees rode through them, eerily erect, balanced by a mass of earth-clinging roots still intact.

That afternoon, going up a stream for water, we stopped to talk with another trapper, younger than Norbert, and prospering: a fiberglass canoe, a big wood-and-canvas freighter, an aluminum boat with a forty-horse motor; several thousand dollars' worth of boats. His dogs were staked along the beach where they could drink. Three small children stayed around a cabin as rudimentary as Norbert's while their father came down to see what we wanted; man's work, protective. We asked about the distance to Arctic Red River, the best side of the river for the currents. He would be going into town in the morning sometime with his boat and offered to give us a lift the last few miles. He kept his word, as it turned out, but by the time he caught up with us, about noon, we were nearly there and I was too depressed to talk to a stranger, and dubious about towing the loaded canoe through the rough water behind his boat. After paddling fifteen hundred miles, I said, I thought we had better manage this last bit on our own. All right. We pushed off from the boat, waving, and he revved the motor and headed on down the river.

There are four other Red rivers on the continent, but this one, for distinction, is the Arctic Red. It has been a summer meeting place of the Loucheaux and Eskimos for centuries, but it was not till the 1870s, with the building of a trading post at its mouth, that it became a permanent settlement. Above the town, the Mackenzie narrows between hundred-foot, cliff-like banks of shale and clay and swings in an eight-mile arc to the west, doubling around to the south before turning north again to the delta: the Lower Ramparts, reversing the curves of the defile by which, two hundred miles upstream, the river makes its approach to Fort Good Hope.

Fewer than a hundred Indians live in the place called Arctic Red River; a long-time Belgian priest; the young manager of The Bay, newly arrived from Glasgow, tall, slender and long-haired, differing in style from the generations who preceded him but with the same innocent delight in profit; and, in winter, a teacher. The RCMP post has closed, moved inland to the larger settlement of Fort McPherson; down by the river, the white board residence and jail weather in the sun, the doors standing open, the windows broken. The church, the mission house, the school, a territorial office, and a few cabins are thinly scattered across the steep, grassy slope, the white clapboard Hudson's Bay store looking out from near the top of the rise. What living there is comes from a sawmill cutting lumber floated down the Arctic Red River and supplying, it is said, all the towns of the northwest Arctic. Here too, however, transformation is on the way. Inland, there is an airport where small, scheduled planes arrive and depart, twice a week. To the south, a new road, the Dempster Highway, crawls north through the Yukon from the Alaska Highway; in time, Arctic Red River will be the junction for this road and the Mackenzie Highway; already across the river a section of highway has been finished as far as Inuvik, though no map yet shows it (that road, with the world's largest culvert, was a matter of local pride until the culvert crumpled under spring ice and flood and a heavy truck; but it will, one day, be rebuilt). On the pastel government bungalows lining the road to the airport, television aerials have sprouted to receive the broadcasts beamed from a hovering satellite known as Anik, an Eskimo word for "brother."

The town when we arrived that midafternoon seemed deserted; a Sunday. We tied up at the dock and, cautiously leaving Jim to watch the canoe, I started up the hill. One man, possibly white, hiked along a grassy track from the church to a building marked as the office of the local airline, and I followed him: Father Colas, the priest; and—travel agent, meteorologist, amateur ethnologist, author of some of the paintings at Fort Good Hope. The rubber boots of an Indian riverman, dark trousers, a heavy black sweater either naval or clerical; he had been up the river with his canoe, cutting wood. I offered cigarettes and we went into his office to talk.

It was not easy. Each question provoked a disquisition. The route across the delta from Aklavik to Inuvik? No, really, don't attempt it, quite impossible without a guide—maps useless, the channels changing from year to year. Our hope of somehow getting out to the coast? Not at all advisable, tides and sudden storms, a tale of a trapper who'd camped out there sixty feet up from the water and lost everything, boat, tent, food; everything. The canoe, now, perhaps we were planning to sell it? Several of the men here would appreciate a canoe like that—the price, of course, he knew nothing of such things. No, I said, it had taken us this far, we were attached to it, like a horse; we would get it home somehow. Ah! He explained the origin of the tribal name, Loucheux, a perfectly good French word, did I know the language, the theory of the Anglican bishop was quite mistaken, and what languages, by the way, did I know? I mentioned French, Italian, German; Latin, Greek; thoughtfully, Provençal, wondering if it counted. But no *oriental* languages? he asked hopefully. Perhaps I should look into the linguistic evidence for the transpacific origins of the North American Indians. He personally did not accept the Bering Strait theory; in the American Southwest, the Navahos, for instance, there were remarkable similarities, the same number system as among the Loucheux, and what did I think of *that?*

I was asking him to recommend a place to camp and he was urging that we push on, not wait: The weather, often stormy between here and the delta, might be dangerous. I looked out the window at the sky: clouds but not heavy, mostly sunny; it would last another day, two days. And if it changed, we would take our chances. Ah! He pointed to charts of the weather on the walls of the office, kept over twenty years: cycles. But of course . . .

Father Colas finished a cigarette and stood up: "And now that I've told you everything you wanted to know!" Yes, I thanked him. But that passenger boat, the *Norweta,* due here about now, did he know? "Oh, no, no, *yesterday,* didn't you see it? At Aklavik by now." Ah! We had not seen it. I had wondered. . . .

I went back to Jim and the canoe and we paddled a mile up the Arctic Red River, looking for clean water, and found it in a cool, clear, reedy stream with a steep mud bank where we could pitch the tent and a thicket of spring-shattered willow, dead and dry enough for fire.

Missing the ship was in fact a relief: one problem at least that no longer spoke for our energy and attention. Jim and I talked a little about the final heading. All right, we would give up on Aklavik, turn off into the East Channel and go straight to Inuvik; the extra distance, with the never remote possibility of bad weather, might take a week, which we did not now have; and the priest, perhaps, was right about the difficulties, the risks, of the route across the delta, much of it upstream. Vacation, I said, which we had not yet had; we could take it easy now, stop early in the day, find a little time at last for fishing.

The morning was bright. We paddled back to the town, climbed the hill to the store, and waited for it to open. Mail: birthday cards; a letter from my wife with papers that had to be signed, reminders of the real world back there, waiting.

The weather was going to hold. The wind had swung around to the south, behind us, for the second or perhaps third time since June, and we were getting beyond the rafts of driftwood. Jim rigged the spare paddles to catch the wind, and in two hours of invigorating speed we had reached Point Separation, sixteen miles, and were stopping for an early lunch. The point is a small one nosing out into the river, named by an explorer, Sir John Franklin, who followed Mackenzie North, divided his party here, and in wintering overland toward the coast was lost and, for years after, searched for. Not only the name expresses finality. The river spreads east and west, opening out in its delta, flowing around huge islands divided and subdivided by intervening streams: What you see from the point is a six-mile expanse of open water and, faintly in the distance, barely distinguishable in this flat, green, almost treeless country, three wide channels; and beyond, forty-five miles northwest, the snowy peaks of the Richardson Mountains, dim in the mist and glowing sun. It is a place for decisions not lightly taken: Given the realities of time, current, distance, weather, whatever choice you make will be absolute; no turning back, no second chance. For us, it meant giving up a part of the trip, a goal, and it was a subtraction I had not yet entirely given in to; but necessary nonetheless.

Mackenzie too had landed here, uncertain what to do, to consider and, for once, talk through the possibilities with his men. The river, he could see, as we did, "here . . . widens, and runs through various channels, formed by islands, some of which are without a tree. . . . Their banks . . . display a face of solid ice, intermixed with veins of black earth, and as the heat of the sun melts the ice, trees frequently fall. . . . So various were the channels . . . that we were at a loss which to take." He took the time for an observation, with discouraging results: much farther north than he had hoped. He had finally to admit to himself that the river's course was north, not west, that "these waters emptied themselves into the Hyperborean Sea." He had failed, then, in the goal that had persuaded his partners to agree to the expedition: the great river did not after all carry through the mountains to the Pacific and the hoped-for wealth of a world-circling expansion of the trade. Why then go on? And if they did, food was now so short, the hunting so uncertain, that it seemed unlikely they could return to Athabasca before winter. The canoemen were for pushing on to the sea; curiosity, if nothing else, having come so far. All right then, the middle of the three channels, biggest and probably most direct. The Indians, however, were still reluctant, nervous of wintering in a strange and inhospitable land. The Loucheaux guide, no longer eager, discouraged them further: He knew the East Channel, where the Eskimo encampments would be, but was fearful of the others. In the end, Mackenzie made a bargain, reluctantly accepted: another seven days' travel north; if by then they did not reach the sea, they would turn back.

Ten miles down from Point Separation, where the East Channel veers off to the right, we entered a new world: after the immensities of the river, a narrow, sheltered stream glazed with images of reflected clouds, blue sky, bright sun, unruffled by the placid current. By the circuitous windings of the channel, Inuvik was still sixty miles off, but already signs of its presence rippled outward across the delta: several camps of Indian fishermen come out for the summer; a boy and girl in a powerful boat, rushing downriver to the town; up ahead, a float plane, spindly limbed and delicate as a dragonfly, alighting on the water with supplies for one of the camps, taking off again. We camped that night on a low-spreading willowy island of sand, which we shared with a big colony of Arctic terns. Overhead, the creamy, angular birds swooped and darted in the bright air, instructing their young in the acrobatics of hunting and survival. The terns noticed us with a rasping, buzzing, polysyllabic cry that sounded like "Why'n't ya *beat* it?" spoken by a midget with a harelip and a nasal Brooklyn accent. We were finishing dinner when an Indian and his three boys crossed the channel and nosed the plywood scow up the beach. He had been lifting his nets, had seen the canoe, and had come over to visit, self-assured and unconstrained. Maybe we'd like some fish? There were several good whitefish in the bow, a twenty-pound cony (a species of whitefish whose name Mackenzie had carefully written out in full, *poisson inconnu*, each time it turned up in the nets). I took a small whitefish—no, have a bigger one, they had plenty; and I accepted.

We built up the fire again and made a fresh pot of coffee, the other gesture, with cigarettes, of northern civility. While we drank it, the boys kept politely silent, and Jim with them; talk between strangers is for the men, the fathers. The Indian, it turned out, had been a mighty canoeist and wanted to know about our canoe, our trip. Ten years back, he had won a race from Aklavik to Inuvik, in a plywood canoe he had built himself, all that remains of the skill of birch bark and spruce; twice he had descended the Fraser, he knew the rapids on the Slave and wondered how our canoe had handled in them.

Like Julius Norbert, he wanted to know what game we'd

seen, and where. Nothing but fish all summer: He and the boys had been cutting wood, on contract with one of the oil companies. I had noticed and admired his work as we came into the channel, foot-thick logs of pine, all of a size and exactly cut to eight-foot lengths, stacked in even cords between standing trees; beautiful—but destined to be ground to chips to fill the artificial islands that were being built that summer off the mouth of the Mackenzie, as bases for oil rigs. While we talked, the boys had wandered off to the other side of the island. Now they came back, whispered to their father: Birds over there, geese, ducks. Could they take the gun? Meat, serious business: The Indian finished his coffee, they climbed into the boat, and we helped them off. They cruised back upstream, into the channel around and behind the island, slowly, looking for game. A couple of distant shots; luck. By our watches, it was midnight, but above us the terns still swooped and darted in the golden sunlight.

The delta had reserved a lesson for the next day. It was toward noon. We had found our way past several doubtful side channels, and I was feeling a little cocky about all the warnings we had had: Nothing to it, I was telling myself; all you had to do was follow the map. Ahead, on the map, was another channel, cutting close inside an island, that would save several hundred yards of paddling. We turned in at what looked like the channel and immediately it seemed wrong, too winding and in the wrong direction, and yet there was nothing on the maps that made sense of it. We paddled, drifted with the current, passing the map back and forth, debating uneasily: Where the hell were we exactly? The thought cut with a sharp edge of panic. This map, which did not quite make sense, was our connection with places, people; once out of relation to it, there were a thousand places on it where we could be and getting back might be days, weeks, and strictly chance. A couple of miles along, the channel narrowed, then opened out in a lake, the source, and I began to see: It was a small tributary; the river was full enough to reverse its flow. We turned and paddled back to the East Channel, moving slowly against the current, still doubtful, properly humbled. Even in this small way, the delta could be deceptive. To large errors, it would be merciless.

For the sake of clear water, we camped that night beside a slow, cold tributary stream. Wet-loving, reedlike horsetail was thick on the bank, carpeting it, meadow-thick, in brilliant green. It looked promising for mosquitoes, but the dragonflies had done their work, and the mosquitoes were scarce. A new butterfly crouched on a pack, fanning its wings dry. Spring and summer were compressed in one, but fall was now only weeks off. After dinner I washed and dug out my least dirty pair of socks, gestures of anticipation. The next day, maybe, we would reach Inuvik; or maybe not, I was through with impatience. Later, in the tent, it was too warm for sleeping bags, for the first time on the trip— seventy, by the thermometer my engineer son had brought so as to be informed of such things. In the night, a light rain fell, and the weather cooled again.

The drizzle lasted into the next afternoon. About midmorning we were astonished to see a blue tent identical with our own, a canoe pulled up on the bank beside it, covered with a tarp, and we paddled over. Asleep? A head looked out: a man from Ontario, with his wife, started from Fort Simpson and bound like us for Inuvik. They had passed our camp in the night, late, and decided to sleep out the rain, go on in the afternoon. See us in Inuvik then? Why not—camped on the beach somewhere within reach of the town, maybe a night in a hotel to clean up. And on down the delta to the coast? If we could manage it—hadn't figured out how, yet. We hung onto the bank with our paddles and sat in the canoe, talking, for an hour, in no hurry now, famished for talk, swapping stories of the birds and animals and people of the river, the weather we'd all been through, the storms; his wife stayed out of sight in the tent. We exchanged names: Steve, remember? In Inuvik, then.

As we came nearer the town, human signs multiplied.

High on one bank was the hulk of a wooden barge, built of two-inch planking and now broken in half, a type as old on the river as the last steam-powered paddle-wheelers, retired in the thirties, which served as passenger boats and freighters till the planes took over. Cabins became more frequent, brightly painted against the prevailing earth browns and dull greens of the northern landscape: strong red gables, brilliant blue doors, the logs plaster-chinked and painted white. Then it was not single cabins but several families banded together for the fishing, radio antenna and flagpole with its maple-leaf flag announcing a settlement.

As the channel winds, you begin to see the town first from ten miles off, and the approach becomes tedious with expectation: small seaplanes landing and taking off on a lake near the airport, disappearing behind the intervening land, leaping up again; then scattered distant houses, a warehouse, a power plant. Behind them all is a line of bare hills, stripped by fire and wood cutting and covered now, in summer, with a purple-pink haze of fireweed; a westernmost outpost of the Barren Lands stretching east across the continent as far as land carries.

The beach below the town, when we at length reached it, looked uninviting: barges loading and unloading, a noisy power plant in process of construction; the town itself lay back from the river, toward the hills. To get nearer, we paddled into a channel above the beach and came out in a lake cut off from the river, with houses and barrackslike apartment buildings high up the bank on one side, a sheltered landing place for boats down at the end: Boot Lake, so named for its shape. Small Eskimo children playing by the water waved and smiled as we entered, welcoming. Moored below the houses was a scow, a cabin built across the bow half for sleeping and eating. We paddled over: a strapping Loucheaux down from Arctic Red to show his three boys the town, getting loud now with celebration. Holiday—vacation! Girls! Did anyone care where we camped? Hell, camp where you like—*our* country and welcome. Come on board, have a beer—have some *whiskey!* We tied the canoe and climbed into the boat. The beer hung on lines over the stern, cooling. The Indian had been drinking beer but was switching to Canadian Club—holiday, by God, not drunk, but *getting* drunk. The boys were earnest, he was kidding them about the snooty Inuvik girls, wouldn't look twice at an honest man, by God—and money! Where had we come from in that little canoe? We talked a little about the trip: Have another beer, you've *earned* it. And it had begun to seem now that perhaps we had. We stayed for an hour, talking, joking, telling stories, then paddled off to find an opening along the lake where we could put the tent. The light was dimming as we hiked up through the half-built town to look for a place to eat. It was the first day of August, a day of endings but also of beginnings. Three or four weeks I had lazily told Don Tetrault back in Hay River. We had done it.

Covered with ice . . . and no land ahead. . . . We landed at the boundary of our voyage in this direction. . . .

CHAPTER 10

To the Edge of Earth

There are three hotels in Inuvik, each with several restaurants and a bar that is usually packed through the noon-to-midnight licensing hours; a territorial liquor store; offices of thirty federal and territorial government agencies; freight yards, warehouses, and docks of the two barge lines; the only news agency in the Northwest Territories (outside Yellowknife), where as usual the girl magazines predominate and the few copies of *Time, Newsweek,* and the Edmonton papers are sold out within an hour of delivery; headquarters for two negative organizations, COPE (Committee for Original Peoples Entitlement) and its newer and less vociferous rival, HOPE (Help Original People Evolve); a few old-time fur traders; a craft shop that collects certified native artifacts, mostly Eskimo, from throughout the North; an airport built to handle the biggest jets; several taxi companies; a research laboratory operated by the federal government, which co-ordinates scientific work of all kinds in the Arctic and, to a degree, in the Northwest Territories as a whole; a colorful primary school known locally as SAM (for Sir Alexander Mackenzie), with a high school and two hostels for students brought in from the northern towns; and a circular Catholic church in the form of an igloo, with walls of preformed concrete panels and a domed metallic roof that glitters in the sun like the scales of a fish. Inuvik is, in short, a city. In the ten years of its official existence, its population has grown from nothing to, at the moment, about four thousand.

More than half these people are white, mostly working for one or another branch of the government. Perhaps a third are Eskimos. The rest are Indians, subdivided into several more or less distinct groups, though in counting heads the government no longer distinguishes. Never having subscribed to a treaty with the rest of the country, the Eskimos are undivided. To have any of the blood is simply to be Eskimo, without qualification.

Inuvik is a city, but in a style that is both Arctic and frontier, twentieth-century and Canadian, with the advantages and drawbacks of a colony. There is much building but no factories, nothing obviously productive; such production as there is, is in the oil and gas camps north and south along the river and on the coast. Everything is new but with an air of being unfinished and provisional, of being simultaneously torn apart and rebuilt. The seven miles of road running south to the airport is black-topped, but in town the unpaved streets blow with dust and turn viscous when it rains, and the boardwalks that line them are slippery with mud. Every building is set on piles, four or five feet off the ground, like a riverside warehouse, so as not to disturb the permafrost; along the main street, false fronts, as in a Western cow town, raise the stores still higher. Through the town snakes the connecting umbilical cord called a utilidor, aboveground water and sewage pipes, also on piles, sheathed in planking and galvanized metal and here and there crossed by stairways, up and over, that look like oversize stiles. In a few places architects brought in from the South have tried to invent an indigenous style: not only the igloo church but a glass-and-shingle pyramid erupting from the roof of the Research Laboratory or a geodesic dome looking out across the river from among the private homes in the direction of the airport; or simply the brightly painted frieze of teepee forms relieving the blank walls of one of the schools.

The overall effect is one of indifferent utility: the three- and four-story subsidized apartment buildings, each to the same plan, thrusting up among the smaller structures like the warehouses and factories of a New England mill town; the rows of attached, single-family houses, identical in form and color as the officers' quarters in an American Army camp.

The morning after our arrival, Jim and I hiked up to town from our camp on Boot Lake, dodging around half-finished apartment buildings and ducking under utilidors, to get a room at the newest of the three hotels, the Eskimo Inn. There was a government boatyard at the far end of the lake, canoes and boats pulled up on the beach and the bank behind, and I'd thought to store the canoe and some of the packs till we knew what to do, carry what we needed to the hotel, but the yard was locked up, deserted; a Friday, the beginning of another of the long Canadian summer weekends. A white family back from an outing and hauling a boat out repeated the universal warning—*leave nothing unguarded*—and offered a lift to their house, where I could telephone a cab.

Fifteen minutes later, I was back at the boatyard and we were loading the packs into the car, roping the canoe onto the roof—the driver had a yard across from the hotel where he could store it. John Blatz: with the blond, muscular good looks and disciplined intelligence that to me said German Army—he would have been the right age. But—no, when I said something about Germany—Alberta, northern Alberta, grown up on a farm, and I did not pursue the question; a fresh variety of Northland frontiersman. The cab fare was figured by the minute. A driver with a car could clear a hundred, two hundred dollars a day, when he worked: not only the constant stream of officials back and forth to the airport, the random visitors, but the Indians for whom the two-hundred-yard ride home from the store or the hotel bar was a pleasure out of proportion to the two or three dollars it cost. (John's feeling for the Indians was the same cool indifference of most whites in the North: drunk and looking for a fight, no problem, backhand them a couple of times across the mouth, knock 'em down the stairs in front of the hotel, and they'd quiet down right enough, next day, sober, be all over you, thanking you; "These guys that drink all the time, you know, mostly don't eat well enough to have much strength.") John had another cab now, had bought one of the fast-food franchises, hamburgers and milk shakes, that were still booming in the North, had built the store across the street from the Eskimo Inn, with an apartment above, air conditioned: That was where we would store the canoe. Clearing seventy-five thousand dollars a year by now; he was starting to think about retiring, to Alberta. In the days we were in town, there was never an hour when he was not around, parked in front of the hotel, cruising the street, overseeing the young whites behind the counter in the hamburger shop.

We shouldered the packs into the lobby and registered. John waited for a moment, looking through the magazines on a rack near the desk. Pubic hair, he remarked, that was the big thing this year, had I noticed? The last frontier.

Steve and his wife were having a late breakfast in a booth of the lunchroom behind the hotel lobby. Jim and I slid in beside them. In the morning, paddling down Boot Lake, we had stopped to talk. They had gotten in after midnight, camped on the channel connecting the river with the lake. His wife was trying to get on a plane home in the afternoon and it looked now as if she'd succeed; Steve was still looking for someone to team up with for the final hundred miles of river to the sea and back. How about it? I considered. Images flashed in my mind of the quirks of strangers let loose by travel, making them and oneself intolerable; impossible without immense forbearance. Here, in the intimacy of canoe and tent and evening cookfire, we would depend on each other, absolutely. I do not take to dependence; Jim and I, burdened with parenthood and sonship, were at least used to each other. It was not a decision to be lightly taken.

Maybe, I said, leaving it open. We could talk about it some more.

In the afternoon I hunted alternatives. The town was clearing out for the weekend. A Mounty, supposed to be a local boy, know everyone, wanted us to hire an Eskimo coming out of jail the next day, going home, probably, to the coast; nothing serious, drunkenness and assault, six weeks. The local outlet of the CBC, broadcasting from rooms in the third hotel, the Mad Trapper, ran an announcement; several people stopped me in the street to ask if I was the canoe guy trying to get out to the coast, but there were no takers.

That night, his wife safely on the plane South, Steve joined us for dinner in the barnlike dining room of the Eskimo Inn. Over buttery caribou steaks from the freezer, brought in by hunters in the spring, he made us an offer: Ship the canoes back by barge to Hay River, combine our gear, and rent something for the paddle out to the sea. To reassure his wife on the trip from Fort Simpson, he had carried a motor, which we could use for getting back; we would fly to Fort Simpson where he had left his truck, drive to Hay River to pick up the canoes, and he would drive us back to Fort McMurray where we had left our car, another thousand miles and, for us, an unsolved problem. It had become inevitable; all right. We would aim for Tuktoyaktuk, the first settlement east along the coast from the mouth of the delta. Twenty-two miles of open water, the people warn you, knowing distances and small boats. T'k-*ty*-k-tk it sounds like, not easily formed by an English-speaking tongue; the Eskimo name, it is said, has to do with a legend of *tuk-tuk*, the caribou, and a rock formation at a place where the fresh water of the Mackenzie meets the salt of the Arctic Ocean—"it looks like a caribou." I finished the caribou steak and ordered another bottle of Edmonton beer. The young Swiss woman who ran the hotel restaurants sat down at the table to share a pot of coffee and argue us into dessert—a slow night, and, what with the weekend, no help; she and her husband had bought 320 acres in Alberta, a farm rented out now to tenants, and in two years would have it paid off, would leave.

Shipping our canoes back to Hay River by barge would take at least two weeks. There were canoes in town to rent, but all taken, nothing available till after the weekend. Steve and I spent the next morning making the rounds and came finally to the store of an old trader at one end of the town. He had started out at Fort McMurray as a trapper in the early twenties, when trapping was still legal for whites, and had worked North, following the trade, to Aklavik, now finally to the new town of Inuvik. The store was like a Hollywood set for the general store in a Western frontier town: a few oak-framed showcases with glass made opaque by time and abrasion; dusty shelves thinly scattered with a lifetime of merchandise—canned goods, mismatched boots, odds and ends of obsolete hardware.

Our business proceeded with oriental indirection. Well, yes, the trader at length volunteered, he did have a freight canoe. Course, it was old, we wouldn't want it. An Indian trapper came in, half liquored, demanding cash, had to have it *right now*—the system of advances against furs to be delivered in the fall, at interest, as old as the fur trade itself; in fifteen minutes they bargained it up from nothing to five dollars, ten, finally twenty, and the trader pulled the bills from the gilt-brass cash register. We pursued. This canoe: It might be a possibility. Was it any good? Oh, sure, it was a *good* canoe, they'd had it out in the spring, ratting; but old. It was stored on sawhorses in the yard in front of the trader's cabin. Steve and I went over to look: a battered eighteen-foot wood-and-canvas freighter with a vee stern where you could mount a motor, probably thirty years old, much patched and repainted, covered ten years back with fiberglass that was starting to come off; coated with mud and spruce twigs from the ratting in the spring. Well, why not? There was nothing else. We went back to the store to bargain over the price.

With the deal made, there were several matters Steve wanted to settle: a split on the cost of the canoe, food, air freight for his motor to Fort Simpson, mileage on his car from there to Fort McMurray. Like a gambler who will bet on anything—toss of coin, turn of card, afternoon rain—he enjoyed bargaining for its own sake; I seem to have inherited some of the instincts. We bargained.

Getting ready to leave took us the rest of the day: an accumulation of dirty clothes to carry to the laundromat and back, food to be bought, the packs to be emptied out and once more resorted and repacked; finally, the canoes to be loaded onto John Blatz's cab and delivered to the freight yard for shipping. Somewhere in the course of all this, the three of us were back in our room at the hotel, eating a lunch of nuts and honey. Steve, it seemed, had theories of diet: sesame seeds, sunflower seeds, soybeans—wonderful sources of protein; this was the last of his supply.

Late that evening, everything at last done, I wandered through the summer sunlight having a last look at the town, stopped at the Anglican vicarage to ask about services in the morning, and stayed to chat. The priest was a man in his sixties, gray and slender, sent out from Toronto the previous fall, with a British polish to his speech and manner; good family and a quick mind, with a respectable degree, probably, from Oxford or Cambridge, tactful in his convictions to the point of diffidence but absolute at the core—the patented model that the Church of England has been turning out since the time of Chaucer. It is a type one still meets with in prosperous churches in the better London suburbs, occasionally on cathedral staffs or in baronial Victorian rectories in the Yorkshire countryside; cures no more unlikely, really, than the western Arctic.

The morning service would be in English, the afternoon one in Eskimo. At Tuk it was the reverse, Eskimos were the majority. I was curious about the language, by reputation almost impossible for a white to learn. Had he managed? Oh, not too badly—it had taken him a month, after he arrived. He got along. Now about the service: If we were leaving early, the regular one, in English, would no doubt be too late, but he could *lay one on* for me, if I liked. Would eight o'clock do?

I did not sleep much that night. It was cloudless and hot, about eighty. Through the bedroom window the sun shone in my face, bright as morning, as long as I was awake.

John Blatz was waiting in front of the hotel when I got back from church, ready to haul the packs and the rented canoe down to the river. He had also solved our final problem, gasoline for Steve's motor for the return trip. We had spent most of Saturday hunting gasoline—the two dealers were off for the weekend, no one to sell it till Tuesday, apparently—but from somewhere John had produced two tengallon drums, at not much over the local price. While we unloaded on the beach, there was a little preliminary dickering about the gasoline: Steve wanted me to pay for it, he could settle later; I thought there'd be less argument if we shared out the expenses from the start. Impatient to be off, I dug out my wallet and we waved good-bye to John.

We had the canoe afloat and half loaded before we realized that there was water in the bottom; a leak. We unloaded, pulled the canoe out, and turned it over. Now that the mud was washed off, you could see, the old paint and glass cloth were coming off, the bottom was honeycombed with possible leaks. I had patching materials, epoxy and several rolls of waterproof tape, in the bottom of one of the packs. No, Steve insisted, he had a waterproof glue that would do the job. I let him try it. We waited for the glue to dry, put the canoe back in the water. Still leaking; the glue, when we pulled the canoe out again, had not set. I patched several of the most likely-looking holes, we tried the canoe a third time in the water, found other leaks, and repeated the process. It seemed, for the moment, to have worked: no more telltale trickles of water between the ribs. I took a few pictures. It was midafternoon by the time we had loaded the canoe and were pushing off down the East Channel toward the sea.

It is not possible to follow Mackenzie's course through the delta with any assurance. Once in the delta his notes become vague. In the multiplicity of interconnecting channels, his distances and compass bearing no longer make much sense. His system of reckoning suited the straightforward trade routes to the south and east but not this maze. In any case, it did not matter much. He had failed in his objective —it was to the Arctic Ocean, not the Pacific, that the river was carrying him, and the record of how to get there would have no practical interest for his partners. Beyond that, the delta has changed. Old channels have filled in, new ones been cut; islands that Mackenzie saw as separate have been joined, others formed out beyond the old river mouths.

It is certain that Mackenzie reached a bay of the Beaufort Sea, but not where. My own guess is that he kept to what is now the Middle Channel, the biggest, to a point where it divides in three, then veered north into a smaller channel and followed it to the northwest side of the delta and a group of high islands that lie near the shore of what is now Mackenzie Bay. But it is no more than that, a guess.

Although Mackenzie knew by now that he had missed his

goal, there were lesser marvels. Whitefish, cony, and the troutlike Arctic char swarmed in the shallow channels, leaping from the water as the paddle strokes frightened them, sometimes flopping into a canoe. On the low islands there were immense flocks of birds in their Arctic breeding grounds, not only the many varieties of geese and ducks but the tan, majestic sand cranes and the pure white snowy owls that summer near the coast and hunt by day; flights of rock ptarmigan, mottled white and brown now in summer, skittered across the willow thickets, startled by the passing canoes. On the tenth of July, camped on a channel somewhere west of the site that would be Inuvik, Mackenzie sat up to note the hour of sunset—and was astonished to discover that there was none. He called one of his men "to view," as he said, "a spectacle which he had never before seen." The Frenchman, seeing the sun high, thought it was time to get up and go on and woke the rest; it was only after much argument that they were persuaded to go back to bed. It would have been about two o'clock. They had entered the season and place of perpetual light.

Several times a day now they passed the distinctive winter camps of the Mackenzie Eskimos: oval lodges dug into the ground, heavy frameworks of driftwood covered with skins and sod, sleeping platforms around the walls inside for several families; beside the lodges, the small sledges of this area, *komatik*, frames of kayaks and the big umiaks in which the people traveled upriver, for warfare or trade, and probably east and west along the coast as well; soapstone pots and neatly carved wooden buckets and eating trays; thick chunks of discarded whale and walrus hide. They saw none of the Inuit. The people, the nameless Loucheaux guide insisted, were on the East Channel; he knew nothing of this part of the delta or of the seacoast ahead. Mackenzie persisted in the course he had chosen. The guide was increasingly restive; Ageena, stiffly on his dignity, resisted any further progress in this fool's mission, and his Indian hunters followed his lead. By way of persuasion, after sitting up to watch the all-night sun, Mackenzie gave the English Chief one of his hooded overcoats and the guide a well-cured moose hide ("original" he called it, mixing the French word, *orignal*), a scarce and valuable present in this country. They were less than a day from the sea.

The guide was truthful. There were three or four thousand Eskimos in and near the delta when Mackenzie discovered it, possibly the most numerous group of this northern people anywhere in the Arctic. As many as half of them were probably gathered for the summer not more than thirty miles off, just beyond the mouth of the East Channel, at a place they called Kittigazuit, "the place with the high bluff." The reason for being there was the same as the reason for their comparatively large population: whaling; food. Kittigazuit is a narrow neck separated from the mainland by a two-hundred-yard channel. To the north, the island spreads out and rises to two-hundred-foot cliffs of sand and clay, forming the easternmost boundary of the delta. In July, when the ice is gone, the beluga whales, twenty or thirty feet long, with a skin of angelic whiteness, come into the bay formed by the East Channel and the island, frisking and leaping, to feed on whitefish swarming in the fresh water of the river, mingling with the herring and small sharks of the salt water. (In the deeps out toward the ice pack there are giants, blue whales big as islands.) On the treeless tundra of the high ground north of Kittigazuit, Eskimo lookouts waited in religious silence for the coming of the white whales. Then there were wordless signals to those waiting on the beach below, and the hunters pushed off in their kayaks, a hundred, two hundred, till the first out was near the land seven miles off and the rest had formed a line across the bay. They paddled into the mouth of the channel, shouting and beating their paddles on the water, driving the whales into the shallows. The oldest hunter was allowed the first shot with his harpoon, coming in close; those who were strong and lucky

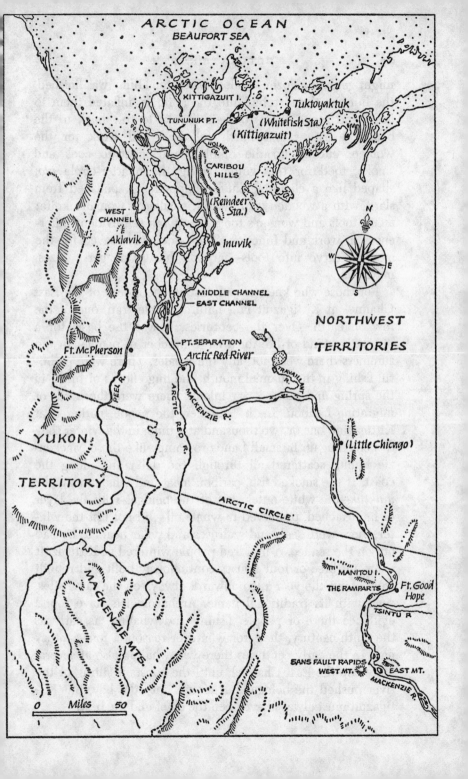

might get half a dozen whales. When the killing was finished, the hunters thrust tubes into the animals, inflated them to float, and roped them to their kayaks to tow back to the beach. Feasting and mirth followed—and work for the women, cutting up the blubber and meat to cook and smoke, food for the winter, using the quarter-circle *ulo*, shaped like a chopping knife, chipped and polished from slate, with a wooden grip, which is called a woman's knife: men's tools and women's tools, signifying self-evident differences in work and function. The bones were saved for the men to carve into tools—harpoon heads, daggers, adzes, mattocks.

For those who knew how to use it, the mouth of the East Channel at Kittigazuit is a natural whale trap, one of the few on earth. Over the centuries, it was the basis for a distinctive kind of life for a large number of people. In the summers there were not only the whales. There were plentiful fishing in the channel mouth, the huge flocks of birds; in the spring and fall, not far inland, there were the herds of migrating caribou. In the summer, the people gathered at Kittigazuit, one or two thousand at a time; in the winter they dispersed again in small bands to camps like those Mackenzie found, scattered all through the delta and along the coast. If the smoked fish, caribou meat and whale meat, the *muktuk*—the white outer skin of the belugas with the layer of fat attached, preserved in whale oil—did not last the winter, there were seals and walruses and polar bears to be had out on the sea ice. A hundred people wintered at Kittigazuit itself, in three or four houses continuously built and rebuilt from about the year 1400 onward, always on the same sites, each with its traditional name. Archaeologists have found evidence there of people, fishing and whaling, as early as the tenth century, then, for whatever reason, a four-century gap. In the early centuries there was whaling also at several places up the East Channel, until the constant silting of the river pushed the belugas farther out into the bay, but Kittigazuit must always have been the chief and the best.

Although the Mackenzie Eskimos formed a distinct group whose life centered on the white whales, they had links with other Eskimos scattered along the Arctic coast from Alaska to Greenland. The language itself varies little, even in its idioms, throughout the area. The first Eskimos had crossed the fifty miles of the Bering strait from Asia around the beginning of the Christian era.* Over the immense distances of the Arctic Ocean, the movement by sea was continuous. There was also trade, overland through Alaska and across the Barren Lands to the east; stories of Cook's ships, exploring the Alaskan coast, were carried back through the mountains to the delta Eskimos; when the Russians built their first trading post on Kodiak Island in southwest Alaska—in 1784, midway between Cook's voyage and Mackenzie's—European goods and iron above all began to find their way up the Alaskan rivers, through the mountain passes and down rivers like the Arctic Red to the delta. Already, when Mackenzie came, the presence of the Russians was known in the area. To his Indian guide, the sea ahead was *Benahulle Toe*, "the white man's lake." The Eskimos, knowing themselves to be Inuit—the people, the human race—invented a name for the strangers, *kabluna*, and a myth to explain their origins: bred from the primordial mating of a human and a dog.

As it had been for all the peoples of North America, trade with the Europeans was the beginning of the destruction of the Eskimos. By the 1840s, whalers were making the im-

* This is the generally accepted view of where the Eskimos came from, and when, but the question is more complicated than it may seem. Over the past century, scholars have developed widely differing theories as to whether or not the Eskimos in fact represent a physical type distinct from the northern Indians; where their traditional culture and its variants originated and how it was diffused across Arctic North America; and when the earliest archaeological findings that can be classified as Eskimo are to be dated. Comparatively recently, sites have been found along the coast of the Bering Strait that can be called proto-Eskimo and seem to be at least five thousand years old. A clear and interesting account of the whole subject is *Ancient Men of the Arctic* by J. Louis Giddings, an archaeologist who was himself responsible for many important finds along the western coast of Alaska (Knopf, 1973).

mense voyage north through the Pacific and into the Arctic
as far as the delta, landing at the summer camps to buy
meat from the Eskimos; about the same time, fur traders
were following Mackenzie's route down the great river to
the summer gathering places of Indians and Eskimos that in
time became Fort Good Hope, Arctic Red River. The Europeans brought not only their tools and weapons, their cloth
and manufactured food, but their diseases—scarlet fever,
smallpox, influenza, measles—which spread among the Eskimos in successive waves; and the people died. In 1850,
there were still at least 2,500 of the Eskimos living in the
delta (some explorers guessed as many as 4,000); by 1910,
there were no more than 150. The last great caribou migration into the area came in 1924. They too were gone, but in
the bay off Kittigazuit the white whales still came, leaping
like fish in the summer sun.

In the five centuries of their life there, the Eskimos buried
their hunters on the rim of the high ground overlooking the
bay, and the narrow beach of Kittigazuit in summer was
crowded with the log-and-earth lodges of the permanent
residents and the caribou-hide tents of the visitors from all
over the delta. The graves were built above-ground of
squared drift logs, filled and covered with turf. The bodies
were placed in them sometimes lying flat as if in sleep,
sometimes in the kneeling crouch of the lookout watching
across the sea for the coming of the whales; differences, perhaps, of character in life or of the authority conferred by
talent in the hunt. On top were placed the men's sledges,
their kayak frames, and the delicate double paddles with
their quick-stroke four-inch blades. Toward the end, when
the people were few and the deaths many, the hunters were
buried several in one grave. The graves remain, the sled
runners and paddles and kayak frames, finely carved and
smoothed with tools of stone or bone, still fresh as if new-
made, unweathered by the dry-freeze climate of the Arctic.
The people have gone.

In time, those Eskimos who survived acquired the white men's immunities as well as their diseases. Today there are about 12,000 in the Northwest Territories, two thirds of Canada's Eskimo population, and of these probably a majority live in or near the Mackenzie delta. They have become town dwellers, a few going out in the winter for the fur trapping, most working at full-time, wage-paying jobs, living in the subsidized apartments and houses, sending their children to the schools—receiving, like the Indians, the mixed benefits of the government's attentions. The differences between the Indians and Eskimos of this region are not obviously physical. From what I had read, I had expected the men to have the heavy, fat-layered bodies of sumo wrestlers, but those I met were slender and tautly muscular, fairer, perhaps, than the most northern Indians, the women strong, compact, smooth-skinned, often strikingly beautiful in a way that might almost be Polynesian.

The important difference is interior, apparent even on brief acquaintance. I never heard an Eskimo refer to himself, diffidently, like the Indians, as "a native." He was *an Eskimo:* too polite for condescension but with no doubts as to the final worth of his race, sharp bargainer in questions of Eskimo rights, adaptable to the world as it has become but tenacious of essentials—the language, the places, the skills and oral traditions of the Inuit. For the people of the delta, many of these essentials center on the summer hunt for the white whales; as they have for as long as there have been people here.

In July and August, the men of Aklavik and Inuvik take weeks off from their jobs, load their families and their gear into boats, and head downriver to the coast. The main camp has moved from the eroding sandspit of Kittigazuit to the northeast end of the island, a place designated on the government maps as Whitefish Station—not a settlement but a camp on a narrow beach like the one at Kittigazuit, named for the belugas that in the Eskimos' English vernacular are "whitefish." The method of hunting has likewise changed. The whales are chased in twenty-foot boats or square-end freighter canoes, powered by sixty-horse kickers; shot with rifles, then harpooned to keep them from sinking, and hauled back to the beach, lashed to the side of the boat or dismembered on one of the offshore islands and brought back in sections for the women to finish. The black meat is dried in the sun, then smoked; the *muktuk* goes into ten-gallon drums, like chunks of fatback, is cooked and covered with oil to keep. One whale yields a hundred pounds of *muktuk*, two or three drumfuls; two will supply a family through the winter. When one man has enough, he stays on, helping the rest. Not much use is made now of the bones. The island beaches are layered with whale skeletons, laid down like driftwood, slowly petrifying as the seawater washes through. Occasionally a whaler, windbound for days on one of the islands, will collect the curving three-inch whale teeth, polish and drill them, perhaps engrave them, and create a necklace to sell to the *kabluna* women in Inuvik; or, seeing in a massive half-fossilized pelvic bone an enigmatic feminine form, chip away just enough to release the face—sculpture.

For a wage-earning man, the whaling has an obvious practical value: Through the long winter The Bay will not get much of his money for meat. But for the Inuit the necessity of whaling goes deeper than saving a few hundred dollars in groceries.

In 1935, after years of bureaucratic backing and filling, the Canadian government introduced the first breeding pairs of reindeer from the Scandinavian North into the high open tundra east of the Mackenzie delta. They were to be the nucleus of large herds. The intention was to convert the Mackenzie Eskimos from whaling and trapping to reindeer herding, providing them with a new local source of meat and cash. The idea was less whimsical than it may sound. Since early in the century, white ranchers in Alaska have raised reindeer commercially by the hundreds of thousands. The imported animals would take the place of the no longer plentiful caribou. The two animals are closely related, so much so that they can interbreed (an unanticipated problem, as it turned out—the reindeer mares tended to wander off with whatever caribou bucks turned up, and the herds steadily dwindled). The reindeer present certain advantages. They are smaller than caribou, more easily managed, and can, to a degree, be domesticated. Their natural pattern of migration is comparatively limited, more human in scale. In the vast reaches of the Canadian North, the caribou herds winter below the tree line, then in the spring just before the ice breaks travel a thousand miles or more north to the Arctic. The area set aside for the reindeer reserve was a rectangle roughly 160 by 125 miles, bounded by the Arctic coast and the East Channel of the Mackenzie; and apparently it was enough.

As the headquarters for this experiment, on the East Channel at the edge of the Caribou Hills, the government constructed a settlement for the herders that was named Reindeer Station; there was a slaughterhouse, and another, thirty miles south near what is now Inuvik. From the beginning, the project was to be modern, managerial, semi-industrial. From their base at Reindeer Station the workers would from time to time inspect the herds from snowmobiles or planes; at appropriate seasons, like cowboys, they would bring the animals in for butchering. Scandinavian reindeer experts flew over the reserve and predicted that in time it would support a hundred thousand reindeer. A succession of Swedish managers came—and went. The herd was never in fact as large as ten thousand. In that summer of our passage down the delta, one of the odd bits of local news was that the government was selling the reindeer grazing rights to a private firm, along with any animals that could actually be caught. The experiment was at an end.

One reason for this failure was that the planners had

never asked the Eskimos whether they *wanted* to herd rein-deer. A few years ago, one of the innumerable government surveys inquired into students' vocational preferences. What did the children of the Northwest Territories want to do when they grew up? After nearly forty years of the reindeer experiment, reindeer herding was at the *bottom* of the list; nothing the children had seen or heard of the reindeer could persuade them that herding them for a living was anything but contemptible. (At the top were jobs like those of airline pilot or stewardess and an adult life in such glamorous cities of the South as Edmonton, Winnipeg, or Saskatoon.)

Earlier in that summer a United States senator had flown into the North to persuade the Eskimos to stop hunting whales. The senator had taken it into his head to be con-cerned about the future of the whale population. Why he should have supposed that the Eskimo whalers, rather than the Soviet or Japanese factory-ship operators, deserved his attentions and those of the constituents whose taxes paid for the air fare and photographers is not easy to imagine, but the Eskimos are, at least, good listeners. They suffered his insolence politely, but the senator might as easily have per-suaded them to swim to the North Pole; or to stop being Es-kimos. It is possible, however, that the senator learned something from his visit—supposing, of course, that a United States senator can learn *anything*. The Eskimos are not unaware of notions of conservation; unlike the Indians in the first intoxication of having guns, they have not, on the whole, slaughtered for the fun of it but have taken only such numbers of animals as balance with their actual needs. They know also that, as the townspeople they have become, those needs are different from what they were a century ago, and less; that there are other sources of meat and fat and that the cost is not the main factor. But the *muktuk* from what-ever source—and elsewhere in the Arctic the people get it not from belugas but from big, deep-water whales, from walruses or seals—is what sets them apart from other peo-

ples; the one item in the Eskimo diet that most whites cannot stomach, but to the Eskimos, delectable. And it is not
simply this end product that is essential, but the hunt itself:
the camps on the summer beaches where the people have
gathered for a thousand years, working together, helping
one another; the pursuit across the wild and often fog-
damped Arctic seas; the capture; the lounging afterward beside the tents, talking, telling stories, joking, while the
women finish the work. It is the same kind of question as
with the Indians: Take from the Eskimo these things, and in
what sense does he remain an Eskimo? It is not a question
that Canadian officials or United States senators are likely to
ask, let alone try to answer.

In the few hours remaining on that first afternoon, we
traveled barely ten miles down the East Channel. After the
hot days in Inuvik, the morning was foggy and raw, but the
weather had cleared by the time we started. Jim and Steve
paddled, *voyageur* fashion, from the heavy thwarts in the
bow of the freighter. Our combined gear, the gasoline
drums and gas tank, the motor, filled the canoe to the gunwales, but it rode high and was, I thought, surprisingly easy-
paddling and maneuverable. Everything, at that start of the
final phase of the trip, seemed marvelous, the camp that
night the best so far, the dinner—a potful of fresh chicken
from The Bay at Inuvik—a feast. We set the tent at the top
of the bank, on a pillowy carpet of moss, sheltered among
the spindly spruce, with serene vistas of the narrow channel
stretching in both directions. Near the water, pale lilac-
colored aster daisies, Arctic natives, bloomed in abundance,
with other spring flowers we had seen along Great Slave
Lake six weeks back; among the trees, stunted blueberry
bushes were thick on the ground, covered with small berries
still green. It was spring here, no country for annual plants;
in the month remaining before the coming of fall, these per-
ennials would have barely time to flower, fruit, and seed.

The light was still strong an hour past midnight when I came out of the tent for a final look: Across the channel, a few scattered spruce rose from a complex tracery of willow shrub, etched against the lavender sky like a pen-and-ink signature of the North.

We reached Reindeer Station the next day in time for a late lunch. Although the formal closing of the experiment was only a week past, the settlement had the look of being long abandoned, with the melancholy of any human place from which the human presence has departed: tall grass covering the boardwalks connecting the scattered houses and workshops; doors sagging open, windows broken out; bare, trampled earth where the reindeer had been penned, but the fences were salvaged and gone. The station had been built piecemeal, blending the styles of the Canadian and the Scandinavian North: a snug white manager's house near the landing; a heavy log food storehouse that had been painted red, where squirrels ran in and out hunting traces of spilled flour; a Quonset-like hut built of plywood, once a school, with children's textbooks scattered across the floor. Back from the water on rising ground stood a big square log building that had been a meetinghouse or church; in front of it, down a trapdoor, a storehouse for meat, carved from the permafrost, the walls glistening with ice and frozen blood, chill as a deep-freeze room. Behind the settlement the Caribou Hills rose five hundred feet, thickly grown down below, almost bare at the top, a few trees, facing the delta, thrusting singly against the sky. Up a dry narrow valley between two hills, the spaced poles of an electric line marched to an outpost of the station in the high, treeless grazing lands. It would have been the natural route for men and animals: Down that valley you could almost see and hear the vanished herds, driving to the slaughter.

Steve, we discovered, was a collector. While we explored the settlement and, finally, waited around for him to finish, he hunted souvenirs: an oversize pipe wrench, glass electric insulators that could be pried loose from the side of a building, a meat hook embedded in the ice of the permafrost storeroom. It is not a mentality I am able to imagine; forbearance, I reminded myself, and said nothing. The pickings were slim; others had preceded.

There are two big oil camps along the East Channel, new, like those farther south, within the year but fully occupied and working now twenty-four hours a day, base camps for the offshore drilling stations: barges and boats moored along the banks, a constant movement of trucks, airplanes, and helicopters coming and going from the landing fields. (One of these, on the point the Eskimos call Tununuk, was doubly linked with Arctic history: In the midfifties, it had been cleared as a DEW Line base, a system still not entirely abandoned, though private contractors have taken the place of the U. S. Air Force; much earlier, it had been an Eskimo winter camp and burial place.) Across from the second of the oil camps the government that summer was making a modest experiment in commercial fishing: three or four Indian families from Aklavik, the men to man the nets, the women to cut up the fish; a white manager contracted in from Hay River for the summer; a portable freezer-room, generator, and workroom, brought down by barge. The place, Holmes Creek on the map, is said to have been the dividing point between Indian and Eskimo "in the time of the grandfathers," an elastic time that might be decades or centuries past; Sinigiyuak, the Eskimos once called it, a "sleeping place"—a seasonal camp for caribou hunting rather than a winter settlement.

As we approached, a seaplane was tied up at the bank, loading cartons of frozen whitefish fillets to fly to Inuvik, and we paddled over to talk. The plane loaded, the bearded pilot topped off his gas tanks, taxied cautiously around the nets across the creek mouth, and took off. The manager, John Mapes, offered coffee in his tent: long-boned North of England face, his father an immigrant, himself a fisherman all his life, an outfitter and wholesaler for other fishermen until the government Fish Marketing Board monopolized the business. His tent with its plywood floor and walls was set up next to the gasoline generator that powered the freezer, and while we sipped the coffee we talked across its pounding: *What?* he said often; *What?* Steve talked on, after something, and succeeded. When we at length pushed off, we were congratulating him on the plastic bag of frozen whitefish fillets he had persuaded John to give him, stowed in one of the packs to thaw.

Other channels had joined, the East Channel was no longer a narrow stream but had widened out to a river, a mile across in places, the banks guarded by wide, reedy shallows. The last of the Caribou Hills was behind us now, we had passed the tree line: The delta spread open and flat around us in all directions. Here and there along the horizon low hummocks stuck out against the sky, shown on the maps as landmarks: pingoes, cone-shaped, heath-covered protuberances of ice, a hundred or two hundred feet high, thrust up from the earth like frozen volcanoes.

We were traveling slowly. Steve had talked lengthily about his lifetime of canoeing and camping, but all his gear was new, bought for the trip; our stuff, some of it forty-year-old canvas packs passed down from my father's canoeing days, looked by comparison as if it had been picked up in the discard room of a thrift shop. With the differences in equipment went differences in style that were becoming time-consuming. If I mixed pancake batter for breakfast, he preferred eggs and fried several while we waited and he delivered a homily on diet; if I cooked raisins in the oatmeal, he topped his off with a double handful instead of sugar, again accompanied by edification; our coffee was unsatisfactory—Steve preferred to boil his up in a bucket with a cup or two of dried milk until the scum had blackened the inside and took twenty minutes to scour. His cooking, when he took a turn at dinner, was the kind that used up half a pound or a pound of butter. It began to look as if our food would not last to Tuktoyaktuk. There were other improvements he wanted to make. He worked at converting us to his noon-to-midnight schedule, running against the strong winds of afternoon; by six or seven I was tired, ready to stop and eat; any more and I lost the evening, worn out all the next day. When I made the fire at night or at noon to break the chill—I make a fire as my father taught me at the age of five, with one match—I had Steve looking over my shoulder telling me how to do it. Finally, late one day, he undertook to teach me how to paddle. I was heading for a point a mile off that looked like a possible camp site. Where was I headed? he wanted to know. I pointed. We would not, he allowed, come within half a mile, the way I was steering. I stuck out the paddle but refrained from hitting him with it: the point! That was where we were going. He could paddle *against* me if he liked, and the current against me, but if I said that was where I was steering the canoe, that, by Jesus, was where we would go. We went.

When we drifted in the canoe, resting, studying the maps, taking pictures, Steve stretched out the time with stories of the women he had known. I wondered why. He had the kind of glib plausibility that excites disbelief; it was only a few years back, past fifty, that he had married, for the first time. Considering the possibilities, I was thankful for having no daughters. The man, I thought, would bear watching.

At other times there were stories of what Steve called his "ungovernable rages," a phrase with a rolling resonance: elaborate revenges for minuscule slights. Again I wondered. The forgivable vanity of an aging man, with the formerly muscular belly beginning to sag? Some kind of threat? It occurred to me that he had looked at a map, concluded that his offer to drive us to Fort McMurray was excessive, and was working at the diplomacy of evasion.

The mouth of the river was complicated by many islands. After the warnings against the open water, we tried to hold to the mainland, to the east, where there would be shelter, but in the low water the channels were too shallow for a canoe, and this one, with its patched and leaky bottom, we treated tenderly. We worked our way around to the west, following the ship buoys, where the channel was kept open by dredging. At length we were through: one low island ahead, then nothing. The sea! The days from Inuvik had been overcast and cool, but now the temperature was up to seventy and felt hot. The sun flashed on the water, dead calm, dappled by a light breeze from the north.

Steve was stripping off his clothes. He wanted to be able to tell his friends at home that he had swum in the Arctic Ocean. A bay of the Beaufort Sea, continuous with the ocean; it would do. He was over the side, paddling beside the canoe. Jim and I lay back, waiting. The canoe drifted with the waves. Steve climbed back in, dug out a towel, and dressed. We paddled on a little farther, but Steve had another thought. He dropped his pants and squatted over a gunwale of the canoe. He had crapped, he explained, in four of the world's oceans; now he was adding the Arctic to his collection. He wet his fingers in the cold, fresh water and wiped his behind.

It was late in the day on July 12 that Mackenzie reached the end of his voyage. All day the canoes had followed the current through the meandering channels of the delta, "the country so naked that scarce a shrub was to be seen"; often, the shallows slowed or stopped them. Now they came to what he thought the entrance of a large lake. *Lake:* It was the word the guide had used, having none for "ocean"; and what lay ahead was not to the eye different from other huge lakes they had crossed, Great Slave in particular. Five or six miles off the channel mouth, the ice began, spreading across the water "as far as the eye could reach." The current carried them to the end of an island that rose to a high point, "the boundary of our voyage in this direction." They landed. Mackenzie and Ageena climbed for a look at what lay beyond: "no land ahead . . . solid ice . . . to the southwestward . . . dimly, a chain of mountains . . . to the eastward, many islands." On the height was the grave of a hunter, with his bow, paddle, and spear beside it.

Mackenzie and the Indian came down the hill again. The men, thinking they had come only to another lake, were disappointed. They were ready, they declared, to follow their chief "wherever I should be pleased to lead them."

Events corrected the impression. The men had set the nets, as usual, upon landing, but now the wind blew up so strong they could not be reached. In the night, wind and the low tide of the delta coast drove the water up under the packs, and the men woke to carry them to higher ground. The weather held them for another day. Mackenzie sat up most of the night, watching, and slept late in the morning. The men woke him: Something strange out there in the water, chunks of floating ice or—whales, Mackenzie realized, white whales! In the excitement of discovery and with no thought, till later, that it was "a very wild and unreflecting enterprise," they got the canoes in the water and set off in pursuit. They were several miles out, the whales all around them, when the wind came on hard from the north. They turned and began to work their way back to land, tacking across the waves. A heavy fog followed, closing them in. In the heavy swell, it was all two men could do, bailing constantly, to keep the big canoe from swamping. They landed, intensely thankful at having "failed in our attempt to overtake" the white whales, "as a stroke from the tail of one of these enormous fish would have dashed the canoe to pieces."

They knew now that it was not a lake they had come to but the shore of the Arctic Ocean; the end of land and absolute limit of their voyage. In commemoration, Mackenzie ordered the men to set up a log of driftwood on the beach beside the tents. On this smooth surface, stripped of its bark by the water, he carved his name, the number of people in his party, the date, and the latitude, which he reckoned as 69°14′ north, probably half a degree short. The place he named Whale Island. Later in that day, as they paddled the length of it, heading east, he guessed it about twenty miles long but very narrow. There is no island in the area now to match that description; it has vanished, along with the wooden post that marked it. The delta has changed.

By now we were well out in the bay. I pointed the canoe east and we started along Kittigazuit island, keeping a mile or two off; Steve grumbled at the course, but in the light, warm breeze we could take that risk to avoid the shallows near the shore. In the far distance north and east a pure white bank of cloud lay along the horizon, glowing in the sun: the beginning of the ice pack, by now, in August, well out from shore; or perhaps only the mass of white fog that hangs over the ice, like a mirage miles off in the desert. We should by the end of the day reach Whitefish Station at the far end of the island. A whaler we had talked to before leaving Inuvik had promised to meet us there, let us come out with him on a hunt, but on the way we had seen him coming up the river again, half a dozen drums of *muktuk* in the back of the boat, all he needed for the winter; most of the people now were getting ready to go home, but one or two families still had not enough.

On the high bank on the seaward side of the island there were low, angular shapes that I realized later were the ancient graves of the Kittegaryumiut, the "people of Kittigazuit." Halfway along, the soft hump of a low pingo rose from the edge of the cliff.

It was late afternoon when we rounded the end of the island into a natural harbor. The high ground fell off here to a low beach, ending a mile off in a narrow spit of sand and sea grass where the channel came through from behind the island. (We had figured to come that way if the sea looked rough, but the weather, so far, had been kind.) There were tents all along the beach and across the channel on the mainland, small, brightly colored umbrella tents, big square trappers' tents with high walls and stovepipes fitted through the roofs. The wind had begun to blow the water to a rough, quick chop, and the canoe disquietingly rode through the waves, not over them, sloshing cupfuls of water over the gunwales; we were about in time. We headed down the harbor, into the channel where several boats were moored, and around behind the beach to the only tent site still open. We tied up and scattered back down the beach to explore and look.

Several of the big tents were set up with foot-thick drift logs set deep in the sand, the heavy root end upright; as tent poles they looked massively out of proportion and, walking past them in the warm sunlight of that afternoon, I wondered at the effort. Farther along, on a table made of sheets of plywood laid across a heavy log framework, a woman was cutting up a whale that must have come in that afternoon, using the same wide, fan-shaped *ulo* that the Eskimo women have always used, but now made of steel. She was working fast, no time for talk now. Behind her on racks set across the same massive logs, big as a cabin, long strips of black whale meat and the shining white fat hung drying in the sun; in a day or two, if the weather held, it would be ready, and the framework would be walled with rough-shaped planks of driftwood, the smoke fires lighted for the meat, the *muktuk* cooked in gleaming new ten-gallon drums waiting around the work table. There were several whale carcasses along the water's edge, still beautifully white but finished with, the yards of pink guts spewed along the sand.

I looked back to where we had left the canoe. Jim and Steve were back there now, unloading, making camp, and I guiltily started toward them. No loss; there was the long evening ahead of us still, tomorrow, other days. Tuktoyaktuk was only seventeen miles off now if we followed the shore line, less if we could take the straight course farther out; a short and easy day of paddling, half a day with any luck.

With the tent up, the canoe out of the water and turned over, the packs stowed, we were ready for dinner and still early. No hurry now. We walked back along the beach to talk with one of the whalers. The woman was still working at her whale, tirelessly, but almost finished now, the drying rack full. A man stood beside one of the tents. I got out my last pack of cigarettes—more to get at Tuktoyaktuk—and offered one. Names: His was Ned. We squatted down to talk. Would he be going out tomorrow? Maybe—he had about enough, there might be others, still, coming out from Inuvik. But the white whales—in the late afternoon they would come in to the edge of the harbor; playing, he said. He pointed across to a pingo a mile or two off at the top of the bank, big enough to be named on the map, Whitefish Summit; climb it and you could see the whales out at the edge of the harbor. I wanted to get in the canoe, *now*, and go, but I restrained the impulse; we had *arrived*, there was tomorrow, there would be other days.

While we talked, from a transistor radio in the tent behind us I became aware of a familiar voice: Nixon; the President. Seven o'clock, prime time, as always. This might, I said, be important. We went over to listen. It was, I remembered, a Thursday by now, the eighth of August. He was explaining, excusing, denying things of which, in the two months we had been on the way, Jim and I knew nothing—mercifully. I did not make much sense of it but he seemed to be leading up to something, and then through the sound of the waves washing along the beach, the wind blowing in from the Arctic Ocean, the desultory talk around us of the Eskimo whalers and their women, I made out what was coming: He was resigning, effective at noon the next day. The broadcast ended. In the tent someone switched to another station, music; we moved off.

"My God," I said, "that means—that means what's-his-name's President now!" I groped for the name and really could not bring it up, it had been that long: "What *is* his name?" Steve thought for a moment. "Ford. Gerald Ford." Of course! I managed a tiny joke: There really had been a Ford in our future after all. We laughed and started back to our camp to cook dinner.

By the time we had gathered wood for the fire, the fleecy cloud bank we had seen that afternoon on the horizon had blown in as wet, chilling mist, behind it the wind, getting stronger. There was no shelter on the open sandspit: The fire streamed in the wind as in a blast furnace, but the fish—a big lake trout John Mapes had thrown in with the fillets—was cold again before we could eat it. That night I put on extra clothes and curled up in the double sleeping bag, warm. Our breath was a visible mist in the tent. The tent walls snapped and rattled in the wind, but it seemed to be holding.

I woke in gray light around four and listened to the wind tearing at the tent; and dozed again, thankful there was no need yet to get up. A couple of hours later an Eskimo camped near us came to the door of the tent: Better get out, the water was coming up; all the people were leaving. We dressed in haste. All along the beach the people were taking down the heavily braced tents, loading boats, to head for shelter. Tide and wind-driven waves were cutting off the sandspit from the rest of the beach, the water already at the packs stored under the canoe and filling the hollow where we had made the fire last night. Mist and rain blew in the air, driven like bullets. We packed up, loaded the canoe, and started back along the inner channel behind the island, using the motor for the first time. Even here, walled off from the ocean, it was rough; the ancient canoe dived through every wave, water washed back and forth in the bottom. Like this, we could not go far. A mile or two along, standing in the bow, I pointed to a possible camp—Steve, running his motor, could not hear above the whine of wind and wash of waves—and we landed: immense piles of driftwood, several places leveled for tents, a hollow dug out among rocks for cooking; people had camped here that summer, the year before, maybe in progression back through the centuries. The rain blowing in the wind was turning to sleet, freezing; my hands ached. I got a fire started and we heaped it with logs, a bonfire, roaring in the wind; built a smaller fire six feet off for cooking; and settled down to wait it out.

This was open tundra now, rising inland, thickly covered with gray-green heath like an English moor and utterly treeless. Not even the dwarf willow and birch remained; here and there, a few flowering plants, undersized lupines with their deep-purple flowers and star-shaped leaves, white-and-red paintbrush and pink wintergreen, not fully open, sheltered among the heath, struggling to survive the season. The ground was thick with ptarmigan: Walk fifty yards in any direction and a flock burst up, skimming along the brush, and dived into it again, invisible.

Warmed by food and the roaring fire, Steve wanted to hike. We paddled across the channel. Several pairs of reindeer antlers, too small for caribou, had been shed on the beach where we tied the canoe. Steve wanted them and deputized Jim to take charge. I protested. How in the hell would we get the God-damned things into a pack, even if we had room? Jim set them carefully in the bottom of the canoe and I held my peace. We climbed to the top of the island and started across for a look at the weather on the sea: Going on to Tuk or turning back to the river, we would have to face it. The surface swelled in spongy, grassy hummocks, wet between, spreading in places into ponds; the mechanism of the pingoes. On the sea side, the island rose in grassy dunes, then dropped abruptly, cliff-like, two hundred feet. The sea spread infinitely to the north, creased with miniature whitecaps under the metallic sky: hard, from that height, to judge, but rough, more than our boat would take; wait it out.

We hiked on along the rim of the island toward the narrow neck that had been Kittigazuit and came to the first of the log-frame graves looking over the sea, then more and more, everywhere. Far off, on the headland across the channel, there were a few log crosses silhouetted against the sky, but these were older than the coming of the missionaries, ancient, monuments to a vanished people. Treasure hunters had broken in: kayak paddles and wide, smooth-finished sled runners were scattered on the ground, parts of kayak frames; skulls and thigh and arm bones lay exposed where the earth had been turned back and hastily replaced. Steve picked up a skull, his collector's instincts aroused. *Put it back!* Why? He's *dead*, what difference could it make to him? I tried other tacks: an archaeological site—for the record of the race, leave it; or tact—people in this area still who would resent any trifling with their ancestors. Reluctantly he gave in. We walked on.

We were near the end of the island. From the beach below, three small children came running up the slope to the highland, two fiercely protective, barking dogs racing ahead. Kittigazuit: a couple of boats, a smokehouse, two or three tents fenced from the wind with slabs of driftwood; one family was camped there now where once, in summer, there had been hundreds. We followed the children down the slope. Their father came out to meet us: Bill Cockney, slender and bespectacled, a maintenance man working for the town government in Inuvik, out for the summer, fishing mainly, but whales too. Tea? The afternoon was late by now. In the main tent, snug from the wind, his wife was boiling water on a square sheet-metal stove. Two small, beautiful, dark-haired girls produced jars of whale teeth their father had collected for them, which they had cleaned and polished. Steve wanted the teeth. Bill was going to help the children with the bargaining: four dollars each you would pay at Inuvik, he suggested with a smile. But for you, here—how about three-fifty? I drank a cup of tea. It was going to take a while.

In the intervals of offer and counteroffer, I asked Bill about the graves. Old, I thought. Did he know? He shrugged, reflecting, working back: What is age? His father had come here, his grandfather. The graves were older than that—the time of the grandfathers; forever.

That night while the wind raged at the tent, we talked through to a decision. The weather might be easier in the morning, but we were at the end of the season, all of us near the end of the time we had. We might make it to Tuk and be caught there for days. All right! We had done it, we had come to the end of the river, we had reached the sea; it was enough, the limit of what we could do. In the morning we would start back, if we could cross the open bay to the mouth of the channel; if the weather allowed.

Late the next morning we left the tundra, crossed the bay, and re-entered the East Channel. It was still cold. The canoe was leaking steadily now. Since that first day at Inuvik, I had patched and repatched it, but there were always fresh leaks, and I was running out of tape and epoxy; nothing to do but bail, with a big sponge and aching, cracking hands. By midafternoon there were a few trees on the banks again, but the weather was unchanged, still the weather of the coast, cold, and we landed to build a fire and eat. Early in the evening we put in at the Holmes Creek fish camp.

The fishermen had come in with a load of fish—with the storm, they were not getting many in the nets—and the girls were cutting them up. Steve collected the livers, stomachs, and roe, John Mapes produced butter, eggs, bread, sugar, evaporated milk from his stores, and we carried the cooking pack a hundred yards down the beach to make dinner. It was midnight before Steve had finished with his cooking. Jim had pitched the tent between John's tent and the gasoline-engine generator. The generator thumped steadily into the night, pausing for a minute or two at a time as the charge built up, starting in again. I walked back to the patch of sand where we had cooked dinner, collected some sticks, and made a fire. "White man make big fire, stand far away," my father invariably observed; "Indian make little fire, stand close." In the long twilight of the Arctic summer night, I lay down on the sand and curled around the fire; slept. Toward morning it began to rain.

We spent the morning cooking breakfast in the deepening rain and arguing about the weather. Early, it had looked to be easing, and we started slowly packing up to go on; now, with the rain, the storm moved up the channel from the coast and the river was covered with whitecaps. Finally: Take the God-damned canoe and I will *give* you the God-damned motor and go! I'll charter a plane. Steve was frantic: I'm supposed to be on a *vacation!* Why in the hell should I try to get myself drowned? He showed me his hands, cracked and painful at the fingertips as mine had been on the Slave: *Look what you've done to my hands!*

No, I said mildly, we would not take the canoe. We would wait it out, together.

We spent the day dozing, waking at intervals to warm by the electric heater in John's tent. Toward midnight, waiting for a final boatload of fish to come in, we sat in his tent, talking, while two of the girls, friends from Aklavik, made another pot of coffee on the Coleman stove. Mary and Martha: both nineteen, Indian, mostly, with that amber coloring, but —Scots, French, Eskimo—all the races of the delta; and beautiful. Mary, one of seventeen children, had quit school at the age of twelve to earn money; Martha had finished, that spring. John joked with them, paternally: I've fuc- — fixed—the electric fish scaler now. The girls laughed. When he talked of far places—the cities of the South, hotels and restaurants, credit cards, crowds of people—their eyes glowed: magic. In the fall, with money saved from the summer, they would fly to Edmonton for a week; neither had ever been farther than Inuvik. Shyly Mary asked if I would take their pictures. Perhaps I could send them prints? They wrote their names and addresses on a slip of paper. We went out into the twilight. High overhead a pair of sandhill cranes flew across the darkening sky, north toward the setting sun.

In the morning, early, we were able to go on. As the trees thickened around us, the weather changed and softened; we were leaving the harsh climate of the coast. We crouched in the bottom of the canoe, wrapped in rainwear against the spray as the bow sliced into the waves, bailing steadily; from time to time I dug out a map to check the course, all the landmarks different now, reversed. Several river scows passed us with their more powerful motors, whalers going home to Inuvik. The people waved. In the battered freighter with the underpowered kicker, the trappings of poverty, we were no longer distinguishable.

In the evening we reached Reindeer Station and landed while Steve stewed another mess of fish eggs, livers, and stomachs in the last of the butter. As we went on, it struck me that the time of farewells was beginning: God knows when, if ever, I would see this country again. I looked back, trying to fix its images in memory: the log buildings translated from a different Northland, behind them the raw hills rising to the edge of the Barren Lands, etched with solitary pines along the top; down the saddle between the hills straggled a phantom herd of reindeer, bells tinkling in the darkening light.

It was early morning when we reached Inuvik. My watch had stopped at two, I had forgotten to wind it. The rain had begun again, gently, the air almost warm, the last light silvering the river ahead. For hours now we had steered for the glow of lights that would be the town, hidden by the windings of the channel. We arrived at last in full darkness. Arc lights bathed the deserted store yards and warehouses along the bank, there were lights on the streets and in the houses all across the slope rising from the river. Inuvik: The season of the midnight sun was past. It had become a town like any other town.

The wind was as strong as we could bear it with the high sail, so that we arrived at Chepewyan fort by three o'clock in the afternoon. Here, then, we concluded this voyage, which had occupied the considerable space of one hundred and two days.

CHAPTER 11

Anabasis

The Mackenzie is like the road to hell: easy enough to go down—you have but to resign yourself to the current and follow it to the end—but not to be ascended without struggle, if at all. *Anabasis:* a journey upriver but also the name Xenophon gave his story of the Greeks' march into the interior of Asia Minor and out again, the type for all time of men's struggle against a hostile geography, human and physical, and their survival. In its smaller scale, Mackenzie's return up the great river combined most of the elements of that epic—suspicion, dissension, the fear and hostility of the natives, hunger and exhaustion, above all the unremitting resistance of the river itself. *Our* anabasis required no heroic qualities. We had only to find our way through the maze of a transportation system that, even when it works, treats its users with studied indifference.

That night of our return to Inuvik, we tied up at the government dock, and Steve hiked up through the darkness to the town while Jim and I unloaded. Half an hour later

Steve was back, with John Blatz and his cab, for the haul to the hotel. Jim was in bed and asleep by the time we'd carried the packs into the room and shut the door, but I stayed up for another hour—a long, hot, slow shower, smoking, reading, making notes—tired but not wanting to sleep, postponing the end. I was up early and back, without transition, in the world of hotel and plane reservations, timetables and obligations, where the machines were fueled and lubricated by money, and the modest talent for endurance that we had cultivated in the months since June was no longer pertinent. My world, it seemed, familiar, continuous: I did not feel changed; only, at moments, a stranger looked back at me from a random mirror, shaggy-haired, disguised by a mat of grizzled beard, the skin darkened by sun, the eyes too quiet; and the hands, holding a menu, writing a check, making notes, hefting a pack—desensitized through layers of callous, the parchment old man's skin fish-scaled with fine wrinkles.

The three-times-a-week jet to Yellowknife left late the next afternoon; overnight in Yellowknife and the plane to Fort Simpson the next morning—no other way, that was how the schedules worked, at rates not much more than double what they would be for the same distance in the South. Two days to wait: They would be filled with trips to the Laundromat, letter-writing, a hunt through the library at the Research Laboratory for anything about the Kittigazuit Eskimos, a visit to the craft shop.

The *Norweta* was tied up at the government dock, awaiting its next complement of southbound passengers. My note of introduction to the captain was still in my wallet, seven weeks old by now. I hiked down the muddy boardwalks to the river. A youth looked out from the ship's lounge. Grant Mackenzie? No—he described the captain; ask one of the barmaids at the Mackenzie Hotel. I headed back to town. The girl behind the bar suggested the Eskimo Inn. I went from there to the Mad Trapper. It was not till next morning that I found him. Back on the ship, I knocked on the door of the captain's cabin, tried the lounge again, let myself in. The remains of a party—full ashtrays, half-empty glasses, forgotten plates of food. A young man asleep on a couch came instantly awake, smiling and alert, and I introduced myself; strikingly handsome, with a ruddy beard of neat, Elizabethan cut, and, maybe, in the deep-set, penetrating eyes, the look of his famous namesake, the trait that those who knew him remembered most and that is present in the one portrait. We talked for an hour about navigating the river: shifting currents and sandbars, bumping across the Sans Sault ledges in low water, the ice at beginning and end of the short season.

As I was leaving, a woman came purposefully across the mud bank and climbed the gangplank—Birgit, the Swedish girl I had last seen, helpless and appealing, grappling with a paddle in the bow of René's canoe, at his camp on the Liard. She had aged a little, unsmiling and travel-hardened: Against the raw day, a heavy, shapeless sweater hid the nubile breasts; a kerchief covered the golden head. She sized us up and turned to the captain. You work here? she asked in her faintly accented English. He admitted that he did. How would he like to give her a ride up the river—to Fort Simpson, say, or Hay River? He smiled faintly. Well, she could work, of course—wait on tables or . . . The smile became dimmer. I left them to negotiate.

Somewhere in the course of the two days Jim and I composed a telegram home: "Paddled to Beaufort Sea our ultimate north. Stopped by Arctic autumn storm delayed our return." For their sake, not ours; let them feel pride, if there was any, but I did not, it was merely that we had done it and were back. What else? "All went well," they would want to know that. And? Yes, always: "Love."

Wednesday, an hour to plane time, our packs drawn up in the hotel lobby like a squad of infantry, waiting for the airport bus. Steve had started to worry about his motor, and

John Blatz produced a large carton and a ball of twine. The bus arrived. Steve and Jim were still working on the carton, winding it round and round with twine. They emerged, carrying the box between them. The bus was off. At the airport the driver wanted another five dollars before he would unload—taking up all his luggage space with our packs and the God-damned motor. I tried to think of anything else I could buy here for five dollars. There was not much.

The airport waiting room was jammed—a couple of planes going out, coming in, all late. We lined the packs up at the check-in desk and began the complicated business of paying for the fifty-five-cents-a-pound overweight. Jim was still carrying the antlers, now wrapped in plastic bags, that Steve had picked up near Kittigazuit. The check-in clerk was positive: absolutely cannot carry antlers onto the plane. Jim slipped them, without a word, under a bench. The last of the packs, our fiberglass food box, was on the scale when the clerk noticed something odd: Your pack seems to be *bleeding*. Bleeding? And rather an unpleasant smell, too— and I remembered: Steve's fish stomachs, more than we'd succeeded in eating, still stashed in a tin in the box and forgotten. Indians and Eskimos in the line behind us were becoming restive. We opened the box, and Jim ran to the men's room with the rotting meat.

The plane left not much over an hour late. I leaned at a window as it climbed, looping north, then east, south: a disoriented flash of river, the eastern hills pink with fireweed in the twilight, then gone, as the plane plunged into the clouds and pointed toward Yellowknife.

From the point at which he left Great Slave Lake, Mackenzie had traveled the whole distance down the river to the place he named Whale Island in fifteen days; something over a thousand miles. The return against the current took them thirty-eight days, to the end of the third week in August. More than a week of this time, they were able to move the big canoe only by towing it with a long line tied at the bow, a method known as tracking, and for the canoemen, with their massive arms and shoulders and weak legs, a worse torture than portaging. Two men took the line in two-hour shifts, walking along the bank, wading in the shallows; the others stayed in the canoe, guiding it with their paddles. The Indian women were kept busy cutting and stitching moose-hide moccasins, which, in these conditions, lasted about a day.

Food had become an anxiety. They still had most of their original supply of parched corn, frugally saved for emergencies, but the pemmican was running low and had turned green with mold. Heavy eaters among the canoemen were always an annoyance to the traders and were closely watched; their food could only be procured by transporting it across the continent with the trade goods or hunting it along the way, consuming time, powder, and shot; both cut into profits. Now, tracking the canoe from the bank or struggling against the current with their paddles, the consumption of meat was prodigious. In one week, Mackenzie counted "two rein-deer, four swans, forty-five geese, and a considerable quantity of fish"—perhaps half a ton—among the four women and ten men (he never counted himself). Alarming, but forgivable—he was hungry too: "I have always observed, that the north men possessed very hearty appetites, but they were very much exceeded by those with me. . . . I should really have thought it absolute gluttony in my people, if my own appetite had not increased in proportion."

Along the lower river, with the breeding grounds of geese and ducks all around them, the caribou ranging along the banks, they were lucky with the hunting. As they progressed, game became scarce, and even the fishing was unproductive—there were mornings when the men pulled the nets in empty, so that, landing in late morning for the midday meal, they had only dry corn and some blobs of fat

to throw into the cookpot. The Indian hunters pushed farther and farther inland, sometimes separated from the party
for two days at a time, but often came back with nothing.

Along the way, there were storms of a violence unknown
on the Mackenzie today: heavy, drenching rains that kept
up for hours, winds of hurricane force. One night, all the
tents were blown down. On another, the massive, three-inch
ridgepole of Mackenzie's tent snapped in the middle and
the wind lifted the stones off the beach and "hurled them
about in the air like sand." The men threw themselves flat
on the ground, as if under bombardment.

Although for many long days there was no alternative to
the line, it is remarkable that for much of the distance up
the river the men were able to paddle against the current.
They kept to the eddies near the shore. Often the constant
north wind helped, blowing behind them now, and they
were able to run up the square sail at the bow of the canoe;
probably at such times they paddled as well—against the
current, the sail alone was not enough. Later, when the
great river had become an established route of the fur trade
and before the North canoes gave way to paddle-wheel
steamers in the 1880s, towing was the norm for most of the
distance. There is still a place, about seventy-five miles
above the Liard, where the river narrows and the current
speeds up, known as the Head of the Line: where the ropes
were coiled and put away and the men took up their paddles once more; lesser men than Mackenzie's, perhaps, and
more heavily loaded canoes, low in the water with their
packs of tightly compressed furs.

Most of the way up the river, Mackenzie and the English
Chief hiked along the shore, keeping to the high ground
back from the river. They could move faster than the canoes, tracking or paddling, and by walking they lightened
the load for the men. Mackenzie, increasingly convinced
that the journey down the river had been a blunder, that he
had missed the passage through the mountains that would

have taken him to the Pacific, was intent on finding natives who could give him precise information about the other great river rumored to lie somewhere to the west. The Indian had his own motives, not least his dignity as a chief—if the white captain walked along the bank, it was necessary that the chief should do so as well.

They found many camps along the river, but more often than not the people eluded them. Mackenzie and Ageena would see them in the distance, men, women, and children, scattering into the woods; or they would come upon the cook fires in front of the lodges, still warm, the people themselves and their possessions nowhere to be seen, untrackable. There were reasons enough for this wariness. Often in the past, big boats coming up the river had been filled with Eskimos intent on plunder; there were, besides, signs that summer of a Cree war party coming down; and by now the caribou herds would be moving in from the Barren Lands, a sufficient reason for the people to go inland even if they were not afraid. Mackenzie, however, became convinced that he was being shunned: the people were in hiding to keep him from learning more about the great river to the west.

When he did manage to surprise a band of Indians before they could escape, the results were not satisfactory. Ageena made long and eloquent speeches. The people responded with tantalizing hints of a west-flowing river that emptied into Belhoullay Toe, the White Man's Lake—at the mouth, white traders who may have been Russians, great sailing ships, a fort; and, mixed with these, fabulous tales of strange animals and birds, winged giants that killed with a glance. Most of the details that were not invented suggest the Yukon River, though there are other possibilities in southern Alaska—Prince William Sound, for instance, east of Cook's River and likewise explored by him, an established trading ground for Athabascan-speaking Indians and south-coastal Alaskan Eskimos, where the Russians had very lately built a fort. There are sources of several Mackenzie and Yukon tributaries not far apart in the mountains, separated by high passes; these the Mackenzie people climbed to the height of land, in late winter and spring, for the moose hunting, as some still do, and there was a guarded trade by Indians and Eskimos, stimulated by the coming of the first whites with bits of iron to exchange for furs, that must sometimes have led all the way to the Alaska coast. The Indians were evasive. Ah, no, unfortunately they knew none of this from their own knowledge but only from stories told by others; if the stranger would only proceed a little farther up the river, undoubtedly he would find people better able to inform him. Mackenzie made gifts all around from his store of trade goods, offered handsome terms to any man who would agree to guide him through the mountains or simply sketch an accurate map of the route in the sand on the beach. The people were most sincerely regretful: Nothing could please them more than to be of service, but they were, alas, unqualified. . . .

Mackenzie was in a fury. At a Hare Indian camp, he got all his men ashore, set up the tents, and determined to stay the rest of the day and all night till the people answered his questions truthfully. Putting on an angry air, he announced that he was on to their tricks and, unless they told him what he wanted to know, would take one of their men and compel him to lead them through the mountains. At this, "they all, at one and the same moment, became sick, and answered in a very faint tone, that they knew no more . . . and that they should *die* if I took any of them away." They now directed their persuasions to Ageena, the translator and intermediary in this negotiation: Their brother, they *loved* him! Why should he lose his life following the mad white man into dangerous and unknown lands? Stay with us and live and we will care for you, O brave and noble brother! Ageena's wives took up the argument. The chief, Mackenzie savagely concluded, was more than half persuaded.

In the morning, half the band had fled. The rest lay in their huts, too sick to rise—but when Mackenzie let them know that he would not take any of them after all, they got up joyfully to see him off, and in thanksgiving sent him on his way with a lavish gift of fish from their nets.

As the two men followed the canoes from the bank, Mackenzie grumbled at the deceit, and the chief caught his bitterness. Slaves! "His heart was set against" these lying and ignorant natives. These many moons now had he journeyed, hoping for booty, young women to carry home, and the vermin hid themselves.

As Mackenzie's venom grew, so did Ageena's stoic indifference, in proportion. Now, when Mackenzie urged him to pursue a band of fleeing Indians, the chief begged off, pleading fatigue. Let one of the hunters follow the track, if someone must—but it would do no good. They would not find these Indians now. Even the canoemen were losing interest. When they reached Camsell Bend, and the southern end of the mountains along the river, Mackenzie ordered an early camp, determined to climb for a last chance at seeing a way through to the west. Ageena and his hunters would not go. The canoemen, exhausted, could think only of getting some meat into the pot for dinner. Finally, one of Ageena's boys consented, too junior to refuse. They hiked inland for hours. Thick woods at the base of the mountains hid the view, tore at their clothes. The boy, his buckskin leggings and shirt in ribbons, begged to turn back, but Mackenzie pushed on, obsessed. The ground began to rise, the trees thinning out, but as they came out in the clear where they could see, the mountains seemed as distant as they had from the riverbank. Now wet ground blocked the way, they were wading across it up to their knees, but Mackenzie was determined: *He must get to the top.*

A few more steps in the failing light and he was into a deep, sucking hole in the slough and up to his armpits in mud and wet and rotting plants and leaves. The muck clung to him; for a minute it seemed he would not be able to extricate himself. Then he was out, stumbling and crawling, hands and knees, back to the solid ground, scared and furiously humiliated. All right, enough! *They could not do it.* They turned and started back toward the river. It was midnight before they reached the camp.

He had missed the chance now. Defeated, Mackenzie brooded on the frustrations of the weeks since they started back up the river. The real problem, he decided, was not that the natives were reluctant but that Ageena and his Indians were working against him for fear he might discover the way to the other river and winter in the mountains, going to it: mistranslating his questions, concealing the answers; deliberately failing in the hunt for meat so there would be no choice but to push on back to the post at Lake Athabasca. Betrayal! In Mackenzie's mood of disappointment and anger and exhaustion, it all hung together, it made sense. Near the mouth of the Liard, when he caught the chief and his hunters looting an Indian camp while the people made off through the trees—strictly against orders, they were *not* to steal, they were to pay a fair price for anything the natives chose to sell them, without exception—the trader boiled over. "I had come a great way," Mackenzie began, "and at a very considerable expence, without having completed the object of my wishes." Why? He proceeded to an extended accusation of bad faith: The English Chief had garbled his questions to the natives, lied to him, refused to hunt. On top of everything else, he was *jealous* of the canoemen, supposing, evidently, that he had not been treated with sufficient deference.

The Indian was wounded to the heart: *"Ill words!"* He spoke at length, denying everything. The speech rose to a climax: He would go no farther. What need had he of gun and ammunition? He was as able to live off the land as these miserable slaves. With that, overcome by his peroration, Ageena burst into loud and bitter tears. His followers, who had gathered around to listen, joined in: five Indians, howling and weeping, rolling on the ground. A little taken aback, Mackenzie glanced at his watch and sat down to listen and observe. They kept it up for two hours. At length—since, after all, he "could not well do without them"—he interrupted with soothing words and summoned his considerable powers of persuasion. The Indians listened, quieted, and after a time reluctantly agreed to go on. In further demonstration of his sympathy, Mackenzie collected the natives' bows and arrows, nets, and fur robes and distributed them among the Indians, leaving some cloth and tools as payment. Ageena scorned these trifles.

That night, camped at the mouth of the Liard, Mackenzie thought it politic to break his custom of dining alone in his tent and invited the English Chief to join him. The flask of rum passed back and forth; "a dram or two dispelled" the Indian's "heart-burning and discontent." He grew confidential. Was Mackenzie aware of a custom among the chiefs of his people? He had shed tears, a woman's weakness. Now, to wipe out that disgrace, it would be necessary for him to go to war. In the spring; he had sworn it. The trader listened gravely. When they had finished eating, he "took care that" the chief "should carry some liquid consolation to his tent, to prevent the return of his chagrin."

Nearing the lake, they traveled slowly. The Indians spent days climbing into the high land north of the entrance to the river, where the buffalo were abundant now, to bring back meat. The canoemen took the time to patch and gum the canoe, carve new paddles—against the heavy current, paddles kept breaking, there were minerals too in the water that Mackenzie thought must be doing something to the wood. Mackenzie himself had time to take several careful latitudes. The lake when they reached it toward the end of August was already boiling with autumn storms. The first day out on the lake, running before the wind, it took two men to bail the big canoe, and the Indians, following, expected to be drowned; two days the wind pinned them down on shore. Then in the distance they saw another sail: Laurent Leroux, the clerk Mackenzie had left near Yellowknife Bay to establish a new post, out on a month's hunting expedition and working toward the river in the hope of meeting his chief. They went on together to the cabin that had been built. Mackenzie sat up through the night, repacking, writing out instructions for Leroux, who was to stay the winter. In the morning Mackenzie and the English Chief exchanged cool farewells. The Indian would stay behind, trading in the country north of the lake, collecting old debts. He promised to return to Fort Chipewyan in the winter.

Mackenzie began that final leg of his return journey from a nameless point on the east shore of Great Slave's North Arm, about a third of the way in from the lake. The opposite shore protrudes in a bulbous conformation called Whitebeach Point, four miles distant. It is the first place where the North Arm is narrow enough to risk crossing in a canoe, even the big North canoe that had carried Mackenzie to the Arctic and back with no more than an occasional leak through its pliable bark seams. To the north, the arm leads through a series of rivers and lakes to the third great inland sea of the Northland, Great Bear Lake and the country of the Copper Indians, another new territory that the traders were beginning to know. Leroux had built his outpost at a natural junction of the trade. Mackenzie was still nearly 450 miles from Fort Chipewyan, but from here on, the way was more or less familiar. He was almost home.

Twenty-five miles southeast of Leroux's camp, Mackenzie

crossed the mouth of a deep bay he had no time or motive to explore. It was a century and a half before anyone but the Indians and a few trappers seriously noticed the place. In 1934, ten miles up the bay, geologists found gold, and a boom followed: not the wild romance of the Klondike or the Yukon but the sober and profitable productiveness, with an eye to the world's markets, of two twentieth-century Canadian mining companies. The bay had been named for the Copper Indians who lived there, for the yellow metal they dug farther north and hammered into tools: Yellowknife. The name stuck to the settlement that grew up around the mines. The gold fluctuated in price but lasted. The mining camp became a town. In 1967, by proclamation of a government minister who flew in from Ottawa for the purpose, the town became the first capital the Northwest Territories had ever had. (Before that, at infrequent intervals, the government met serially at older settlements along the Mackenzie, sometimes arriving by dog sled over trails half a winter long.) In 1970, legally and officially, it assumed the dignity of a city. Yellowknife: That was where the jet was taking us, a capital to the extent that you cannot readily get from one point to another in the North without going there. Our overnight change of planes allowed us a morning for a quick look.

More than any other town in the Northwest Territories, Yellowknife has the look and feel of a city. Along the main street half a dozen new buildings have the square, spare anonymity of the commercial skyscrapers that have transformed the cities of North America since World War II: hotels; offices of the federal and territorial governments; a gold-and-silver metal-sheathed shopping center, still building that summer, that in this climate is compact and vertical, unlike the spreading suburban fairgrounds, in their seas of asphalt, that now ring most other cities on the continent. The tallest has seven or eight stories but in this landscape seems to press against the sky. Land for private use is controlled to prevent speculation—and therefore scarce and expensive, supporting the only real-estate agents in the Northwest Territories; the surrounding land belongs to "the Crown" (so long, at least, as the Indian treaties stand) and may be leased under various well-intentioned conditions but not owned. The official population on record in Ottawa is sixty-five hundred, about two thousand less than the on-the-spot estimate—another reason for the pressure on the available land. Since the federal money that on the whole supports the city's ambitions is in proportion to population, the exact count is a focus for local sensitivities. A top-heavy elite —the heads of the sundry government offices, the local managers of the airlines and trucking companies and mines— sets an urban style, but its roots are elsewhere. It may support a respectable book store and buy the tickets for the orchestra or acting troupe that flies in occasionally from the South for a one-night stand in the high school auditorium, but its lifelines are the air routes that lead to Edmonton and Toronto, Seattle, San Francisco, or New York. Work supports these links and contract and custom assure them, with periodic leave and air fare to the outside world.

The city is also a small town, where the people, walled in by a million miles of almost empty land, know each other and their doings; and a neighborhood in the thin-spread Mackenzie community. On the dot of noon, the government offices lock their doors and the officials go home for an hour's lunch. The man driving a cab back and forth to the airport sits on the city council. The young Indian standing next to you in a bar expresses interest in the camera slung over your shoulder and turns out to be a Hare from Fort Good Hope who has spent the summer traveling up and down the valley on a government grant, making a movie; his movie camera sensibly locked up in a hotel safe before he set out to cruise the Yellowknife pubs. The engineer collecting a machine brought in by air freight, blond and, for all you can see, white, is an in-law of Lou Norwegian, the chief

at Jean Marie River. In the sandwich shop at the Yellowknife Inn, crowded with long-haired summer wanderers from
the South, a young man introduces himself, Northland fashion, with a capsule history of his life. Five years up here,
now, driving a cab in the winter, guiding at one of the fly-in
fish camps on the lake for a couple of months each summer.
I am interested in the fishing. I want to know how they do
it, where they go, but he has not much to tell: Run the boat,
get the fish off the hooks for the guests, clean 'em, cook 'em.
He thinks about it for a moment: "Kind of a shitty job,
really, you know." I finish my coffee in silence.

The small-town city is also, finally, a transient human
camp surrounded by a wilderness as immanent and indifferent as it was when Laurent Leroux built his first cabin
on the shore of the North Arm; you can get behind doors,
not look at it, but the wild country is always out there,
waiting, and close. The original mid-thirties gold miners'
settlement is still there, on a humpbacked granite peninsula
reaching out into Yellowknife Bay to form a sheltered
cove for seaplane landings, but the new capital city has
been built on a rocky hill that climbs inland from the
bay and faces toward the airport and the highway; a terminus, another of the jumping-off places. These links with the
settled country to the south are tenuous. More often than
not, the planes operate on an elastic schedule that stretches
an hour's delay to several, then half a day, a day, and no one
seems to know why. The road outwinds north to cross the
North Arm, then along the northwest shore of the lake to
the ferry crossing above Fort Providence, but Edmonton,
the real beginning of the outside world, is still another eight
hundred miles down the Mackenzie Highway. In May and
November, when the river is thawing and then freezing
again, the ferry does not run and there is no way of crossing
("dependent on ice conditions" is the official phrase). In
summer, low spots in the two hundred miles of gravel road
between Yellowknife and the ferry dissolve into quagmires

when it rains, and the trucks and cars sink axle-deep or slither sideways into the ditches—and wait till a road-crew tractor turns up to pull them out. Winter is best. The river is frozen thick, the ferry crossing an ice bridge; the cold is, at least, reliable.

The tall new buildings that line the cement pavement and the wide city sidewalks of Yellowknife's main street are a narrow band between the airport and the highway. Within two or three blocks on either side, the streets are gravel again, muddy in season, the sidewalks are gone, and the wind-stunted spruce and aspen and willow of the subarctic forest mingle tolerantly with the human landscape. And everywhere the rock breaks through, rounded in soft forms by a billion years of weather: the same beautiful pink granite that runs north in a line from Lake Athabasca to the east end of Great Slave, not quite as ancient or enduring as the gray-green mass of the Canadian Shield but older than anything human; as old, almost, as earthly life itself.

Our collective mass of baggage, perfectly adapted to a summer's travel in a canoe, was turning into a nearly insupportable burden now that we had returned to civilization. At the Yellowknife airport, with the packs heaped in the middle of the terminal waiting room, I wondered if we could avoid hauling everything into town; the essentials for the night were in one small pack, all we needed. I looked around for a check room, a bank of steel lockers, then tried the young man behind the airline check-in counter. Maybe we could leave the stuff there? or in an unused office somewhere, a broom closet? check it onto the next day's flight right now, tonight? No—as if I'd made an improper suggestion; and that was that.

The packs, with Steve's motor in its carton trailing strands of twine, filled two cabs. We piled them on the sidewalk at the hotel entrance and took turns standing guard. It was an hour's work with a handtruck to get everything up to our second-floor room. Beefy private guards, in police-style uniforms, guns at their belts, circulated importantly in the crowded lobby: There seemed to be a little old-fashioned excitement in one of the bars tonight. Rumors whispered through the crowd: a fight, a knifing, an arrest? drunks turning rough, Indian or white? No one seemed to know.

In the morning we dispersed, Steve to tour a gold mine, Jim to visit the museum, another capital-city amenity, I to climb the granite hill down toward Yellowknife Bay. We regrouped in the lobby after lunch for the sortie to the airport. Again the handtruck, borrowed from the front desk, the piling up of packs. Steve had acquired a set of tie-on labels for his packs and was busily filling them out while we waited for the cabs and once more loaded up.

The terminal building was ominously crowded when we arrived. We humped the packs one at a time through the swing doors. A back-up, as from a clogged drain: No planes seemed to be coming in or going out. As for Fort Simpson, the government had closed the airport. Someone said this week had been picked to rebuild the runway, someone else that it had simply collapsed, a big hole opened up in the middle—the rain, you know, it had rained a little in the past day or two. Cabdrivers watching with interest from the edge of the crowd were refusing two-hundred-dollar offers for the run to Providence or Simpson, a dollar a mile: Somewhere forty miles north of town, the road had broken down, no way of getting through—lose the God-damned car. One of them suggested we might be able to get on the bus, there was one scheduled to start south tomorrow night, at midnight. Of course, with the road . . . I pushed through to the check-in desk: the same harried young man I had talked to last night. They knew where we were staying, we had given the telephone number. Why the bloody hell didn't anyone tell us the God-damned flight was canceled? Now we didn't even have a place to stay. The young man gave me a baffled look. *Notify the passengers?*

On the runway outside the terminal, a four-seater was warming up, waiting for the signal to take off. Steve was talking earnestly with the pilot. Jim and I went out to listen: one seat to spare, flying to Fort Simpson—only the commercial planes were bound by the closing. Steve talked himself on board. He would reclaim his truck, meet us in Hay River; we would get ourselves and the packs across the lake somehow. The hatch slammed shut. The engine revved and the plane moved off down the runway.

I went back to the airline desk. Ah, yes, a flight in the morning to Hay River at ten thirty-five, the young man said. Could he sell us tickets? Well, really, he didn't know how to write the tickets. Besides, it was almost five o'clock, quitting time. I made a speech. Oh, all right, maybe he could get on the phone to someone in town who could tell him how to do it.

We loaded the packs into a cab and went back to the hotel. Luck: a room for another night.

We were in a cab again and headed back to the airport a little before ten the next morning. Charter flight? the driver delicately inquired. No, I said with unwarranted confidence, just the regular plane to Hay River, ten thirty-five. Ah! He refrained from correcting me.

We hauled the packs back into the waiting room. Deserted. A boy and girl were waxing the floor. Would we mind waiting till it was dry? Only twenty minutes, the boy added in an aggrieved tone. Jesus Christ! The young man was still behind the desk. Flight to Hay River? Well, actually, the plane hadn't left Edmonton yet. Estimated time of departure was now four o'clock.

Jim had had enough and decided to sit it out with the baggage. I started back to town. The cabdriver, still waiting outside, commiserated, advised collecting expenses from the airline, and wrote out a handful of cab-fare receipts for the purpose. Sue the bastards! another man suggested. He had been waiting all summer for a vital piece of equipment that the airline had lost; he was now, as a result, paying penalties on an unfulfilled construction contract. A woman offered a ride to town and entertained me on the way with stories of the airline's incompetence. Pacific Western Airlines, PWA, which people transcribe variously as "Please Wait Awhile" or "Pray While Aloft"; but stoically endure as merely one more hazard of life in the North, like the mosquitoes and the long winter night. What could they possibly do about it?

I thought I might at least try, and found my way through to the territorial director of tourism about the time the office was closing for the noon break. By the time we had eaten our respective lunches, my thoughts had moderated from lawsuits to a few modest suggestions for improving the plane service. The official, a well-fed, cheerful, fluent man, had answers for everything, but unlike those of an American PR man, they were all negative. Everything from a set of twenty-five-cent storage lockers at the airport to scheduling the planes to make it possible to get from one place to another without an overnight stop was economically unfeasible. The federal government put up the money and called the tune. What could *he* do about it? I thought it looked like a country at the beginning of a boom—growing population, unlimited resources barely touched; investment would pay off. No, really—economics, the country would never be self-supporting. Even if they had the money, the people doing the jobs were incompetent, though the management wasn't so bad. He gave me the name of an airline vice president with an address in Edmonton. I could write to him if I liked. He would probably answer.

I tried, finally, life in the North. Did he like it? Well, actually—not much interested in hunting or fishing, and what the hell else was there? Really, no place for cultivated people—like ourselves. He had stood it now for twenty-one years, remembering like everyone the anniversary date; but only because he'd managed to spend about half the time elsewhere, working, vacationing—keeping in touch with what was really going on.

I thanked him and went out onto the street to hitch a ride back to the airport. The plane left finally about five o'clock. The jet flight across the lake to Hay River, at seventeen thousand feet, took twenty minutes. In the day-old Edmonton newspapers on board, part of the service, the premier of Alberta was announcing that he (or at any rate the province) had bought the airline. It was not clear why he had done this, but the passengers received the news with gloomy zest; things had been bad enough without nationalizing the God-damned thing.

We loaded the packs into a cab, drove to the mouth of the river, and camped on the beach. Steve had said he would meet us here in the morning. In the night, a storm blew in from the lake. The surf boomed. In the soft sand, the tent stakes tore loose and we went out in the darkness, gathering driftwood to weight them down. Overhead, for the first time since June, there were sharp points of starlight in the black sky, and out over the lake the northern lights pulsed in incandescent sheets of cold fire.

In the morning we drifted along to the main office of the barge line to find out about retrieving the canoe. It was two weeks now to the day since we consigned it at Inuvik; about time. The girl at the switchboard telephoned the freight yard, then handed me the phone. There was a familiar voice at the other end: Steve had beaten us to it. The barge with the canoes was still on the river somewhere, maybe another week. A tug broken down at Norman Wells or Fort Simpson, someone said, a violent storm around the Providence Rapids, but Steve probably had it right: The freight manager at the other end had promised to ship the canoes out the next day and had simply forgotten; and, oh, sure, people said agreeably, with the depressed cheerfulness of the North, that must be it, he was that kind of a guy, sure.

Nothing to hurry for, now. We went back to the beach and moved our camp into a public campground back from the river and sheltered among pines, with an open field of ripe raspberries along one side; the wind still blew in hard from the lake but we were out of it. Steve had parked his truck in one of the tent sites. There was no one else. The rain that had closed the Yellowknife Highway had rutted the road to the campground a foot deep in mustard-colored clay. Later, Steve drove us into town to buy food. He had a suggestion. Since there was time, why not go to Fort McMurray and get the car? *Of course* he'd drive us there when the canoes turned up, if we could still spare the time, but he'd have several stops to make along the way. . . . I had not expected him finally to keep that part of the bargain and had been wondering how he'd disentangle himself. But why not? The trip would take up some of the week; I take badly to waiting. And bringing the car back would spare us a little of Steve's company and save a couple of days besides; by the time we had the canoe, we would just about make it home for Jim's return to college.

There was a bus leaving at dawn the next morning: twenty-four hours by way of Edmonton, a thousand miles; slow torture. It was also possible by plane—with an overnight change, at twice the bus fare.

In the evening, as Jim and I were finishing dinner, Steve stopped by our camp to settle accounts. He had remembered a rather surprising number of odds and ends, $1.00 here, $2.95 there, that he had spent on the trip to the delta. I wrote down the numbers and divided them up while he looked over my shoulder: "Good thing you're a writer and not a mathematician," he said cheerily and redid the arithmetic, getting it wrong. I worked it out again: I owed him $16.77 and got out my checkbook. No, really, he wanted cash. I wrote the check and handed it to him. He said a rather formal good-bye and left. I did not expect to see him again.

I did not sleep much in the night, nervous of missing the bus, and was up in the predawn dark, making a fire to warm up. I slung the pack over one shoulder—sleeping bag, poncho, a little food for the trip, a Bible—and stopped at the tent door: Good-bye, Jim, and God bless you. He did not stir.

The Alberta Government that summer was asphalting the Mackenzie Highway north to the sixtieth parallel, the border of the Northwest Territories, but was still 150 miles short. For 150 miles south from Hay River the highway was sand and gravel—"Finest gravel road in the world!" Steve was saying the night before I left, in an outburst of Canadianism —and for a while the old road of the late forties runs beside it, a narrow track, grass-grown, separated by the deep regulation ditch strewn with the stripped hulks of wrecked and abandoned cars and trucks. Fifty feet farther, on either side, the yellow-green trunks of aspens rise straight as flagpoles, even-spaced as pickets in a fence, each with a banner of leaves waving at the top. The gravel was succeeded by oil and sand, holding down the dust, then intermittent patches of the new asphalt, already breaking up under weather and trucks and heavy equipment; and, finally, solid pavement all the way to Edmonton. The truckers carry heavy chains in their cabs and when they sink in the unpaved stretches of the road take turns at trying to pull each other out.

There are named places along this highway, Indian Cabins and High Level and Grimshaw: gas stations and motels and Chinese diners built around a muddy parking lot like a medieval inn yard. Gradually their style changes from northern to western. The men slopping through the mud wear high-heeled boots and stovepipe jeans; posters tacked to the gas station walls advertise a coming rodeo. As the road angles south into Alberta the forest is broken by patches of cleared land where the sparse wheat grows a foot high—already ripe in that late August, hand-cut and raked into small sheaves, grass-tied.

The bus that morning when I hiked into the bus station in the old town of Hay River was a small, silvery Greyhound that awakened a remote memory of a childhood bus ride somewhere. ("Made in Calgary," the station operator had said, as if that were sufficient explanation, when I asked if he had any problems keeping the buses going, getting spare parts. "Finest buses in the world!") There was a cardboard sign at the front ("Your Operator, Safe—Reliable—Courteous"), with the driver's name slipped into a slot: Scotty Ballantyne. He closed the door and delivered a series of announcements, not asking but telling, the captain now: We were permitted to smoke, in seats provided with ashtrays; there would be a fifteen-minute break at nine, thirty at noon; since the run to Edmonton would be seventeen hours, we were to be tidy. Any questions? There were six of us. An elderly Swiss tourist in a bright green tweed suit, with an air of having traveled everywhere, seated himself confidentially behind the driver, for the view ahead, the answers to questions. I nestled into a seat, parka over my shoulders, the pack beside me—cigarettes, raisins, chocolate, the Bible to read. The time would pass somehow. I sorted through old memories, looking for any bus trip as long as this—once through the Austrian mountains, or earlier, up the Rhone Valley, or farther back still a long haul through eastern Quebec—but none qualified. Watching nervously as the driver hugged the high center of the road—I would be driving this myself in a day or two—I tried gravel roads and drew the same set of places, then a childhood trip through central Kansas to a relative's farm: the yellow dust rising behind the car—and osage hedges along the fields, in summer the swarms of tortoises migrating across the road, from one dry ditch to the next; dirt-poor, but even that road had been crushed stone, they would not have stood for less.

Six o'clock. Dawn at Fort McMurray: An hour back, there was a stop to inspect another bus lying on its side in the ditch, from yesterday's trip North, but the people have been taken somewhere by now and the run goes through on schedule. I hike the last mile into town, feeling good, stretching the stride, grateful for the pack warming my back in the raw chill. I have arrived, I am on the move again, on my own. The puddles along the road are sheathed in ice, the grass white: the first frost; already the garden patches beside the houses are beginning to droop.

Almost three months now: The town has gotten out of focus; not just memory slipping, buildings have been torn down, rebuilt, others are filling up the vacant land along the main road into town. Among the oil men and builders and construction workers I treat myself to an elaborate breakfast. The Chinese waitress, daughter of the house, is overworked and slow but it is still early when I telephone Bob Braund, who comes to get me in his tow truck. Over the summer he has grown a bushy beard—a contest, a centennial coming up, not for this meeting place of rivers, which is older, but for the province. Bob is apologetic: Someone has gotten into his locked storage yard, broken into the car. I brush it aside. It does not matter; I have come this far, I have arrived. For an hour we sit in the kitchen of his small, neat house at the edge of town, drinking coffee and talking about the summer, the trip. After the prolonged dose of Steve's whimsical jingoism, it is a relief to be reminded that most Canadians are not crazy; or not, anyway, in the North. It is enough here to be a man.

Mackenzie left Leroux's camp on the first day of September and in two days was back in the Slave River; in June, the passage had taken two weeks. There was no ice now and

the weather was kind. His notes became telegraphic. Except
for a wounded Cree, separated from the war party, there
was not much to record; the course was known and familiar.
At the portage around the Pelican Rapids, the canoe, nearing the end of its life, broke on the men's shoulders and
there was time lost repairing it. Heavy rain stopped them
for a day, but except for that they traveled as fast up the
river as they had coming down. One day there was snow in
the air, then hail, and in the night a solid freeze. On the final
day, crossing Lake Athabasca, they caught the wind, "as
strong as we could bear it, with the high sail," and were
back at Fort Chipewyan by midafternoon. Life there had
gone on. Getting ready for winter, McLeod, the clerk, and
five of the men were "busily employed in building a new
house." That night, back in his own cabin, Mackenzie
counted up the entries in his journal and wrote a final note:
"102 Days since we had left this place."

In the spring, Mackenzie went out to Grand Portage to
deliver the year's furs, pick up a new supply of trade goods,
and confer with his Montreal partners. They must have read
the journal but were unimpressed. One can hear the Scots
voices: the Hyperborean *Sea?* Ay, but where's the *profit* in
all this grand expense? They were not more critical than
Mackenzie himself. The idea remained: the way through
the mountains to the Pacific; and he had failed. In a letter to
his cousin Roderic he spoke of "the river Disappointment."
The following spring, 1791, driven by the idea, he went all
the way out to Montreal, took ship for London, and spent
the winter there, buying an improved set of instruments for
reckoning latitude and longitude, learning navigation, and
studying accounts of the exploration of the Pacific Coast. I
think also that in those months he had his journal copied,
showed it around, and talked with a London publisher who
proposed bringing it out with an account of the new voyage
of exploration that Mackenzie was now planning; a further
motive.

Mackenzie returned to Fort Chipewyan in 1792, and in the fall built a winter camp to the west on the Peace River. In early May, with two of the Canadians who had traveled with him to the Arctic but no women this time, he went up the Peace to near its source, portaged over the divide to the Fraser, and descended to the Pacific, caching the canoe and hiking the last two hundred miles to the sea with a party of coastal Indians. He had demonstrated that it could be done, the first white man to do so, twelve years ahead of Lewis and Clark at the mouth of the Columbia. The year was 1793.

Again, depression followed. In the silence of the winter back at Fort Chipewyan, prompted by his publisher's advice, he tried to convert his journals into a book and could not do it. There were days when he sat down at his desk to work and found himself, hours later, staring into space, the page empty and no recollection of what had been in his mind. "It is a work, I find, that requires much more time than I was aware of," Mackenzie concluded, in a letter that spring to his cousin Roderic, now stationed at a new post at the west end of Great Slave Lake:

> The greatest part of my time was engaged in vain speculation. I took such a habit of thinking so long on a subject that I sometimes walked backward and forward, musing, for hours, at the end of which I could not tell what it was about. . . .
>
> Did I sit down and write, I was sure that the very things I ought not to have been thinking of would occur to me instead of what I had to do. This one calling me to the garret, another to the cellar, and others to the shop, kept me so busy doing nothing . . . my mind was never at ease, nor could I bend it to my wishes. . . .

The writing would have been difficult enough even if the two voyages, valorous, informative, but not obviously useful, had succeeded, but the feelings here sound as if they had a physiological base. Probably—after the waist-deep wading through icy rivers, the smashed and rebuilt canoes, the miles of portage trails cut through the mountains—Mackenzie was experiencing the beginning of the nephritis, slow, gradual, and incurable, with symptoms of drowsiness and stupor, that eventually killed him. In the spring he went to Montreal as a trading partner, no longer a winterer, and, as his life unfolded, never returned to the Athabasca country.

There were rivalries within the company, divisions, recombinations, new partnerships. Mackenzie himself was becoming famous. The great river of the North that he had discovered had become Mackenzie's river, as the bay was Hudson's, the Alaskan inlet Cook's; Mackenzie used the name himself, diffidently. He resigned from the North-West Company and went back to London for business that included publication. An editor worked with him, asking questions, clarifying, revising the rough notes of the two journals into workmanlike and sometimes graceful prose, eliciting the knowledge of the fur trade that became an extended historical introduction to the book. It came out in 1801 with the selling title page of the time:

The book did well in that expansive and romantic age hungry for knowledge of far places; it was reprinted, translated into several languages (Napoleon bought a French copy). Mackenzie became friendly with a son of George III sent out to Montreal—dukes no less than *voyageurs* responded to the genial spirit, the compelling energy—and was knighted the year after his book was published. He was in and out of the North-West Company, invested in the rival Hudson's Bay Company, promoted a consolidation of the trade. Through all of this, the fur profits accrued; the two voyages had not realized all the glories of his imagination, but they had made his fortune. Mackenzie went home to the North of Scotland, married the well-born daughter of an impoverished Scottish laird, another Mackenzie, and bought the family seat, Avoch, on Moray Firth. Eight years later, in 1820, he was dead. He was fifty-six.

VOYAGES

FROM

MONTREAL,

ON THE RIVER ST. LAURENCE,

THROUGH THE

CONTINENT OF NORTH AMERICA,

TO THE

FROZEN AND PACIFIC OCEANS;

In the Years 1789 *and* 1793.

WITH A PRELIMINARY ACCOUNT

OF THE RISE, PROGRESS, AND PRESENT STATE OF

THE FUR TRADE

OF THAT COUNTRY.

ILLUSTRATED WITH MAPS.

_____

BY ALEXANDER MACKENZIE, ESQ.

_____

LONDON:

PRINTED FOR T. CADELL, JUN. AND W. DAVIES, STRAND; COBBETT AND MORGAN,
PALL-MALL; AND W. CREECH, AT EDINBURGH.

BY R. NOBLE, OLD-BAILEY.

·M.DCCC.I.·

Even before Mackenzie left the North for good, the trading posts were pushing out from Great Slave Lake and down his river. In 1851, another trader, Robert Campbell, found both the connections with the Yukon River that had eluded Mackenzie: up the Liard and through a pass, then down the Pelly to the Yukon and north to the Porcupine, which led up through the mountains to another pass and, finally, the head of the Mackenzie delta. The Northwest Passage, dreamed of since the sixteenth century, had at last been achieved, though like most goals too long desired it proved less valuable in possession than in anticipation. Campbell's two routes were used for perhaps twenty years, but the human difficulties—paddling and tracking and carrying the big canoes from the sea level of the Mackenzie further hundreds of miles upriver and through high mountain passes—were more extreme than on any other part of the continent's trade routes. The whole of the Yukon was now within fingertip grasp of Montreal, but distance and the iron limits of the season made it impossible to seize it tightly. And by now Russian posts were well established on the Alaskan coast— overland across Siberia or by sea around Africa and Asia —and American traders had followed Lewis and Clark to the mouth of the Columbia. The railroad brought the Pacific within reach of the American seaboard and made San Francisco the natural base for the fur trade in the west and north. In the moment of their fulfillment, the transcontinental canoe routes were becoming obsolete.

The storm that drove us off the beach at Hay River kept up, a source of some anxiety: The river mouth was for a time too rough for the barges to get in or out. It was exactly a week after we flew across from Yellowknife that the canoes at last turned up. Steve, grumbling about important business affairs that were suffering from the delay, had after all stayed around. Early on a Friday morning we met for the last time at the freight yard to collect the canoes and pay up. (The bearded young clerk in charge turned up late, re-

fused a check, and then wanted exact change; a final twist.)
With the canoes loaded, Steve and I said a cool farewell,
shook hands, but did not exchange addresses. Jim recorded
the moment in a photograph.

Nothing remained now but the long drive home: thirty-
eight hundred miles. With luck, we could do it in a week; it
was all the time we had. In camps along the river we had
talked about the trip home: a leisurely swing west into the
Rockies, then across Canada and down through New England, taking our time, visiting friends, doing a few odds and
ends of business. Now we could only push, up at dawn for a
cold breakfast that took no time to cook, driving into the
twilight to build a fire, make dinner, and camp in the dark.
We would make it home just about in time for Jim to get
back to college. I had obligations of my own: work—a book
to finish, already past due, two more to start, half the royal-
ties by now spent paying for the trip. It was not going to be
an easy fall.

As we travel east, Steve's compatriots become more con-
sciously Canadian, with frequent little pinpricks of difference
—we are merely Americans; strangers, marks. Finally, at a
Toronto gas station while we wait around with the car up on
the rack for grease and oil, an apple-cheeked mechanic
points out a screw embedded in one of the tires, triumphantly plucks it out with pliers, and the tire deflates. That's
an *American* screw, he tells me, there are none like that up
here—as if one of the good Canadian screws would not have
made a hole in my American tire. I consider. Friend, I tell
him, you are bloody well seeing one now. We have been in
your country since the beginning of June. If there is a screw
in the God-damned tire, it is a God-damned Canadian
screw.

In a park beside the Niagara River, a couple of miles
above the falls, we spread out a hasty meal on a picnic table.
It is getting dark. Below, where the falls go over the drop

and the spray leaps at the sky in clouds, pink in the sunset, throngs of people stroll the walks under the perpetual mist or lean on the guardrails, looking, but the park is deserted. The rapids draw me, the tactics of surviving them in a canoe: The river is no wider than the Slave at Fort Smith, but rougher, with sharp ledges near the shore, a wrecked barge lodged farther down, on rocks in midstream. It would be possible, I think, if you were strong and lucky enough: Take it just outside the ledge, then cut in to shore and paddle like hell for an eddying bay where an ornamental stream comes in, an outlet now for a power plant. An exacting course, which you could not afford to miss: *We are not dead but live*. Canoemen did it for a while, I remember, impelled by furs—that would have been the landing, going downstream, and then the steep, terrible carry (later, there were wagon teams, a rope lift). The portage up was longer, coming out above where we are sitting, beyond the rapids. The canoes could get down them but not up.

We were in the driveway and coasting down to the house late on a Friday afternoon, in the steaming drizzle of a Philadelphia summer at the end of August. It was only ninety-six days since we drove off from here and started west, the one respect in which we'd improved on Mackenzie. Home: much touching, awkward hugs for the three sons who had stayed at home, kisses for my wife, but not many words; there was more than could be said, connectedly; it could only come out, their months and ours, in quick memories starting the flow of words, through the fall and winter and spring ahead.

Weeks back in one of her letters, my wife had asked what we'd like for our homecoming dinner, but the question was a conundrum. I didn't, I answered, much care what she gave us as long as it was *a lot*. Dinner that night was that kind of meal. She had remembered.

Jim and his next younger brother still had a day in which

to clean up and pack for college; our timing could not have been closer. Over the next weeks, while I cleaned and patched the clothes and packs and tent to store for the winter and scrubbed the last traces of the Mackenzie mud off the canoe, I discovered that it was almost impossible to talk to anyone of what we had seen and done in our months in the North. As every returned traveler from a distant place has learned, people ask only such questions as they can best answer themselves, from whatever they already know. But even the simplest question is answerable only with the entire experience: It is a connected whole, a web in which you cannot take one strand between your fingers without drawing out the whole; as such, not good for conversations. That is one of the reasons why books are written: for memory, certainly, for the sake of places known and become parts of your life, and for their people, above all, living and dead; for all, the whole. You can have no rest until it is done.

I think back, trying to ask and thereby answer my own questions. Jim and I, my son: not even a symbolic death between us, and whatever changes those months together have made are subtle. He will answer for himself one day. In myself I find a taut quietness, deep silence, long contemplations. These are of the mind, the soul. My body, I think, is attuned to a different weather and feels cold less; through the winter of work, writing this book, confined to a house, it misses the fresh touch of moving air, it feels closed in. In the mornings I examine the sky, the light, the stir of wind through the trees, for one day's weather and the next, the cycle, but am walled off from it now. On the cold days, warming the house, I kneel like an Indian before the fireplace to make the fire, and am quiet and at rest; this matters now. The hands setting the logs in place are ridged with muscle, the fingers thick, shaped to the shaft and grip of a paddle, stained with the weather of the North, but they no longer ache much.

It is not over, then. I would be there. There is rain on the window now, as I write these words, forming in silver drops on the branches of a stand of aspens outside, where spring is returning and buds are about to burst into leaf. Beyond the trees it is a different landscape that I see, where the great river stirs and coils in its ceaseless flow, the rain patters lightly on the tent and the wind riffles under the tent fly. The two landscapes fold into each other, and I cannot tell you which is the real, the actual; for me, now. For as long as I live, I think, I will inhabit both.

APPENDIX

Practicalities

Some account of the food and equipment my son and I relied on, the books and other sources of information, may be useful to others who attempt a comparable distance in the northwest quarter of the continent. What follows will also, I hope, be of interest in itself, as a record of how two people set about solving a problem in survival which, for us, was without precedents.

Supposing You Go

You won't try it on your own until you feel within yourself the right balance of skill and experience, in canoeing and camping. Up to a point, the two qualities are equivalent: You make up by the one what you lack in the other. This book is a record of quite modest abilities made good by the sort of usually sensible judgment that you form unconsciously from a lifetime of experience. I will never win prizes for flat-water or downriver racing, for slaloming a complicated course through rapids. I *do* know what to expect in most such situations and how to get through or around them, effectively if not elegantly.

Except in the series of rapids at Fort Smith on the Slave River, the Mackenzie system is nowhere supremely demanding: Pure skill counts less than judgment. Its sheer scale, however, is a third dimension. It is remote and long; it is also *big*—crossing one of its connecting lakes or simply getting from bank to bank, when the distance may be two or three miles across and the current strong, must be a very considered act. To canoe these waters requires not only skill and experience but a large measure of endurance. Weather is part of this factor of size. The weather of the northern summer is not the howling icescape one may imagine, but it shifts abruptly from chill to warmth to storm and back again. Of the sixty-nine days it took my son and me to canoe from Fort McMurray to the Arctic coast and back to Inuvik, fewer than half were sunny and more or less warm. The rest were cool or rainy or windy (or all three), and for seven of those days we were pinned down by winds too fierce for canoeing. (Mackenzie's weather in 1789 was worse. He was windbound for seven of the forty-four days he took from Fort Chipewyan to Whale Island—and stopped by Great Slave ice for eleven days.) You will plan your equipment and food for extremes of weather; and in figuring time, you will allow the weather a tithe. I have tried to do both in the suggestions that follow, correcting what we planned beforehand from what we learned in the course of the trip.

Routes. On the Mackenzie itself, the distance from Fort Providence to Inuvik is 938 miles by my log. It took us a month, including three windbound days. If you plan such a trip yourself, allow an extra week, partly for bad weather but mostly to give yourself more time than we could afford to visit the towns along the river, explore some of the interesting tributaries (the North Nahanni, the Willowlake, the Keele, the Bear, for instance), perhaps climb the beautiful mountains around Camsell Bend. From Inuvik to the mouth of the East Channel is about 95 miles, another 20 from there to the Eskimo coastal community of Tuktoyaktuk—at least a week and probably twice that for the return by paddle, which is feasible against the moderate current but tedious and tiring (or there's a scheduled plane service between Tuk and Inuvik). Except on one of the long summer weekends, you should be able to rent at Inuvik a satisfactory freight canoe, with motor, for the trip to the coast and back: say a twenty-foot Chestnut freighter with vee stern (not too bad to paddle); a twenty-horse motor would be more than adequate.

If you have time for only part of the Mackenzie, the most interesting section is that between Fort Simpson (for now, the end of the Mackenzie Highway) and Norman Wells (scheduled flights back), with fine mountain scenery on both banks most of the way. The distance is 350 miles, which you can canoe in ten days—and allow another week for weather and exploring.

If you're sure of your ability in rapids, several of the western tributaries of the Mackenzie offer good possibilities for trips of two or three weeks: the South Nahanni (to the Liard, thence to Fort Simpson, much of the route in Nahanni National Park), the Keele, the Mountain; one would use a charter plane from Fort Simpson (or Fort Norman or Norman Wells) to the starting point—on the South Nahanni, probably to just below the spectacular Virginia Falls, though you could start farther up and portage around the falls (arduous!). A possibility to the east of the Mackenzie would be to start from Fort Franklin on the southwest side of Great Bear Lake and descend the Bear River to Fort Norman (one big rapids but not too difficult except in late-summer low water)—or continue on down the Mackenzie. Perhaps the most interesting and varied canoe trip in the Northwest is the Camsell River, a river-and-lake system, comparable to the Churchill, connecting the North Arm of Great Slave Lake with Great Bear Lake. One would start from Yellowknife (or the small Indian community of Rae farther north, equally accessible by road). Getting back is a difficulty: The paddle from Conjuror Bay in Great Bear Lake will take at least a day to Port Radium for a charter or scheduled plane back to Yellowknife; or arrange to be met by a chartered plane at Conjuror Bay (but that would require setting, and meeting, an exact schedule).

The Peace and Athabasca rivers are part of the Mackenzie system and are canoeable from near their sources in the Rockies west of Edmonton—largely wilderness country with occasional small settlements, as on the Mackenzie. Fort Smith on the Slave River would be the natural terminus for the Peace River trip, Fort McMurray for the Athabasca (the section of the Athabasca from Fort McMurray to Fort Chipewyan is the least interesting part of the river). The rapids above Fort Smith are *not* canoeable, but the channels and portages around them along the east bank, which Mackenzie followed, still exist and can be taken (the west bank route around the rapids was never designed for canoeing). Mackenzie's description of the portages and their approaches did not seem to me clear enough to trust, and I found no local information that could be relied on. After getting back, however, I discovered one old description of the Mackenzie route that I believe would be adequate if I were to try it again—which I'll cover in the next section.

Maps and Other Sources of Information. Nearly all of Canada is covered by the 1:250,000 series of government maps, to a scale of about four miles to the inch. A free index map for this series is obtainable from:

> Map Distribution Office
> 615 Booth Street
> Ottawa K1A 0E9 Ont.

This series is not entirely up to date but is better in that respect than the comparable U. S. Government maps. The scale is satisfactory for most river canoeing, but where following a precise course is important, one of the larger scales might be preferable: 1:125,000 (about two miles per inch) or 1:50,000 (about .8 mile per inch). These two series are still quite incomplete, but index maps showing what's available may be ordered from the same source.

Canada's Wild Rivers Surveys project has sent teams of canoeists down many of the remote rivers of the Northwest, and their multilithed reports provide exactly the kind of firsthand information a canoeist needs on several of the Mackenzie Valley rivers (but not the Bear nor, curiously, the South Nahanni). For copies, write to:

> Information Services
> Conservation Group
> Department of Indian Affairs
> Ottawa K1A 0H4 Ont.

The provincial governments of Alberta and Saskatchewan publish admirable guide booklets, with maps, on canoe routes in their areas, including such great fur-trade rivers as the Athabasca, Saskatchewan, and Churchill, which still provide long-distance wilderness canoeing of the first order. Write to:

> Alberta Department of Culture, Youth, and Recreation
> Canadian National Tower
> 10004 104th Avenue
> Edmonton T5J 0K5 Alta.

> Saskatchewan Department of Tourism and Renewable Resources

P.O. Box 7105
Regina S4P oB5 Sask.

The government of the Northwest Territories has, so far, little to offer on canoeing, but general information on travel there and some advice on canoeing (including a brief description of the South Nahanni) can be had from:

TravelArctic
Division of Tourism
Government of the Northwest Territories
Yellowknife XoE 1Ho NWT

To get by road to any of the possible starting points in the Northwest Territories, Alaska, the Yukon, or northern Alberta or British Columbia, you should probably have the current edition of *The Milepost,* an annual guide to the roads and facilities, such as they are, with a road map. Order from:

Alaska Northwest Publishing Company
Box 4-EEE
Anchorage, AK 99509

Incidentally, before venturing onto these gravel roads (at Edmonton, say), I'd advise putting a bug screen across the front bumper to protect headlights, radiator, and windshield from flying gravel; protection for the gas tank is also sensible, though that was not a problem we had. We carried two spare tires and emergency gasoline but didn't need them. If you emulate the natives, you'll have snow tires on your drive wheels for traction, though we got through without them.

Two general guides to Canadian canoeing are worth knowing about. Neither is satisfactory, but there are no others—in going into the northern wilderness, one wants whatever information one can get. *Canada's Centenary Journey* describes an east–west crossing of the country by teams of canoeists in 1967, with some (unreliable) historical background (Canadian Camping Association Publications, 102 Eglinton Avenue East, Suite 203, Toronto M4P 1E1 Ont.). *Canada Canoe Routes* is a compilation published by its author, Nick Nickels, of material on canoeing in most parts of the country, nearly all of it from sources such as those suggested above (Canoecanada, Lakefield KoL 2Ho Ont.).

The Appendixes of my own *Canoer's Bible* (Doubleday) contain what I modestly believe to be the most comprehensive available and, for the moment, up-to-date list of sources of information on canoeing throughout the United States and Canada.

Finally, for the rapids on the Slave River, I'd suggest an article by Amos Burg, "On Mackenzie's Trail to the Polar Sea," carefully collated with Mackenzie's own account (*National Geographic,* Vol. LX, No. 2 [Aug. 1931], pp. 127–56).

Equipment. The canoe I chose for the trip, after months of study and trying out, was the Old Town Chipewyan Tripper, a seventeen-foot, two-inch canoe with a thirty-seven-inch beam, made of layers of vinyl and ABS (a tough and resilient plastic) vacuum-formed over a naturally buoyant compressed-foam core. This material is, I believe, substantially more durable than aluminum, fiberglass, or wood and canvas—the outer skin will scratch a bit on rocks, but in any conditions I can imagine, the canoe is virtually indestructible. It proved to be a nearly ideal choice for the conditions. Its depth (twenty-five inches at bow and stern, fifteen inches amidships, about three inches more than standard for most canoes of that length) gives it a good load capacity and enough freeboard so that we rarely took water in storms on the lakes and rivers that would have swamped most canoes. We carried a weight (cargo and ourselves) of about seven hundred pounds (theoretical capacity: nine hundred), never with less than six or eight inches of freeboard, which is plenty. The design is moderately fine in the bow, fairly full behind (for riding over waves), keel-less, and rockered (curving from end to end, not flat-bottomed), so that it is highly maneuverable; I had thought of this quality mainly as an asset in rapids, but it was valuable also in storms, where one must zigzag in quick turns between waves to keep from swamping. With a total weight of seventy-five pounds, the Tripper is a little heavier than I like to portage, but not too bad.

If I were buying a canoe solely for the Mackenzie, I might think seriously about a bigger canoe than our Tripper, up to twenty or twenty-two feet—one of the big Canadian wood-and-canvas Chestnut canoes still much used in the North, perhaps even one of Ralph Frese's fiberglass North canoe replicas, though for that I'd want at least four paddlers (for details, see *The Canoer's Bible*). The extra capacity and freeboard of a big canoe are an obvious plus in big waters, but the main advantage is speed: It's axiomatic that a long canoe will move faster with the same effort than a shorter one of the same general design and proportions. The disadvantage is that you would not get much use from it later unless you made another trip on a river of comparable size and length—the Yukon, say; the weight of a canoe that big would make it a killer on portages, for me and for most other men of average size and heft.

Getting your canoe back from the end of nearly all the possible canoe routes in the Northwest is a major difficulty. The barge service is not too satisfactory, where available; air freight or a charter plane is expensive and in a cargo plane will require crating, a further expense if it can be managed at all. Selling the canoe at the other end is a nuisance, and buyers are likely to expect a giveaway price. An alternative is to rent a canoe from the Hudson's Bay Company's U-Paddle service. The canoe will be a standard-weight Grumman (a good canoe but not first choice if you're looking for the ideal for the conditions) and can be picked up at the start of the trip and left at the end for a rental that is currently fifty dollars per week; there is a branch of The Bay in just about every settlement in the North. Since the canoes will often have to be hauled in over winter roads, arrangements should be made the previous fall, by writing to:

Hudson's Bay Company
Northern Stores Department
77 Main Street
Winnipeg R3C 2R1 Man.

We alternated two pairs of fiberglass paddles: a big-bladed, heavily built pair with comfortable T grip made by Sports Equipment, Inc. (moderately priced as such paddles go); and the very light Kruger Permapaddle made by the Sawyer Canoe Company (also not too expensive). The former, with its thick vinyl-covered aluminum shaft, is heavy enough to be tiring toward the end of the day, when we often switched to the Sawyers for relief. The Sawyer paddle does well also against strong wind or big waves; it proved to be a little fragile, but the light weight (the lightest paddle I know of) is a real energy-saver. The blade area is about two thirds that of our others (and the same as a standard wooden paddle), but it seemed to move the canoe nearly as well as the bigger blade—we stepped up the beat only slightly in order to maintain the same speed.

Of our six packs, two were old and much-used standard-size Duluth packs, which carried clothes, bulk food (flour and sugar), and canned goods. Everything connected with night and sleeping went into one oversize Duluth pack—sleeping bags, tent, books, lamp, candle lantern, and so on—which was convenient but so big and heavy (about a hundred pounds) that it would have been a trial if we'd done much portaging. For cooking equipment—pots, a folding grill, cutlery, plus the food for our modest daily lunches—we used a small Alpine frame pack simply because it's the right size. We also tried two new ideas in packs: the molded polyethylene Rec-Pac, which successfully protected from wet and knocking around cameras, film, tape recorder and tapes, emergency medicines, and repair materials; and a molded fiberglass tote box, or *wangun*, made by Gerry, for freeze-dried food, bacon, sausage (the Gerry box is out of production and there is no other ready-made *wangun* that I know of). Although the four canvas packs shed rain quite well, they'll soak through if they stand in water; for convenience in sorting and for protection from damp, we packed everything in all the packs in Gerry plastic bags (the plastic bags available in supermarkets are not heavy enough to stand up).

Our tent, like the plastic packs, was also an experiment: a Gerry four-man nylon tent, the Fortnight. We chose it for size (seventy-two square feet—enough room for ourselves and all the packs on wet days—and six feet high at center, so that we could dress and undress standing up) and for its self-contained aluminum poles and stakes (it was not always possible to cut poles and stakes as needed). It's a good tent, though I dislike the low entrance that seems to be a feature of all tents designed for backpacking (awkward for getting packs in and out) and found the light aluminum stakes inadequate in a storm (we supplemented them with heavy plastic I-beam stakes, which were effective). The chief advantage of nylon in any tent is that it's light and compact compared with canvas or poplin; its disadvantage is that it's vulnerable to sparks—you need to be rather careful about making your campfire well downwind from the tent.

Our sleeping bags were a three-season weight (rated to about +30° F), one with goose down, the other with the new Fiberfill II insulation (about as effective as down and doesn't absorb moisture). We also carried light summer sleeping bags to serve as outer bags on cold nights—which I needed rather often, my son never.

We chose our clothes for warmth and protection against mosquitoes and flies: heavy wool shirts, heavy duck trousers with fitted cuffs (field trousers made by L. L. Bean—no bugs up the legs); ordinary work pants and shirts for warm days and, for the coldest weather, old ski pants, which also tuck into boots, and long underwear (half-wool union suits and, less effective, cotton net). I treated myself to a new pair of calf-length Dunham boots, silicone-tanned and waterproof, which I recommend. A ten-inch rubber boot would have been as effective and much less expensive but chilly on cold days. To keep the mosquitoes off the back of my neck, I wore a bandanna, which looks odd, perhaps, but does the job. We also had head nets but used them only once—they interfere with vision and with eating and smoking. We tried a variety of insect repellents but found Cutter's liquid the most effective, and even that we no longer bothered with from about mid-July on; the number of insects diminished as the season progressed—and, apparently, we got used to them.

My son and I both had windbreaker jackets and heavy sweaters. For wet days we relied on knee-length rain shirts of rubberized nylon, with elastic cuffs on the sleeves—which sweat inside and do not keep you dry below the knees or down your boots (a wick effect from tucked-in trousers). A rain suit, with waterproof trousers, would have been better—but also a nuisance and, by my standards, excessively expensive. (A new material, Bukflex, is best for the purpose if you choose a rain suit; it's waterproof but "breathes"—doesn't condense your own body moisture inside—which sounds too good to be true but really works.) On any canoe trip, rain is likely to turn up often enough in the weather cycle so that you can't afford to let it stop you. Comfortable and effective rain gear is a necessity.

The only serious omission in our clothing list was waterproof gloves. Anyone canoeing in the North would do well to provide himself with a pair of rubber lineman's gloves—or else the sort that goes with a kayaker's wet suit, more expensive but better-fitting.

Food. For dinners, we relied on freeze-dried stews and vegetables, with a few heavy canned meat stews for emergencies, which we were usually able to replenish at Hudson's Bay stores in the settlements. For breakfasts, we had two sides of double-smoked bacon (which lasted, though it got moldy toward the end), oatmeal, pancake mixes, freeze-dried and, when we could get them, fresh eggs, and dried fruits. Our lunches were processed cheese, small smoked summer sausages that also keep well (the kind the Germans call *Jägerwurst* [hunter sausage]), and dry breads, such as Rye-Krisp; chocolate bars and huge quantities of raisins. The freeze-dried dinners were a problem—filling but short on meat protein, so that by the end of the first month we had worn down noticeably. I had expected this but chose them anyway to be sure of being able to carry enough (they are, at least, light and compact) to last the summer. We should have fished more than we did but were too often short of time or simply tired—one more reason for building extra days into any plan for canoeing in the North. Time would always, I think, rule out serious hunting—and on the Mackenzie itself game is scarce in summer. Nuts or dried soybeans, perhaps a supply of a concentrated cereal such as Granola, would have filled out our protein needs to some extent, though I'm skeptical of fad foods, and most are bulky as well as overpriced.

For the time and distance, probably the best solution would have been the one the *voyageurs* and most Indians used when on the move: pemmican. If I were attempting a comparable trip again, I would use it, by itself and as a nourishing addition to the freeze-dried stuff. In the quantities needed, one would have to make it oneself—the commercial versions I know of are not genuine and are ridiculously expensive. Pemmican can be made from beef or other red meat. The meat is sliced thin and cut into narrow strips—say an inch wide by eight inches long—and sun-dried ("jerked") for two or three days (a clothes line will do, but dry weather is a must). At that point it will keep and is not bad to eat. The next step is a day or two of smoking—the meat is hung on racks over a low fire, the heat and smoke kept in by a covering tarp (an oven at a low temperature would do). It is then crumbled, mixed with an equal quantity of rendered fat, and sealed in waterproof bags, in which form it should keep for up to a year; raisins or any dried berries obtainable can be mixed in to improve the flavor and nutrition (the Chippewas of northern Wisconsin and Minnesota used maple sugar). With or without the berries, pemmican is a complete food. For a person of average size, two and a half pounds per day is enough for the heavy work of canoeing.

People. Three weeks after Jim and I got home, an RCMP constable telephoned long-distance from Fort McMurray to find out if we were safe: we had not reported in at our intended destination, Aklavik, and the Mounties were about to send out a search party. We registered at each RCMP post along our route—names, address, telephone number, next of kin, description of canoe, expected arrival date at the next post—and the information was passed on so that we were always expected when we turned up. The system is voluntary but is used throughout the Northwest (there's a comparable scheme in the wild parts of the western provinces). The practice is strongly recommended to anyone canoeing there: In emergencies, relatives at home could get in touch through the RCMP; in case of accident, one would be looked for. Beyond that, in the settlements the local constable is usually well informed and can provide introductions to the people who live there, white and native. The Royal Canadian Mounted Police have been one of the nation's glories. I found their modern representatives very much up to reputation.

Although we had that system as a buffer against disaster, I carried in my pockets, along with insect repellent and a small tube of liquid soap, several emergency items: waterproof match case backed up by a butane lighter; compass; a short, flexible saw blade; twine; an eight-by-ten-foot sheet of light plastic, folded to handkerchief size; and a set of Versa-Ties, plastic grommets that with the twine would convert the plastic sheet into a small tarp or tent or a secure waterproof roofing for a lean-to shelter of boughs. With these, the knife on my belt, and a modicum of woodcraft, we would have been proof against any loss we might have had to face.

With precautions like these, it's not imprudent for two experienced canoeists to travel the Mackenzie system alone, as Jim and I did. At the same time, the risk increases in proportion to the number of rapids on the route and the scarcity of settlements. The smaller rivers, such as the South Nahanni, are best attempted with at least two canoes, as insurance against accident. Needless to say, the group must be chosen with care, not only for skill and experience but for compatibility—the physical stress can bring out weaknesses that in the normal course of life would never appear but in real wilderness would be dangerous as well as unpleasant. A larger party increases this risk as well as the range of abilities and is likely to be slow-moving; and the country is still wild enough so that finding camp sites to hold several tents is likely to be a problem unless someone is very energetic with an ax.

Books

Both before and after the trip, I read as widely as I had time for. The following comments record my indebtedness to authors whose books I have found useful, and that rather subjective standard should be borne in mind by any scholars who happen to glance at these notes; I have not attempted a definitive bibliography. These sources are meant, simply, to be helpful to other amateurs who venture, as I did, into the North.

Mackenzie's *Voyages* is still, after 185 years, the most practical canoer's introduction to the Northwest. University Microfilms publishes a facsimile of the first edition (there are other versions in the United States and Canada). A very small number of details is added by an edition of his journal of the 1789 voyage, from a manuscript that was evidently an intermediate stage toward publication, under the title *Exploring the Northwest Territory* (T. H. McDonald, ed., University of Oklahoma Press). This appears to be an accurate text, but the editor's explanatory notes are mistaken or misleading in nearly every particular. With two exceptions, all of my Mackenzie quotations (including the chapter headnotes) are from the published *Voyages* rather than the journal.

For those who take pleasure, as I do, in the imagination of the past, I have included on the endpaper maps my estimates of Mackenzie's probable camp sites, from Fort Chipewyan to the Arctic Ocean. In doing so, I have tried to match the explorer's descriptive notes, his estimates of distances, and his corrected compass bearings, with my own observations. I do not know of another published source that has attempted to show his whole route in detail. My reconstruction is, however, a diffident one, no more than probable. Except in a few places—the sites below Roche Qui Trempe à l'Eau and at the foot of East Mountain, just above the San Sault Rapids—Mackenzie's descriptions and the modern topography do not make for certainty; within range of each Mackenzie camp, there was usually more than one possibility, and his route through the delta and back again, with the location of Whale Island, remains a riddle. A *voyageur*, like an Indian, can put his tent anywhere.

There is no satisfactory biography of Mackenzie. I preferred M. S. Wade's *Mackenzie of Canada* (Blackwood, 1927) because it included material derived from some of the explorer's immediate descendants who were still living when the book was written. Of the same date are Arthur Wollacott's *Mackenzie and His Voyageurs* (Dent) and Hume Wrong's *Sir Alexander Mackenzie* (Macmillan, Toronto). Two children's books about Mackenzie are, for the moment, in print. One is a tissue of fiction and carelessness. The other, *Alexander Mackenzie and the Northwest* by Roy Daniells (Faber, 1969) is honest work so far as it goes. Mackenzie's letters to his cousin are preserved in archives in Ottawa, but in an odd form—Roderic apparently transcribed and improved them, they were translated into French and further improved by one of his descendants, then retranslated back into English; and that is the version we have. My quotations of these letters are from Wade's biography.

The definitive account of the fur trade in North America has yet to be written; it's a big subject—and indispensable to understanding the exploration and settlement of the continent. Harold A. Innis's *The Fur Trade in Canada* (University of Toronto Press) reflects the author's firsthand observation of the trade in the Northwest toward the end and is something of a Canadian classic; but is clumsily written and, in my view, vague on some crucial matters of the economics of the trade. E. E. Rich's three-volume *History of the Hudson's Bay Company* (McClelland & Stewart) is a company history based on The Bay's immense archives but perpetuates errors and confusions concerning the discovery and exploration of the Athabasca country.

Eric W. Morse's *Fur Trade Canoe Routes of Canada, Then and Now* (Queen's Printer, Ottawa) describes the trade routes, with maps and useful background material, and has the recommendation, in the present context, of the author's having canoed many of these waters himself. Harold A. Innis's *Peter Pond, Fur Trader and Adventurer* (Irwin and Gordon, Toronto, 1930) is just about all that's been published about that obstreperous Yankee colleague of Mackenzie; Pond's own memoir of his life has been published by the Yale University Library (1955) but is virtually unobtainable. Peter Fidler's journal of his youthful winter among the Chipewyans of the Athabasca country (1791–92–he was surveyor of the Hudson's Bay Company) is included in Volume 21 of the Publications of the Champlain Society (Toronto, 1934); Fidler is my authority for the names of Mackenzie's canoemen and of the English Chief, all of whom Fidler met. For some light on the late period of the fur trade in the Mackenzie valley—the steamboat and paddle-wheel era—one might look at Leslie Roberts' *The Mackenzie* (Rinehart, 1949) or F. L. Waldo's *Down the Mackenzie Through the Great Lone Land* (Macmillan, New York, 1923).

Many books have been written about the search for the Northwest Passage, of which I take Mackenzie's two voyages to have been late if not final chapters. One that I found helpful is Nellis M. Crouse's *Search for the Northwest Passage* (Columbia University Press, 1934). The journal of Captain James Cook's voyage to the Alaska coast, with posthumous notes by his lieutenants, was originally published in 1790 and is available in a modern facsimile (Cambridge, England: The Hakluyt Society, 1955).

For background on the prehistoric Indian culture of the Northwest (that is, before white contact), I have relied on Harold Driver's *Indians of North America* (University of Chicago Press); generalizing and synthesizing but comprehensive, and trustworthy in every detail I have been able to check by other research or by direct observation. Most accounts of the Eskimos describe the people of Alaska or the central Arctic and Greenland rather than the important and interesting Mackenzie delta subculture—they apply only in the most general terms. Robert McGhee's *Beluga Hunters* (Memorial University of Newfoundland) admirably describes his archaeological work at Kittigazuit and opens with a brief but authoritative account of the Mackenzie Eskimos. Vilhjalmur Stefannson's many books and papers on his explorations in the Canadian Arctic, including the Mackenzie delta, are reliable for their record of the country and of the Eskimo culture as he knew it in the second decade of this century. The Danish anthropologist Knud Rasmussen, like Stefannson fluent in Eskimo, explored the Arctic coast in the early 1920s (*The Mackenzie Eskimos*, in English, Copenhagen, 1942).

Sigurd F. Olson's books on canoeing the northern wilderness are classics, setting the standard and inspiration for the rest of us who follow in his wake. His *Runes of the North* (Knopf) in particular treats the *Pays d'en haut*.

Bradford Angier, an American long settled in British Columbia, has written voluminously and well on woodcraft and wilderness survival (all books published by Stackpole). I am indebted to his *Survival with Style*, if for no other reason than that from it I learned to make the small net that provided us with most of the fish we actually got.

E. B. Nickerson's *Kayaks to the Arctic* (Howell-North Books, 1967) is a gossipy account of a family trip down the Mackenzie from Fort Providence to Inuvik and is true to everyday white life on the river as it was in 1965. That life has evolved considerably in the decade since, but the book is nonetheless worth a look.

I am very far from being a proficient bird watcher but was never at a loss in finding names for the rich variety of winged life that we saw along the Mackenzie—with the help of the paperback Golden Field Guide, *Birds of North America* (Chandler S. Robbins et al., Golden Press). As a handy field guide to the wild flowers of the Mackenzie Valley, a large and interesting subject in itself, I would suggest *The Alaska-Yukon Wild Flowers Guide* (Alaska Northwest Publishing Company)—many species in the area covered are common to the Northwest Territories. The book includes a bibliography; there is not, so far as I know, a comparable guide devoted exclusively to the Canadian Northwest.

On every aspect of North American Indian canoes—and the fundamentals of canoe design in general, for all conditions—the last word has been written by Edwin Tappan Adney and Howard I. Chapelle in *The Bark Canoes and Skin Boats of North America,* with an abundance of informative illustrations (Smithsonian Institution/U. S. Government Printing Office). The reader interested in classic sport canoe design can do no better than to consult Atwood Manley's *Rushton and His Times in American Canoeing* (Syracuse University Press), which concerns the work of the great nineteenth-century Adirondack designer and builder, J. Henry Rushton.

Thanks

The people who appear in this book are real. To all who helped us survive our journey down the great river and make a beginning at understanding its country, in ways by now apparent, I here express my gratitude. I thank in particular Richard Hill, director of the Inuvik Research Laboratory, who gave generously of his time, knowledge, and the use of his institution's library; Bishop Henry G. Cook, co-ordinator of historical programs for the goverment of the Northwest Territories, and Alex Stevenson, chairman of the NWT Historical Advisory Board, both of whom provided abundant bibliographical assistance; and the librarians of the Free Library of Philadelphia and the University of Pennsylvania, who have helped me get the books once I knew what I was looking for. Robert McGhee, the author of *Beluga Hunters,* answered a number of specific questions about his findings at Kittigazuit; Paul Fenimore Cooper, who in *Island of the Lost* has written of another Arctic explorer, Sir John Franklin, helped me ascertain Eskimo place names and their English meanings. Ralph Frese, the Chicago canoe builder, gave useful pointers at the outset on canoe design. My friend and neighbor Nancy Ulrich has labored at deciphering and typing my book's manuscript.

And I thank, finally, my father, James Mead, the ultimate inspiration of our journey and of this book; and my wife, to whom the book is dedicated, and our sons, Jim and his three brothers, without whose love and forbearance neither book nor journey nor life are, for me, imaginable.

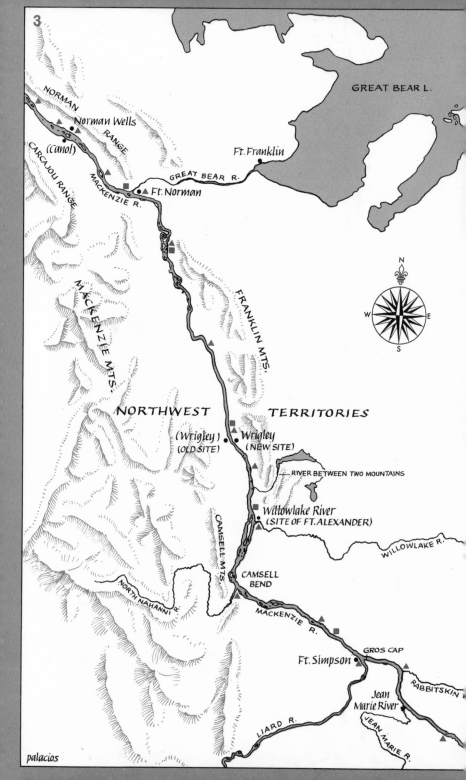

3

GREAT BEAR L.

NORMAN RANGE

Norman Wells

(Canol)

CARCAJOU RANGE

Ft. Franklin

GREAT BEAR R.

MACKENZIE R.

Ft. Norman

MACKENZIE MTS.

FRANKLIN MTS.

NORTHWEST   TERRITORIES

(Wrigley)
(OLD SITE)

Wrigley
(NEW SITE)

RIVER BETWEEN TWO MOUNTAINS

Willowlake River
(SITE OF FT. ALEXANDER)

CAMSELL MTS.

WILLOWLAKE R.

NORTH NAHANNI R.

CAMSELL
BEND

MACKENZIE R.

GROS CAP

Ft. Simpson

RABBITSKIN

Jean
Marie River

JEAN MARIE R.

LIARD R.

palacios